ILL
FEELINGS

ALICE HATTRICK

THE FEMINIST PRESS
AT THE CITY UNIVERSITY OF NEW YORK
NEW YORK CITY

Published in 2022 by the Feminist Press
at the City University of New York
The Graduate Center
365 Fifth Avenue, Suite 5406
New York, NY 10016

feministpress.org

First Feminist Press edition 2022

First published in Great Britain by Fitzcarraldo Editions in 2021.

This book was made possible thanks to a grant from the New York State Council
on the Arts with the support of the Governor and the New York State Legislature.

First printing May 2022

Cover and text design by Drew Stevens

Library of Congress Cataloging-in-Publication Data is available for this title.

PRINTED IN THE UNITED STATES OF AMERICA

'How well one has to be — to be ill!'
—*Alice James's Diary*

¶ Dredge

The day after her fifty-fourth birthday, my mother and I walk through a field near her house at dusk, a small pair of scissors tied to a long string around her neck. The dogs are on their leads because it's getting dark and she isn't brave enough to let them off 'because of the rabbits'. She has already been signed off sick for a year and three months. As we walk, my mother starts to sing the folk song 'She Moved Through the Fair'.

> My love said to me
> My mother won't mind
> And my father won't slight you
> For your lack of kind

My mother mostly sings songs she learnt at musical theatre college, or Norwegian songs from choir, but this one is different – it belongs to her. The lyrics, and the tune, make her voice melancholic, and more relaxed.

> And she smiled as she passed me
> With her goods and her gear
> And that was the last
> That I saw of my dear.

We walk quite far that evening, further than I expect. My mother wants to walk further still, but she is worried about walking back, about me walking back. She is used to negotiating the length of these walks in her own mind, depending on how she is feeling in her body, and the things she still needs to do that day, or even the next day, like go and see her father at the care home, or finish filling out another form relating to her 'Ill Health Retirement'. It is a careful calculation that, once decided upon, can and most probably will be ruefully ignored – she just has to face 'the consequences'.

1

My mother has moved to mid-Norfolk, where the River Nar crosses the Peddars Way, to be near my grandfather, who has vascular dementia and Alzheimer's. He is convinced she lives in Burnham Market, a posh town near the North Norfolk coast, where no one in our family has ever lived, and none of us could ever afford. My mother will move away from here just as quickly, once he has died of leukaemia. The village she has moved to is an ancient land of crossings. When she first arrived, a woman told her she would be healed by the power of the place itself.

My mother had to reschedule her last meeting with HR because it was at 9 am on a Wednesday.

'I was in bed all morning,' she says, as if they should know that someone who is about to be signed off sick forever will never make it to a meeting first thing. It's like the time she was annoyed at the ME/CFS service, who kept calling her when she was asleep, without warning.

What she means is: *I am in bed all morning every day.*

'Dear Dr,' reads a document on her desktop back at her house, 'I have muscle weakness in my hands (holding a pen, lifting a kettle) and legs and breathlessness and palpitations on activity are problematic. Processing and translating information is very difficult and slow, which makes research, publication and teaching impossible.'

'I've had enough of my shit,' she says to me, on our walk. 'I'm wasted.'

When my mother says she's *wasted*, does she mean she *feels* wasted – ill, fatigued, sick – or does she also mean her working life is wasted, her potential is *spent*?

A long time ago, my mother sought a diagnosis. Upon relapsing into full-blown illness again, unable to go to her job as a lecturer in History of Design, she has found only *more work*: phone calls and confusing meetings with HR, days spent compiling documents with names like 'Letter to Sussex Wide ME service.doc' and 'Ill Health Retirement Factsheet.pdf'. My mother must write her own medical history, over and over again, like a doctor, except she is also the patient.

'ME also causes severe impairment of my cognitive functioning including extreme difficulty in focusing and concentrating for any length of time on a task, conversation or text,' she writes. She suffers with 'impaired and interrupted sleep and extreme irritability and mood swings', wakes extremely fatigued, has ear pain, breathing difficulties, frontal headache, sore throat, nausea, heart palpitations, unrefreshing sleep, and even 'orthostatic intolerance, anxiety and of course extreme fatigue'. She cannot 'function', has trouble 'processing and translating information', including 'knowledge of her subject' and 'events in the past'. She must describe her ill feelings – not being able to stand for very long, feeling sick, feeling tired and sore – as if her body is not a body at all, as if her body is a machine malfunctioning, like she is faulty, or broken. If she were a computer she would have *crashed*.

If 'illness is the great confessional', as Virginia Woolf wrote in her essay 'On Being Ill', why is my mother writing like this? Where are the 'things said, truths blurted out, which the cautious respectability of health conceals'? There is the impossibility of speaking through pain, which Woolf also wrote about – 'let a sufferer describe a pain in his head to a doctor and language at once runs dry' – but that is not exactly true. It is as if my mother is writing against the possibilities of a literature of illness entirely.

My mother does not speak to me in the way she writes in her 'Details of Illness'. She speaks like Woolf in June 1919, writing a letter to her sister Vanessa: 'Did anyone ever suffer as I did? You might have seen my soul shrivelling like a – I cannot remember the image exactly, but it is something one does by rubbing a piece of scaling wax and then everything else curls up – as if in agony.'

When I am touched, I feel like those fish that twist up in the heat of your hand.

'Fuck all this fucking paperwork,' she says. 'I'm wasted.'

Audre Lorde wrote *The Cancer Journals* so that, in her words, 'the pain *not* be wasted'.

Is feeling *wasted* the same as feeling worthless? I do not need to ask her. I'm not her therapist. I am her daughter, her biographer, and I know how she feels. I have always been like her, and, for most of my life, she has felt ill.

With the onset of illness, there is a 'before and after' instead of a beginning, a middle, and an end. There is before you got sick, and then there is after – your life forever changed. My mother has a small black-and-white photograph of herself, taken when she started her BA, a copy of which would have been pinned to the notice board during her undergraduate course at the university where she would eventually teach students about archives, material culture and queer histories: her 'before'. On the back, she has written: 'Taken in 1994. I am 29. Pre-ME – JUST'. She has short hair and is wearing a white wide-collared shirt and a dark coloured waistcoat. She is young: thirty-one, not twenty-nine, unless she got the year wrong. Either way, she is younger than me, except she has two young children, a girl and a boy. She is on her own, when it comes to childrearing and homemaking at least. She isn't ill, yet.

The following year, my mother collapsed with mycoplasma pneumonia, which causes flu-like symptoms, such as fatigue, headache, chest pain and fever. I don't remember how long she had pneumonia for – it wasn't even the kind of illness that requires hospitalisation, which is why it's commonly called 'walking pneumonia' – but she never fully recovered and was eventually diagnosed with ME/CFS two years later. Five years spent in her bedroom in the dark followed; ten years of carers in and out most days.

I remember her still lying in the dark of her bedroom in our ground-floor flat in Brighton when I got home from school, if I myself had been well enough to go. She got chest infections all the time, which she would read as a sign of something else more deeply wrong with her, but then she would not get at all sick, and explain that this was because of her 'overactive immune system'. At night, she slept lightly, if she slept at all. Her legs and arms felt heavy all the time, like they were weighted down at her hands and feet. She would often shudder as if electrified, at even the smallest noises or movements, sometimes nothing at all. She struggled to remember things – mainly nouns. She would get this awful ringing in her ears. She had digestive problems, pains in her chest and difficulty breathing. Sometimes her throat would close up, and she'd cough and cough, as if there was something poisonous in the air.

Since that time, some years have been better than others, just like some days are better than others. My mother's initial bouts of pain relieved, and her fatigue got worse. She got well enough to finish her degree, eventually, and then her MA and a PhD, to teach part time, but hers is not the kind of illness you ever really recover from. 'Fatigue' is not the main problem anymore, not that I can ascertain what the main problem is, or where it is: her heart; her head; her sleep; her whole body. She still has muscular pain and light sensitivity, a lot of weakness, the feeling that her muscles 'don't have power'. More recently, she has taken to calling it the vapours.

The day my mother collapsed in 1995, I found her on the kitchen floor. 'Alice witnessed this,' she later wrote, as if I had observed a crime and needed a new identity. I had told my brother to stay in the living room and went to our neighbour for help. According to my mother, it was then that I became 'insecure about leaving the house', and 'became angrier and her schoolwork suffered'. Was this enough of a reason to contact the already-over-subscribed mental health service? Did I just not want to leave our flat knowing that if I wasn't there, no one would be there if she collapsed again? I also developed symptoms of illness. My mother reported to doctors that I felt ill on waking, with sore throats, tummy aches and headaches that seemed to last all day; that I said I needed to rest and wanted to sleep during breaktimes at school; that I had pain in my arms and legs after sport, dancing and 'just the normal walking and standing of the day'; that these symptoms felt heightened when I lay down to sleep; that I had mood swings and emotional symptoms; that I was 'full of anger' which was often directed at her because she was ill; that I got upset because I felt ill so much of the time and could not cope with what was expected of me. I was eventually diagnosed with chronic fatigue syndrome by the doctor at the local children's hospital, where I was being monitored for my size and weight. I remember feeling almost pleased with my diagnosis, even if I was not entirely convinced by it. It made me feel closer to my mother.

'It was awful when you first got ill,' my mother said to me, during that same trip to Norfolk. 'They told me we had a shared hysterical language.'

Hysteria – wasn't that a nineteenth century diagnosis? Did a doctor really tell her that our symptoms, our pain and fatigue, were, in fact, not symptoms of an illness at all, but a – gendered – language that only we could speak and no one else could understand?

'They made me feel so guilty about you,' my mother recalled, 'and at the same time I had to prove my own illness was real. It was an awful time. They told me I was making you ill.'

My mother and I have symptoms of illness without any known cause – according them the status of feelings, confined to our bodies, or our sense of them as ill. Ill – *bad, sick, wrong* – is also how I learnt to feel about my diagnosis. Those ill feelings were not really my own, but reflections of societal ones, which deemed people with ME/CFS as fakers, scroungers, lazy and privileged, and indeed all chronically ill and disabled people as less-than-human, deserving of fewer rights, less pay, and less security and care.

Ill feelings were always something we shared. I never went to support groups or had a friend with the same diagnosis. If I did talk about it to someone else, it didn't feel real, or mine. It is that kind of illness: somehow ubiquitous, or at least recognizable, continually reported on, and always inexplicable. The NHS website describes the main symptom of ME/CFS as 'feeling extremely tired and generally unwell'. It made it all sound so vague – the feeling of being ill, without a reason – no biomarker or treatment or explanation. It is often referred to now as an 'invisible illness', but I don't remember that term when I was growing up.

If illness was our problem, separation appeared to be the only solution. At the suggestion of my grandmother, I even went to a boarding school – my place funded by charity – in the Sussex countryside. I had just turned eleven. Away from my mother, I was unable to *pick up* symptoms off her. I recovered, for a time, but I am not well now, and we are further apart than we have ever been. My grandmother was right about one thing: my mother's illness and my own ill feelings were inexplicably intertwined.

The day after my grandfather collapsed with what would be diagnosed as leukaemia, many years after my mother's first illness, she told me her 'old ME symptoms' had come back. Her mother had already died, and she had taken on the role of her father's primary carer.

'When I lie down in bed my heart feels heavy,' she said to me, 'as if it's been straining to pump blood to my legs all day.'

She had felt the loss of her mother in her body as illness, and now, over the time caring for her father, it was as if that loss in her body had tired her heart. She still had no language for her feelings, besides the terms she has managed to steal from medicine – a form of subterfuge.

'What is fatigue anyway,' she continued, 'your heart not pumping hard enough?'

My grandfather had begun lining up all the tools he could find in his house, from screwdrivers to biros, in rows on the kitchen table. Losing his own grasp on reality and time, he tried to make order out of chaos, a vast chasm or void. With my mother, this disorder was happening in her body: it felt like there was something wrong with her chest or her heart or her legs. These were disturbing sensations that couldn't be measured, tested or diagnosed, let alone treated.

It had taken the doctors at the hospital a few days to diagnose my grandfather with leukaemia as well as dementia. Apparently, he hadn't had a blood test for a long time. The consultant said to my mother that he'd had cancer for months, but he says it like 'for *months*' to make her feel bad for not caring for him properly, as if his health was her responsibility, as if she could diagnose disease with the power of a daughter's duty itself. 'He was wearing an *Yves Saint Laurent* belt,' she told me on the phone, which seemed to prove something, to her at least. We could not speak for too long because using her mobile made her ear hot, to the extent that she thought her brain was being 'zapped'.

'Once you're diagnosed with one thing doctors attribute every problem you have to that one disease,' she said. 'And we know all about that, don't we?' When she speaks to me, she speaks to herself, or to the both of us at once.

In 1868, Alice James's mother called her daughter's teenage affliction 'a case of genuine hysteria for which no cause as yet can be discovered'. Alice's 'nervous turns' were 'not in the least degree morbid in character'; she never seemed to dread an attack and seemed 'perfectly happy when they are over' – the tell-tale sign of nervousness, rather than an underlying physical ailment. The lack of reason for Alice's symptoms was frustrating for both mother and daughter: 'It is a most distressing form of illness, and the most difficult to reach, because so little is known about it.' Alice spent the majority of her adult life in bed or on a sofa, propped up by cushions, known as the invalid sister to her two famous – and prolific – brothers, who often suffered with their own ailments, to the extent that as a family they shared the same body: 'my nerves are his nerves', she wrote of Henry, a devoted brother, 'and my stomach his stomach'.

After Alice's mother contracted bronchial asthma and died in 1882, everyone had expected Alice to get ill. Daughters were known to be affected by the deaths of their parents because of their lives spent at home. Instead, her Aunt Kate reported her 'taking up of household duties that her mother laid down', which 'brought new life to Alice'. Alice and her father moved from Boston into a 'little' three-storey cottage at Manchester-by-the-sea that summer, built in an English country style. Henry Snr got up between 5 and 6 am every morning and wrote until 1 pm, while Alice managed the house, the meals, the workmen and the visitors – 'just as her mother had done'.

'I feel like I've lost my partner,' my mother said, after the death of her father, having returned to care for him. She sounded like Alice, who became her father's replacement wife: 'I used to think I loved my dear Mother & knew her burdens,' she wrote, 'but I find I only knew half them, & that in losing her I am only nearer to her than I ever was before; it is such a happy thought that her dear, tired body is at rest . . . Instead of having lost her it seems sometimes as if I had never known or loved her before.' A singular loss is always experienced as more than itself: it is felt as *total*.

For Alice, becoming a wife, carer and nurse to her father was preferable to another stay at the nursing home for nervous women. It was a way to hold herself together, to stop herself breaking down, or, in her words, 'going under'. Like Alice, we were told we were hysterical, that we were inventing a language of our own demise, that for some reason we needed to be ill to get the attention we desired. My illness could be explained by my mother's. It was as if our personalities were sick.

In July 1890, writing in her diary, Alice recorded that she took a very small amount of morphine, the first in three years, during her last and 'rather excessive and comic' prostration. Taking such a slight dose of opiates, Alice was consequently able to steady her nerves and *experience* the pain (toothache, rheumatic gout and a very bad crick in her neck) 'without distraction', for there is, she thought, 'something very exhilarating in shivering whacks of crude pain which seem to lift you out of the present and its sophistications (great Men unable to have a tooth out without gas!) and ally you to long gone generations'. The unmedicated generations Alice writes of suffered toothache 'such as we can't dream of', but also gendered illnesses lost, not recorded, unheard. When my mother and I enter the doctor's surgery, our symptoms are still opaque and illegible, real and unreal. They are still ours alone to record, and, often, self-medicate.

To relapse is to return, to fall back, or fall off; to *fall from grace*.

When I started to explore my childhood diagnosis, I cycled everywhere, I went to work, I stayed out for late dinners with friends without needing to rest for days before and after. I still had days in bed and knew I couldn't do as much as other people, like work as many days, or do much in the evenings. I knew I got muddled and confused often. I spent most weekends in bed. I got angry and I didn't know why. I knew if I kept trying to keep up with everyone else, I would crash. But I also knew these things were not the same as being ill. Ill was not how I identified. But then: I had never known what 'well' felt like either. As a child I was often very tired, always had a headache and complained of my legs hurting.

When I told my mother I was resigning from my full-time job because I could not manage the hours, and that my relationship had broken down (again), she was strangely surprised. She had thought I was well enough to work, to have a long-term relationship and a social life. I had somehow kept my ill feelings from her too. In fact, they were largely invisible even to myself. It was as if illness was lying dormant in me as a sense of unease, or mistrust in my own feelings.

As time passed – sick time, the time of relapse and re-diagnosis, naming and categorization, treatment and advice – I grew increasingly aware of how many women, and their mothers, I already knew with some form of unexplained illness. These people confided in me, as a fellow sufferer. A friend emailed to tell me she had been diagnosed with 'burn out' after months of suspected ME/CFS. A collaborator told me her sister, who was in her twenties, was still being cared for by her mother at home. A school friend did not realize her mother's fibromyalgia had no known root physical cause, and another's was coming off strong opiates for hers. Someone else told me her mother had once forgotten everyone's names and was still living without a diagnosis for what appeared to be neurological problems with no neurological cause. My own partner's mother revealed it was many years into her marriage before she realized not everyone had pain all the time. They had been there all along, but I had never really seen them. It was as if we had become invisible to each other.

And then I got ill: less and less able to get out of bed before the morning became the afternoon, less mobile, less able to walk very far or stand without support, concentrate long enough to read a book, or go to work for a whole day, or sit at my desk. Less able to control my mood, my anger.

And I got *sick*. I got sick of reading about how mothers 'spread' their borderline personality disorder to their children, stories of 'fatal mothering', and teenagers being detained in psychiatric units because of their diagnosis. I got sick of reading theories that chronic fatigue had something to do with mitochondria, or mice leukaemia, or nematode worms, or that it had nothing at all to do with any of these things after all. I got sick of hearing how half of all people with a diagnosis of ME/CFS also have Lyme disease, and that the bacterium *Borrelia burgdorferi*, which causes symptoms such as tiredness, pain, memory loss and confusion, is also found in seventy per cent of people who have died of Alzheimer's. I got sick of reading about how the ill feelings and strange sensations I had always felt

10

to be real are actually a cry for maternal affection projected onto a female lover: Vita Sackville West, who was 'tender and affectionate to Virginia Woolf in her illness, and making herself more valuable by the threat of absence'. I got sick of reading about some kind of as-yet-unknown 'familial susceptibility' in cases of ME/CFS, about the sort of influence that does not allow space for care and love. I got sick of *all this fucking paperwork*. I got sick of hearing about the relation between mental illness and maternal neglect or absence, which of course sometimes involves the total loss of a mother. I write through this sickness, or sicknesses, knowing all these things are true, and not true, because they are not known, they are felt.

I began writing before the existence of the novel coronavirus. With a global pandemic, and hundreds of thousands of deaths, comes something even stranger, more nebulous: life, post-viral, which does not mean sickness when it has gone away, when the original disease has been cured, and the patient recovered. Within weeks, ME/CFS advocacy groups warned of the coming uptick in cases amongst patients that had recovered from an initial Covid-19 infection. Doctors already studying the biology of ME/CFS started research into coronavirus patients as they recovered. There were reports of people – some of whom had never been tested for corona-virus, because there were so few tests available to begin with – whose symptoms still cycled after months. They found that their family and friends, and even doctors, could not understand why they were still fatigued, suggesting that perhaps it was anxiety, or depression, or deconditioning – terms borrowed from the ME/CFS playbook. When they tried to exercise, they found that it set them back in their recovery, if that was even the right name for it. In 2009, six years after the SARS virus infected around 8,000 people, forty per cent of patients who recovered reported a chronic fatigue problem, and twenty-seven per cent met the modified 1994 Centers for Disease Control and Prevention criteria for chronic fatigue syndrome. What if they never recovered fully?

ME/CFS and FM had not historically been studied enough. Funding had been syphoned off to other diseases in the US, and patients felt abandoned. In the UK, a group of influential psychologists, many of whom had ties to private CBT providers and insurance companies, had misreported that graded exercise and 'cognitive behavioural therapy for erroneous illness beliefs' were effective treatments for ME/CFS in the results of a trial costing the taxpayer £5 million. The NICE guidelines still advised these treatments because they hadn't been reviewed for thirteen years. People with ME/CFS were hopeful that studying coronavirus would shed light on the biological processes underlying their own condition, and devastated by the lack of support after years spent in their beds, at home, with no treatments or financial support, told they could not work or study from home, told it was all in their heads, that they *needed to be ill*, that they had a *shared hysterical language*.

'We'll go as far as the river,' my mother says, having quietly completed her calculation. 'I have to see my river every day.'

Standing at the water, watching one of the dogs walk very carefully across the small rocks on the riverbed, I think about what she said to me the day before, when we were sitting in her garden: that no matter how far she walks each day, she never feels any stronger.

Later, I will read that some researchers have found markedly reduced cardiac mass and total blood volumes, causing orthostatic intolerance and cardiac arrhythmias, including tachycardia (racing heart) or palpitations, in patients with ME/CFS. One study in Japan suggested people with a diagnosis of ME/CFS had smaller hearts, and another suggested that 'non-compliant veins' – veins that were not moving enough blood around the body – were the problem and could explain 'post-exertional malaise'. Maybe my mother was right, and her heart really wasn't pumping hard enough after all.

I want to tell her, to confess, that I have been reading the documents on her desktop and in the paper folders on her dining table, which she has been writing and gathering for her application for Ill Health Retirement. I want to tell her I have been asking her about how she is feeling, and what it was like when I was much younger, when I was also ill and she was even more ill, and nobody seemed to believe us, because I want to know how she is feeling, but also because I want to tell our story. Except I don't.

Dredging a river imposes a brake on the ability of the river to heal itself. When a low-energy river is dredged, it cannot recreate its meanders, pools and riffles; sediment is deposited across the full width of the channel creating excessive and unfocused plant growth. It happened with the Nar, which is a chalk, and therefore relatively rare, river system. Riparian land in these reaches is mostly semi-wild wetland, scrub or meadow. I don't know if dredging up the past makes her less likely to recover from this relapse into illness.

That evening, as we walk back to her house through the fields, she seems stronger to me than she ever has, like she could walk for as long as it was still light. It feels like I am holding her back, willing her to turn and walk home with me.

¶ Basically furious

My mother does not have a letter from the children's hospital confirming my ME/CFS diagnosis, but she does have letters she wrote to doctors and services asking for help. She also has all the appointment cards and the letters relaying negative and normal test results, and the responses to her pleas. She keeps them all in a folder labelled 'Alice – Health'. She calls it my 'health archive'.

'Alice gets exhausted very easily,' my mother wrote to one consultant. 'Alice does not sleep easily but has never been a good sleeper. She gets an ill feeling in her chest region when she is exhausted.'

In rhetoric, but also in medicine, a report by a medical doctor is called an epicrisis, meaning 'a second crisis' from the Greek word for judgement or decision. Epicrises serve an explicit purpose as a contribution to medical knowledge, destined for other 'men of science' to study and learn from. Epicrises are also, by definition, a work in progress – a text that might be re-worked or returned to at any time, written for posterity. In his books on hysteria, Sigmund Freud wrote epicrises in order to share information with his colleagues and the public, to transmit his findings across generations, and create a community of knowledge. Epicrises are written by doctors, but there is also anamnesis, the account the patient writes themselves.

'We just go from crisis to crisis with Alice,' my mother wrote to the local child and adolescent mental health service.

As a mother, when you feel ill and your child feels ill, your instinct is to ask: *what has caused these ill feelings?* You think it might be something in your blood, or your bones, or your brain, or your lungs. It could be a pesticide in the air or a chemical in the products you use, a parasite, a dormant infection. If there is nothing wrong with your blood or your bones, your brain or your lungs, if all the tests come back negative or normal, that means you, as mother and daughter, are made to feel like you are bad for each other. From the outside, this kind of influence can seem dangerous.

Sometimes it is impossible to find an origin for ill feelings. I had contracted Giardia aged two, and my mother says I verbalized my persistent symptoms from when I could first speak, but it seemed my ill feelings were all read through my mother's: they even sounded like the symptoms of atypical pneumonia, the trigger for her chronic illness. It was as if I had watched and learnt how to be ill from my mother.

The doctors wrote back to my mother, and she has kept those letters too. They refer to me as if I was another symptom of my mother's confounding ill health. A letter from an ME specialist in London to my mother's GP confirming her original diagnosis also refers to her 'remaining concern for her daughter Alice', who 'has some difficulties in adjustment and has anxieties and a variety of symptoms that superficially resemble those that her mother has'. Another letter, addressed to my mother, reads: 'My interest in the matter' – the matter being *her* concern for *my* health – 'would be on the basis of a general wish for your situation to be helped by improving hers.' The specialist writes of the unclear extent to which my symptoms reflect 'the use of the common symptom language' with my mother, which he refers to as 'a familiar element in chronic fatigue syndrome', and asks whether these symptoms are in fact 'a way of expressing (my) distress or difficulties'. I found a copy of this letter in a pile of papers relating to her own ill health, on which she had written the phone number for the 90s television show *Changing Rooms*, and a note to herself: 'Alice is angry'.

My anger is a common theme in my mother's letters – her anamnesis of my medical history. 'Alice is full of anger which is often directed at me because I am ill,' my mother writes. 'She gets upset because she feels ill so much of the time and she can't cope with what is expected of her.' This is confirmed in a letter from my GP: 'On direct questioning neither Alice nor her mother felt that she had been depressed although she undoubtedly has mood swings and has at times been low, angry and frustrated by her illness.'

If pain is a kind of evidence, anger is its antidote. 'Art is the guarantee of sanity,' reads the text stitched to the covers of a metal bed in *Cell I* (1991) by Louise Bourgeois. The second half of the quote goes: 'Pain is the ransom of formalism.' There is no mattress on the bed, just the covers, and it is surrounded by wooden doors, and what look like surgical instruments and glass containers. A piece of cotton in a

15

drawer underneath reads 'RAGE'. Bourgeois had her own language for her pain, but also a means to interpret it: her unconscious. In her sculpture and installation, the body is a site of suffering, made of marble, latex or cloth, stitched, bent, twisted and broken. 'The subject of pain is the business I am in,' she said. 'To give meaning and shape to frustration and suffering. The existence of pain cannot be denied. I propose no remedies or excuses.' Why remedy pain, and why excuse it? Pain is evidence of suffering, its marker. Without it, that suffering can be denied.

'You were basically furious and wouldn't speak to him,' my mother says to me, about the doctor at the children's hospital who first diagnosed me with chronic fatigue syndrome in the spring of 1998. 'Our GP said I "needed to be ill" and you were "naughty",' she says, as if these were our real diagnoses. 'She asked you to draw a picture and you refused.' ME/CFS was not even my first unexplained illness. The first was called an 'apparent failure to thrive' – another kind of refusal, all appearances and no evidence.

I was naughty, but I was also ill. What did *drawing a picture* have to do with it?

I could ask why the child my mother described in her letters was so angry, but I am more interested in the question of what constituted that anger, or what seemed to be enacted in its expression.

Our diagnosis – and the symptom language we spoke – contained the histories of two centuries of gendered illness. It was as if that history was inside our actual bodies. As Adrienne Rich wrote in 1969: 'My politics is in my body, accruing and expanding with every act of resistance and each of my failures. / Locked in the closet at 4 years old I beat the wall with my body and that act is in me still.'

Was I sick of feeling angry all day, or angry at feeling sick? I always hated being told to do things. What if I wanted to stay angry, to stay *basically furious*? What if I still do?

My health archive is a record of the help my mother *tried so hard to get me*, and by extension, herself. It is a paper trail, an archive of care and desire, anger and disbelief. This was a woman who had already advocated for her case to be referred to a Professor of

16

Immunology, and was now advocating for her daughter, a child. Still, every attempt was doomed.

'I am writing to you because I am very concerned about the wellbeing of my daughter Alice,' my mother wrote to a consultant at Great Ormond Street Hospital for Children in London, Dr M.J. Dillon, on 10 November 1997. I was ten years old. She was in her mid-thirties. 'Alice has been unwell both physically and emotionally for about two and a half years, which is the same length of time that I have had ME,' she continues. 'Before this she was fairly well, although since the Giardia bug she had when she was two, she has had tummy aches, upset tummies and leg pains. She was under our local children's hospital because she is very small and underweight for her age. She was discharged nearly two years ago when regular visits proved that she was growing and putting on weight.'

She no longer took me to the GP; 'nine times out of ten' she simply let me have a day off school in order to rest. The GP did finally agree to refer me to the children's hospital, but we would have to wait five months for the appointment and my mother was desperate. She went on to explain more about our situation, how my being ill was making her more ill, which was in turn affecting the emotional and mental health of my brother, aged eight at the time, who was 'caught up in the middle', and found the situation distressing too.

'I have tried to do what I can to get help for Alice but just as it has been a battle to get appropriate care for myself it has been equally difficult to know what to do. I try and get her to school most of the time and often go against my gut feelings because of what my family and GP think about our situation. Even if Alice's illness is the result of emotional stress, she is still suffering chronic physical symptoms and something must be done to help her and in turn me. The confrontations and trauma surrounding the situation make it impossible for me to avoid stressful situations which exacerbate my own symptoms, therefore making it very difficult to make a recovery of my own.'

Despite being advised by the GP not to contact Dillon, she had done so anyway. She wanted to ask if he thought I too had chronic

17

fatigue syndrome, and if not, whether he would be able to point her in the direction of a therapist who could help my emotional state, indeed 'the emotional state of the three of us as a family unit'. She enclosed a letter regarding her own health from the specialist, which explained her 'circumstances', details of her illness. It had taken a great deal of persuasion to arrange for her case to be referred to an immunologist in the first place, she adds. Finally, she apologized for taking matters into her own hands, but felt the situation had gone on too long. She had to 'take steps to try and get help.'

During a symposium at the Royal Society of Medicine in 1978 on the subject of 'epidemic neuromyasthenia', the same Dr Dillon had reported on an outbreak of the illness at Great Ormond Street between the beginning of August 1970 and the end of January 1971. 145 patients had been admitted – all staff at the hospital, the majority of them nurses – with headaches, sore throats, nausea, pain in the back and neck and limbs, malaise, vomiting and depression, and some with sensory symptoms, faintness and blurred vision. Their symptoms lasted two to three weeks and then gradually resolved during the next two to three months, but Dillon observed the occurrence of symptomatic relapses over a prolonged period in at least 28 patients. No children who were in-patients during this period were affected, but several were referred in the years following the outbreak: five boys and two girls, aged nine to thirteen. These sporadic cases of what appeared to be the same disease amongst children showed Dillon that the condition was not limited to young adults (103 of the cases he encountered in 1970 were student nurses), and that it might have been more common in the community than was realized at the time. It also highlighted the possibility that adults and children with the disease might have 'already been labelled as psychiatrically disturbed'. One particular symptom was too 'difficult to quantify': 'rapid fatigability reported on exercise' – the defining symptom of what would later be known as ME.

Dillon did not believe the illness he witnessed at Great Ormond Street in 1970–71 had a hysterical basis. Nevertheless, he deliberately limited the number of investigations undertaken in order to prevent fear and anxiety around the illness spreading to a theoretically susceptible population, knowing that this would foil attempts to discover the aetiology of the illness. Despite the fact that no specific infective agent could be isolated, evidence pointed to a possible infective cause: undoubted physical signs in many patients, some abnormalities in their blood serum and lymphocytes, and an observable biphasic pattern, which suggested infection followed by immune response. Dillon thought he might be able to find the infective particles within patients' lymphocytes, some of which grew and multiplied in vitro, similar to lymphoproliferative disorders and infectious mononucleosis, but his investigation into these immune responses was cut short by the loss of the cultures at a relatively early stage: they all perished owing to an incubator failure. However, he felt that these techniques might be the basis of further attempts to define the cause of this disease in future outbreaks.

In January 1997, my mother received a letter back from Dillon. He was sorry to hear of my problems and indeed the problems that also afflicted my mother, 'and hence indirectly her other child', but, he replied, he was unable to review my case. 'This certainly would have been something that I would have been prepared to undertake in days gone by,' reads his letter to my mother, 'but there have been rearrangements in my service to the Hospital such that my ability to provide the type of opinion you are requesting is officially unavailable and because of this I do find requests such as yours very difficult to handle.'

Unable to give a 'clear view' on my case from reading her letter, Dillon added that some of the features I had described to her 'might well be those that one sees in youngsters with chronic fatigue syndromes', but also could be due to 'manifestations of childhood migraine' and 'other factors that might not be in the category of physical that could be contributing in view of the circumstances in which Alice finds herself.' On the top right-hand corner of the letter, sent 15 January 1998 (dictated 1/12/97), is an illustration of a small child in the arms of their mother, with the phrase 'The child first and always.'

What had happened in those two decades between 1978 and 1997, to make Dillon confident that my case probably had no physical aetiology, when he had been so convinced further lab testing of affected patients' blood in vitro would uncover an infectious agent? The only conclusion available to me reading through my health archive was that the 'circumstances' in which I found myself were at least in part due to these 'rearrangements'.

Michael Dillon is now in his eighties and is the Emeritus Professor of Paediatric Nephrology at UCL Great Ormond Street Institute of Child Health in the Faculty of Population Health Sciences. I emailed him to ask if he would be willing speak to me about his experiences at Great Ormond Street. 'It would be lovely to meet you,' I added. Despite the message of his letter to my mother – that he would not be able to help – he seemed kind from his comments at the 1978 symposium, and yet he remained unreal to me, alive only in correspondence and documentation, limited in his action by medical ethics but also bureaucracy. He would be very old by now; his experiences would disappear with his memory. I really wanted to speak to him before that happened.

He replied, saying my plan to write about my and my mother's experience of unexplained illness sounded like 'a major project', and he hoped that it all went well, but was sorry to say that he was not willing to talk to me about his experience at GOSH for a number of reasons. 'Firstly, I'm now an octogenarian, having retired in 2002, and detailed memories of disorders that at one time I was familiar with are now far from clear. Secondly, many years ago, I decided, on principle, not to become involved in such activities on the basis that I was so far removed from the front line of clinical care and current thinking that I would be at risk of misleading those asking for information.'

There was no way to tell him I didn't want information about his patients. I wanted to know what he experienced, and how he felt about it.

'I am really sorry to disappoint you but hope that you understand my dilemma.'

I had already fantasized about going to his house and noting down all the objects on his writing desk – I imagined he had one, for replying to emails at least – and about him telling me the story of those twenty years of lost time. I wanted to know if he was ever excited about the prospect of being at the forefront of a disease, or whether research into ME/CFS was doomed from the start. I had so many unanswered, or unanswerable, questions. And I still wanted to know: what had changed at Great Ormond Street in the 1990s; what 'rearrangements' had occurred so that a doctor with twenty years' experience of ME/CFS in children was officially unavailable to offer an opinion on a case of a child with the diagnosis? Had he just said there were 'rearrangements in the hospital' to let my mother down gently? What had happened to make this man, at one time able to consult on cases of ME/CFS in children, maybe even the first person to assert that children could have the same symptoms, unable to do so? In 1978, at the RSM symposium, those who had observed the illness concluded their patients were not fabricating their illness and expressed concern that they were being treated psychiatrically. Nevertheless, my mother and I, and many others like us, were still being called *hysterical* twenty years later.

Like my mother, I went against my gut feelings, and sent him another email. He did not reply again.

When I first read the doctors' letters in my 'health archive', I felt like I was reading about someone I didn't know, or vaguely remembered. I always thought my mother was trying to get me diagnosed with the same illness as her, an illness that she was convinced had a physical cause, but that wasn't true at all. My mother remembers correctly that she was blamed for making me feel angry and ill, but she has forgotten they also suggested the opposite: I was making her sick. If they fixed me, they would inadvertently fix her. These circumstances were, of course, impossible to untangle, just like our 'shared language' of 'common hysterical symptoms'. It wasn't our symptoms that seemed to have no physical cause, it was our 'circumstances', to quote one of the doctors when referring to our relation to one another, that made both of us *very difficult to handle*.

21

The health archive she gave me was the first archive. But there were so many more.

- A sick diarist's letters to her famous brothers, and the diary she dictated to the woman she loved
- My teenage diaries, which somehow didn't get destroyed
- An academic's letters to scientists, physicians and journal editors on bad medical trials that numbered into the hundreds, all stored on his colleague's blog
- A bank of anonymized blood, and a database of hand grip test scores and consent forms
- An inaccessible paper archive in a house in Scotland that hadn't been dusted since its custodian died
- Outdated guidelines, twice postponed – and then again
- Hundreds of research papers and trial results that cannot be compared because of sprawling definitions

There was always more being added, but there were also so many gaps, so many conferences undocumented and YouTube videos deleted, and accounts that never got written, let alone saved and stored and protected.

Then there was the question of piecing together an archive of illness. As anyone who works with archival material knows, as soon as you think it holds together pieces fall away. My mother knows this well. She is a collector, an archivist, a lover of the objects loved by other people. The archives I have access to are generally not made of dusty paper and books, or clothing, like the archives my mother cares for. My archive of illness is made up of digital scans, and websites hosted on university servers, accessed mainly from bed, cheap books I can get sent to my house, and photos on my phone.

There is a copy of Carolyn Steedman's *Dust* on my mother's bookshelf, annotated, probably, with Post-it notes sticking out of the pages. In my memory, the book is about the material of archives, of being choked by your own dusty desire, of the muck of it getting in your hair and skin and mouth, how inhaling it can make you fall in love, inflict archive fever or *mal d'archive*, as Jacques Derrida famously called it in a lecture he gave in 1994, around the time my mother first fell ill. It can make you so sick you burn with passion, 'never to rest, interminably, from searching for the archive right where it slips away'; 'an irrepressible desire to return to the origin, a homesickness, a nostalgia for the return to the most archaic place of absolute commencement.' In this sense, archive fever is a kind of *relapse*.

¶ Unknown aetiology

The first outbreak of what was then called 'epidemic neuromyas-thenia' occurred in the Los Angeles area in May 1934. There had been an unusual prevalence of poliomyelitis, commonly referred to as polio, in California for the season, of which localized epidemics had begun to appear around 1900. Medical and nursing staff of Los Angeles County General Hospital began to present with what initially appeared to be polio – a systemic infection in the membrane surrounding the brain and spinal cord, affecting the whole body of the patient – but their symptoms were inconsistent with the disease, suggesting this infection was somehow related to polio and yet altogether new. Double vision, constipation and retention of urine were more common in these new patients, and weakness occurred without the usual severe atrophy; pain and muscle tenderness, tingling and excessive skin sensitivity persisted for longer. Members of staff admitted to the hospital also presented with mental disturbances, loss of concentration and lapses of memory, sleep disturbances, fatigue after walking short distances and what was termed 'emotional lability with hysterical episodes and trophic changes'. Recurrences of systemic and neurological symptoms were frequent, and, in some cases, patients were more disabled by a relapse than by the original illness. The main feature that distinguished this new infection from polio was its death count: although a high number of those affected fell ill – a total of 198 staff at the hospital, a case incidence of four-and-a-half per cent – none actually died.

There was, however, clearly something wrong. Pathological changes found in patients dying from polio in the 1934 Los Angeles epidemic, and in monkeys inoculated with the Californian strain of the virus, showed differences from those previously reported in polio. Destruction of neurones was reduced and there was more marked diffuse perivascular round cell infiltration – or inflammation – in the samples. Observers of this epidemic concluded that the disease was spread by direct personal contact, and not by contamination of the hospital milk or food supply, but they couldn't find a definitive cause – either the strain was new, or they were dealing with a disease of unknown aetiology.

24

As members of the hospital staff most closely associated with patients and more likely to live in hospital residences, student nurses were the most affected, which meant three quarters of those affected were women. Considering many men have a diagnosis of ME/CFS, I have always wondered where the association between the diagnosis and women had actually come from. Perhaps it arose from the likelihood of nurses being affected in the early outbreaks of the disease, and of those nurses being women. The LA County Hospital outbreak might have been the first outbreak like it, but it was not the last.

In October 1957, Medical Staff of the Royal Free Hospital, then located on Gray's Inn Road in London, reported an outbreak of an 'obscure illness', which had occurred two years earlier. On 13 July 1955, a resident doctor and a ward sister were admitted to hospital. Within two weeks, more than seventy members of the staff were affected. The hospital was closed because of the threat to the health of patients of what appeared to be an infection affecting the nervous system. Besides, a large number of nurses had taken sick, making it impossible to keep the Royal Free operational. By 24 November, 292 members of the medical, nursing, auxiliary medical, ancillary and administrative staff had been affected by the illness, and 255 people were hospitalised. Cases seemed to vary, both in the content of the extensive range of symptoms and signs, and the speed with which the illness evolved. Patients presented with malaise and headaches, but also sore throats, dizziness, nausea and pain in their abdomen, limbs and back. As in LA in 1934, extensive investigations done in the hospital and many other institutes, including potential toxic causes, failed to reveal an aetiological agent of an infective nature, and no characteristic biochemical changes attributable to the disease were found. In many patients, the symptoms waxed and waned in intensity over a long period. These symptoms, the most characteristic of which was prolonged painful muscle spasms, were frequently associated with what the doctors treating them called 'disproportionate depression and emotional lability'.

To *obscure* is to not express yourself clearly, but it is also to *keep from being seen*, to conceal.

Two nurses aged nineteen and twenty-four, both with recorded histories of psychosis, appeared to present with 'hysterical features'.

25

They were also found to have abnormal electromyograms, which measure the electrical signals sent by the brain to nerves and muscles. In one case, partial paralysis was unaffected by hypnosis and remained unchanged for twelve years, while other symptoms disappeared. Both nurses were diagnosed as cases of 'benign myalgic encephalomyelitis'. Their doctor, R.E. Kendell, stressed the lack of evidence of mental instability his patients had shown, even when coming to terms with the limitations their disease imposed on them, which sometimes necessitated giving up their occupations. 'The issue is important because other young women have been, and will continue to be, diagnosed as hysterical under similar circumstances with the resulting risk of their treatment being misdirected and their doctors' attitudes to them altered in unhelpful ways,' he said. 'As a result of the widespread impression that they are "neurotic" some have received scant sympathy or understanding from their doctors.'

The outbreak at the Royal Free was not confined to Gray's Inn Road and was only an indicator of its presence in the wider community. Dr Melvin Ramsay was a consultant physician in the Infectious Diseases Department of the Royal Free Hospital during the outbreak. He saw fifty-three patients admitted to the hospital from the community between April 1955 and September 1957, suffering from 'epidemic neuromyasthenia', meaning the condition was endemic in the general population before, during and after the outbreak among the staff of the hospital. He also observed similar cases in the population of North West London before the outbreak at the Royal Free, and sporadic cases that continued to occur afterwards. 'Epidemic neuromyasthenia' also occurred in Dalston, Cumberland in February 1955, but Ramsay and his colleagues were not aware of that when they began to admit the substantial number of very puzzling cases two months later. He found mental changes were a feature of a considerable number of cases, and emotional lability and impairment of both memory and concentration were common. Vivid and terrifying nightmares were often reported. There were sometimes marked changes in personality. Many patients over-elaborated the recital of their symptoms and this was associated with impairment of judgement and/or insight, rather than hysteria. Mental as well as physical exhaustion could be severe.

By the time of the RSM symposium in 1978, Melvin Ramsay had encountered well over 300 people incapacitated to varying degrees. He had seen cases coming from all over the UK: Edinburgh, Manchester, Stockport, Wigan, Guildford and Lancing in Sussex, all of which seemed to commence with some sort of infection, often respiratory, but also gastrointestinal. In some cases, the illness came on suddenly, and in a few insidiously. They presented with abnormal muscular fatigability which often had a 'diurnal perio- dicity', a circadian rhythm with primary expression during daylight hours, meaning they may have been fresh in the morning but by mid-afternoon they were compelled to rest. Tingling in the limbs and around the mouth were common, but Ramsay had also encoun- tered two patients who complained of complete deadness in a limb, so they felt like 'a block of ice'. In these sporadic patients, he saw symptoms like those at the Royal Free: severe muscle spasms and twitching, impairment of memory and inability to concentrate, increased sensitivity to cold (practically all of them complained of coldness of the extremities), severe sweating (usually at night) and frequent urination. In many patients the phenomenon of the appear- ance of a 'ghastly facial pallor' was noted by friends or relatives. Two doctors with the diagnosis had found they had difficulty in getting their words right, saying 'hot' when they meant 'cold' or 'right' when they meant 'wrong'. One said she found she began a sentence but could not finish it. Some had blurred vision, and occasionally, true double vision. Ramsay had seen a vast number of people incapaci- tated on account of profound muscle weakness.

Confusion over what to call the disease had lasted decades. Outbreaks of 'Epidemic neuromyasthenia' had been so remarkable that they got their own names, such as 'Iceland disease' and 'Royal Free disease', confining them to specific historical moments and the places they originated, despite the consistent documentation of sporadic cases outside close-knit communities and confined envi- ronments such as schools and hospitals. A single name was needed, but it was impossible to agree on whether these were all cases of

27

the same disease. The term 'neuromyasthenia' itself was medically incorrect, suggesting a relation to myasthenia gravis – a chronic autoimmune, neuromuscular disease that causes weakness in the skeletal muscles – rather than what was more accurately described as 'muscle fatigability'. Some had taken to calling the disease 'benign', because no deaths had been recorded, but that too was misleading. Doctors, including Ramsay, who convened the symposium, had encountered a vast number of incapacitated people with biological markers of disease, including myelopathic lesions and irritable cerebral phenomena. Some patients were so 'impressively sick' that they had to be tube fed.

According to Mair Thomas from the Epidemiological Research Laboratory, who also presented at the symposium, the problem with finding the cause was that there was still no co-ordination of basic standard studies, diagnostic tests and long-term survey of patients, meaning many cases outside of the known outbreaks had most likely been missed entirely. Outbreaks of 'epidemic neuromyasthenia' had not been running a regular or predictable course like that of measles or whooping cough. Clustering at twenty-year intervals, he noted, was perhaps due to the way scientific research is shared: one account had stimulated the publication of others. 'This may itself be related to the uncertainty of diagnosis,' Thomas suggested; 'A precise clinical description of the disease concerned greatly assists epidemiological studies. The syndromes of "epidemic neuromyasthenia" described have features suggestive of an organic disease of infective origin, perhaps better described as epidemic myalgic encephalopathies', or inflammation of the brain and spinal cord, typically due to acute viral infection.

What first struck me about the research presented at the symposium at the Royal Society of Medicine in 1978 was the ease with which doctors who had encountered incapacitated people during these outbreaks believed the illness affected both mind and body, rather than one or the other. Strong evidence seemed to support an 'organic basis' for the disease, from both neurological findings and immunological findings, including high incidence of serum anti-complementary activity and the presence of ill-defined aggregates on

28

electron microscopy of acute-phase sera (lymphocytes from patients could proliferate and survive in vitro for up to nineteen weeks, which was a perplexing finding, suggesting the possibility of a persistent viral infection). Despite the assertion of an organic basis, it was agreed that some purely psychiatric symptoms could well occur, particularly in patients entering the 'chronic' phase, and that in an epidemic, some hysterical persons could simulate the symptoms of the disease.

None of the doctors who treated cases of 'epidemic neuromyasthenia' during the Royal Free epidemic believed patients were making up their illness or suffering with hysteria. Although psychological disturbance was recognized as a component of the illness, many of them had been investigated by psychiatrists who found they did not fit into any recognized psychiatric category, and only in a few cases was the disease itself considered to be psychogenic in orgin. Besides, the repeated occurrence of low-grade fever, lymphadenopathy, ocular palsies and facial palsy rendered a psychological source untenable. Even so, in 1970, two psychiatrists, Drs C. P. McEvedy and A.W. Beard, had put forward the hypothesis that there was never any infectious agent at the Royal Free, 'mass hysteria' was the only explanation for the outbreak. Despite the fact that some people were still disabled by their initial illness, McEvedy and Beard insisted the disease 'proved relatively benign and though a few of the affected suffered some disability for up to a year, no one died of it'. They also ignored the existence of the sporadic cases in London before and after the outbreak at the Royal Free. They made these assertions in the *British Medical Journal*, fifteen years after the outbreak, the same year the Great Ormond Street outbreak occurred, by consulting case notes, and without speaking to any of Ramsey's patients. They based their argument on the following notations: the intensity of the malaise compared with the slight fever, the presence of similar subjective features as those noted during a previous epidemic of over-breathing, numbness in the hands and legs, normal findings in special investigations and the high attack rate in females.

Despite various disagreements, the RSM group settled on a new name for the syndrome many of them had seen during outbreaks at the Royal Free in 1955 and GOS in 1970, and in epidemic and sporadic cases since: myalgic encephalomyelitis, or ME. The description of what they agreed to call ME reads much like the one we have for ME/CFS today: 'One characteristic feature of the disease is exhaustion, any effort producing generalised fatigue. Often there are psychiatric abnormalities, especially emotional lability and lack of concentration. The clinical outcome may take any of three courses: some patients recover completely, some follow a relapsing course, and some are permanently incapacitated.' It was the first time ME was defined as a 'distinct nosological entity', or a category of disease, without a clear putative agent.

There are no records of the 1978 symposium at the Society's archive, which sounds remarkable considering its role in the history of ME, but is, apparently, not altogether unusual. A librarian at the RSM told me he has never been able to find any material relating to it, but that at the time symposia were – in general – more likely to be reported on by the medical press rather than documented by the society itself. Indeed, the papers given that day were reproduced in the *BMJ's Postgraduate Medical Journal* and it was also written up in the *BMJ*. 'We still know nothing about the nature and cause of epidemic myalgic encephalomyelitis,' the article concludes, 'but outbreaks are still occurring.'

Many ME/CFS patients live without a diagnosis for years, in part because there is no reliable treatment for it anyway. In one survey, more than seventy per cent of ME/CFS patients reported seeing four or more doctors before receiving a diagnosis. 'The victims of ME should no longer have to dread the verdict of, "All your tests are normal. Therefore there is nothing wrong with you",' writes Ramsay, as he reaches the end of his account of the 'saga of the Royal Free disease', published in 1986. 'The basic essential in treatment is correct diagnosis. That is a truism which might be said to apply to all human ailments but I have never seen it so vividly illustrated as in victims of ME.'

If the basis for treatment is correct diagnosis, as Ramsay said, the problem remains: no one knows its cause. What if ME/CFS is not an exception to the rule, but proof that the rule itself is faulty, broken?

Before she wrote about archives, Carolyn Steedman wrote a book about her working-class childhood, and her experiences of growing up in the 1950s with a mother who desired material things. Her story didn't sound like the accounts of working-class childhoods written by men, who associated their class experience with a lack of materialism: her mother wanted everything money could buy, including the 'new look' skirt and a timbered country cottage. Neither does Steedman find her story in Freud's case histories, or in middle-class autobiographies of girlhood and womanhood, which use the outlines of conventional romantic fiction to tell a life story.

Who else has lived lives that challenge dominant narratives – about class, and family, and race, and illness? Who has stories to tell to make sense of the place we currently inhabit that cannot be absorbed into the central one, both a disruption and an essential counterpoint?

Diagnosis is a naming exercise. It groups you together with others 'like you', turning your singular experience into one of many. But it is also a condemnation. Some have called ME/CFS the 'trash can' of diagnoses. My mother's diagnosis was not *rubbish* because of the prognosis, or wide-ranging symptoms, including for the most severely affected, many years in bed, which is indeed awful in and of itself, but because the name conferred something else: that you couldn't be helped, that there was nothing to be done for you, except what you could do for yourself. You had to adjust your own erroneous symptoms and beliefs, stop speaking that hysterical language, build up your exercise tolerance even if your body screams 'No.'

It was not that I didn't want to be disabled. There was no shame in that. The shame arose in encounters with able people, specifically when their idea of me and my inherent bodily knowledge of my own needs and limitations did not align with their intellectual assumptions. Growing up, I soon found that when I felt too ill to be a 'normal' teenager, I was told I was not deserving of 'special' treatment, and when I behaved as a 'normal' teenager, I betrayed their idea of a sick one. After all, how was I to know what was best for me, I was only a child. But we – disabled people – will always be treated like children.

'My mother's longing shaped my own childhood,' wrote Steedman. Living in a Lancashire mill town, wanting more than she had, material things that were withheld from her by a class system, her mother blamed the world. This made her mother's stories into political analysis and allows a political interpretation to be made of her life. It is not just the facts of history – however personal, or familial – that influences a life, but how you tell it, how you recover and rework it.

My apparent mimicry of my mother's symptoms – and my anger, mood swings and emotional outbursts as she describes in her letters – reflected badly on her as a mother. She appeared to create the conditions in which this mimicry occurred. She looked like a bad mother, a bad influence. I was certainly made to feel guilty for my ill feelings by my grandmother, who suggested I was mimicking her symptoms, that I was faking it, and I needed to 'give her a break'. I imagined my grandmother attacked my mother in the same way, blaming her for my ill feelings.

My mother. She sang with me. Held me and bathed me. She placed foldout books around me like a full-body halo. She was my primary caretaker. For a while it was just she and I together – she often likes to remind me of that. I do not know why my grandmother thought I must be faking my mother's equally unexplained illness – I never asked her. I always knew my illness was a form of love.

My mother's illness – perceived as a need, or a longing to be ill – shaped my childhood, but it was me who spread the blame around, directed back at her, and myself, as well as the doctors and services my mother pleaded with for help. We were both powerless, with no one to help us. And we were the fortunate ones. We were white, poor but middle class. She knew how to advocate for herself and me, even if she did not have the energy to do so. I suspect the vast majority of people cannot.

I am writing about my mother, and in writing about my mother I am looking for her, but I am also writing about myself.

The shared hysterical language between my mother and me, our way of speaking to one another, was incomprehensible to others for a reason. It was a potentially powerful means of resistance, of subversion, even, to the structures that deemed us sick, and therefore worthless, something to be feared. Our anger, our rage, threatened to demolish discourse. If we couldn't speak then we couldn't relate to one another, sustain the shared hysterical language that protected us and gave us power. If we were silenced long enough, we might even forget how to speak altogether.

I do not have an answer for my ill feelings, but I think the shared hysterical language between my mother and I had something to do with sharing our pain, as well as our influence on each other. It was the movement outwards of something contained within me – 'the equivalent loop now projected into the external world', as Elaine Scarry put it in her book on pain and language. Ill feelings were the way I could make my self-contained, private, obscure pain, and my imagining of it, visible. It was the way I could share my pain with my mother and share my mother's pain.

Along with my health archive, my mother sent me some diary pages I must have written in my first year at boarding school.

'As I have said before,' I wrote, on a diary page titled 'School', which implies that I wrote more often than I remember, 'there is no one I can talk to here.' My theory appears to be that no one can take me seriously 'because I am so small': 'People only listen to me when they ask how big my feet are. All they can do is measure them up to me.' I recall a time from 'my old school', when I was measured by the other pupils in my class to see if I was a metre tall. 'I felt like an object,' I wrote, 'being used to play jokes on.' On the page titled 'Boys', I seem to have anticipated being 'left out' in social situations, seemingly without putting myself into them in the first place – perhaps I hadn't really been interested in boys that much at the time? – and make excuses for not doing things. 'I am on bed rest any way most of the time,' I wrote, which is also why I am 'so behind with my work'.

Even when 'let off' sports, I had to earn my favour, passing out oranges at the end of the steeplechase. It was implied that there was no question that I could not run, but that I seemed to refuse to run. When I was suddenly ill with a legitimate problem, the sympathy I received far outweighed my experience. I felt worse with chronic fatigue syndrome than shingles, or flu. Those things I could recover from. 'All I want to do right now is go home and go to bed.'

The 'ME' page of my school diary details my parents splitting up – apparently, my dad 'buggered off', which is not exactly what happened – and my mother being ill with ME, 'but it's not catching'. The sentences on illness – my attempt at narrating my own experience of feeling ill – come off as impersonal. It's if I am writing in character: 'Alice is the name, having ME is the game.'

Separated from my mother at school, I begged to be let off my lessons two, three times a week. I had most of the symptoms listed on the meningitis poster on the wall in the waiting room. 'Sleep is the only thing I'm good at. Being ill is one of my great pastimes.

Having a crap life is my hobby. My bed is the best place for me, not boarding school.'

After my Meningitis C vaccination, I woke up to my bed spinning, unable to speak, to shout for help. I got out, the bed still spinning, and dropped to the floor. I wasn't scared, I knew I had to wait there until it passed. I knew I had to believe that it would pass. The next year, I got shingles. The doctor at school seemed almost pleased with me. Unlike my case of mysterious – and dubious – fatigue, headaches, and inability to concentrate or remember basic information, he could prescribe me drugs to reduce the risk of post-herpetic neuralgia (nerve pain that can last for years if untreated) and ointment for the burning skin around the base of my ribs from spine to navel, exactly half the circumference of my torso. For years I could feel an odd tingling on that part of my body. It felt medieval, a witch's disease, a kind of punishment. I had this image of the virus moving towards my skin in gentle streams, the skin flaring pink when it got to the limit of my body, like that photograph of lightning flowers. If the rash joins up that means you're going to die, or that's what my friend and I told everyone.

I read the way this virus attacked my body, like the bad reaction to vaccines, as evidence of my wrecked immune system. It was all part of the illness I had, something that filled me up to the edges of my body, flowed invisibly with the blood underneath my skin. The way I got used to the ache in my head. Flinching when touched. Pain in the front of my legs I couldn't remember not having, like someone slicing open the muscle encasing my shins, and the strain in my arms when I raised them above my waist, as if they were being pulled back down, or I was weighted by my hands. Everything was always worst when I woke up, unrested, the prospect of a day of lessons ahead of me, and at night, no distractions, sleeping bodies all around me.

I was forced to 'rest' in the afternoons at an allotted time each day, rather than whenever I needed, or wanted, to. And I wasn't allowed to rest in my own bed in the dormitory, I had to go to one of the rooms in the infirmary, where you went if you had something infectious and needed to be looked after by a nurse. I was not permitted to miss any lessons. Rest felt like homework, a different kind of lesson, or punishment. I had to be supervised in case I got it wrong or I was just faking it. I crept around the hallways inventing my own secret narratives, or sneaked in books so I had something to do, which only compounded my feelings of guilt, and fraudulence. I acted out scenarios. Plays just for me. In other words, I resisted, like Virginia, who, in her recumbence, performed an alternative to 'the upright masses' who go to work every day, and, in writing rather than resting, opposed the doctors who prescribed total rest – on their terms – as a cure for her physical and emotional ailments.

'Lessons are hard for me,' I wrote, 'especially when they are easy for everyone else. I am not going to lessons tomorrow, even if it means going to the infirmary. No one is more ill than me in the hole (sic) house.'

I felt shame when I got things wrong, but also when I asked for help, when I made myself visible to others who refused to see me as anything other than a problem – as someone who did not fit in to the world of the healthy or the sick. I went to the infirmary so I did not have to go to lessons. I often felt too ill to go to classes, where the fluorescent lights made my headaches worse, and my mind could go blank at any moment. I went to the infirmary to make myself absent: to *absent* myself.

'I suppose I have gone mad, talking to paper,' I wrote.

You write a diary to say something to yourself and for yourself, but it is also for posterity. Because I felt ill, and the illness I was diagnosed with had no apparent cause, perhaps that unseen, future reader was my future self. The last sentence, in parentheses, reads, 'I know none of this makes sense, but it just helps me to let it out.'

I wrote my mother a letter from my bed at school: 'I drew a picture for you, so you can look at it and remember me.' (The picture on the other side of the page is of two winged figures, drawn in light coloured pencil – yellow and blue. I must have copied it from somewhere.) I told my mother that matron had got me a pass for hockey and swimming: 'I have been off all day today because I have felt horrible. That's why I had time to draw this.' It was as if I knew I

36

needed an excuse, a reason to spend my time drawing pictures and writing letters, rather than going to lessons and sports.

I am sad for the child who wrote those diary pages, and that letter to her mother, who was clueless that the structure of care surrounding her was built on mistrust.

I realize now that I felt shame that I was not ill *enough*.

'But I supposed all the trouble of body, soul and spirit had been too much for me,' wrote Rose la Touche in her 1867 diary-cum-autobiography, recalling her relatively recent 'child-life', 'for on Monday morning I had a terrible headache and before evening was very ill. It was a strange illness – I can't tell about it gradually but look back upon it – I know I suffered terribly. (I was in bed about four weeks). Everything hurt me. People coming in and talking however kindly, used to give me tortures of pain – I seemed to think through my head, and every thought hurt me.'

I know that feeling, of every sound or touch hurting. There is no metaphor for *everything hurts*.

'I used to sit up nights and pray, more for the sadness, which I could not bear to see, than for the wickedness which made me tremble to think of,' – Rose was nineteen, sick with nervous illness. 'It was a most terrible time for I got utterly puzzled and the terrible feeling of wickedness haunted me like a nightmare.' She found refuge in the psalms. (Rose recalls how her mother refused to go to her Holy Communion because it had rained, which she said was a sign.) 'I was angry sometimes but not then, only so tired I could only rest,' she wrote, as if still exhausted by the experience. Light hurt her, and food hurt her, to the extent that she seemed to hurt herself. Even the doctors were frightened, but not Rose, who never minded being weak, 'only the pain'. My mother and Rose speak almost in unison: *It was a terrible time.*

'She was a marvellous little thing when she was younger,' John Ruskin told his friend Charles Eliot Norton in 1863, the year of Rose la Touche's 'terrible time', when her parents were arguing over religion, and whether or not she should be confirmed. Rose's mother had asked the artist and writer to give her drawing lessons in 1858,

37

when Rose was nine years old. Ruskin became infatuated with Rose, who, he wrote, 'walked like a little white statue through the twilight woods, talking solemnly'. Rose had already become ill, and a teenager. She was no longer a child due to her illness; 'but there came on some over excitement of the brain, causing occasional loss of consciousness', continued Ruskin, 'and now she often seems only half herself, as if partly dreaming.'

Ruskin – already divorced on the plea of 'incurable impotency' – had proposed marriage when Rose was eighteen, but Rose refused. Rose was living between nursing homes and the expensive Shelbourne Hotel, which Tim Hilton, Ruskin's biographer, calls the 'best in Ireland'. Rose's mother, Maria, found Ruskin's affection for her young daughter intolerable, especially in light of her 'tendency to cerebral disease'. Ruskin dreamed of a beautiful, innocent snake with a slender neck and a green ring around it, which became a fat thing, like a leech, and adhered itself to his hand. Maria was the serpent monster of his dreams.

Only half herself – Where did the other half of Rose go, and did it fall away or disappear in retreat; did it willingly escape? In her diary, Rose leaves a clue to being only 'half herself': she was only 'half-believed' by doctors that she was actually sick, and, as a result, was 'obliged as it were to work half against myself'. *Only half herself* sounds like a refusal to be present, it sounds like disassociation. Resisting wholeness, Rose absented herself in sickness, too. Perhaps it took all her energy to be any part of herself at all.

Rose's ill feelings sprang from the sense that she was bad. 'I can remember distinctly feeling naughty when I was about two or three years old, or rather perhaps I should say, being wicked – I used to get angry, and pinch my brother and sister and would rather destroy a thing if I did not want it than give it to them.' As she grew older, Rose explained in her diary, she became ill out of an obsession with trying to do Right. She loved Religion, listened to and absorbed her father's Baptist doctrines, fasted and prayed and read God's Holy Word. She read the Bible, but 'not ostentatiously', hiding it under the table whenever her brother or sister came in the room. Her father told her that the things that concerned God were 'the only real and important things', which meant she lost pleasure in almost everything else. To Rose, 'games and pleasures seemed to get utterly small and tasteless'. Everything she had once liked she soon thought was wrong. This struggle, between being good and enjoying her childhood, made her 'irritable and unchildlike', and precipitated the demise of her health. 'So I got ill and things used to make my head ache constantly,' she wrote, 'and it was a weary period, all that of childhood. I was not often happy.'

What remains of Rose's diary contains scant mention of the doctors who treated her for nervous illness. When she does write of them, it is to remark on their restricted view of her case, thinking so much more about her body than about her head. The treatments prescribed included forced feeding, which only caused more pain: 'They made me eat, but I could not, for it hurt me so'; 'I did what they told me but suffered dreadfully and seemed to get worse'; 'I knew I ought to lie quiet and not think and I did it.' Her doctors seem to oppose her for being in her own – childish, female – body. She had to fight, like my mother did for me. 'I saw clearly what was the matter with me' – but the doctors would not believe she knew what was best for herself. 'They said I could not know, and went their own way . . . if only they had known how they hurt me sometimes and how the pain pulled me down worse than the weakness!' But it was not only the doctors; she even knew that people talking to her, even people she loved, made her worse, and said so. 'But it was very hard to make them understand and that tortured me.'

Rose thought she must have been a dreary pupil to her governess, with a 'strange heavy aching' in her head that put a stop to her enjoyment and study. Besides, when she was well and 'really brightened up', Rose felt she could understand things better than her governess, 'and that was uncomfortable'. Her governess always spared her if she confessed to a headache, but she didn't often, because 'it was almost always there'. Rose's headaches were my headaches; headaches that *seemed to last all day*. Like mine, Rose's doubts would multiply in the evening. At night ('always the worst time for trouble of any sort') her head used to 'seem *alive* with pain'. Her second maid was, by contrast, 'a great help'; 'nobody else sympathised', she wrote, '– only laughed at me'. Rose obeyed her father, but it was with her mother that she had stimulating debates – her mother, who read to her every morning.

Rose's account of her strange illness is, like most writing of sickness, retrospective. You cannot tell about it gradually, only look back upon it. I am Rose, 'in the middle of writing the history of my Child-life', the time *I got ill* thinking I was bad, naughty and wrong, realizing I am so much the same still, 'so entirely the same I might say', 'finding new Wrongnesses, without'.

As a child I too *got ill*, never fully well, or full of energy, never sleeping through the night, or waking up rested. I looked ill, and too small. I complained of headaches and pains in my limbs. As an adult, my ill feelings are not so different, but I am less likely to be called naughty or disobedient. I take my prescription medication, and sometimes other drugs obtained illegally. I take zinc and vitamin C, valerian hops, magnesium and vitamin B12, when I remember. I stretch and roll through sets of movements learnt from YouTube videos. I even go to hydrotherapy, even though it is cold and humiliating. And yet, I am still as angry as my ten-year-old self, still *basically* furious. I am still disobedient, still made to feel responsible for my ill feelings, as though I have brought them on myself.

How do you unlearn that ill feelings are bad?

The first time I kept a diary, I was around nine years old and already knew better. In it, I wrote about my frustration with my mother, along the lines of, 'Why can't she be like everyone else?' – rather than queer, separated and ill in bed all the time. I left the diary at my grandmother's house. She found it, and read it, and then my mother read it. I'm sure my childish spite proved something to my grandmother. I'm sure my mother was furious – I had betrayed her, written things I didn't even believe. From then on, if I ever wanted to write something down, to *let it out*, I wrote on loose sheets of A4 paper, as if they were just notes or a draft, and could be easily disposed of.

I don't know how or when my mother got hold of all the diary pages, only that she 'found' them, and kept them. She didn't want to send them to me at first, but not because she felt embarrassed at having invaded my privacy – her reluctance was her way of protecting me. It was as if reading my writing, hearing the small voice that I had somehow briefly found in myself before throwing it away, would have upset me. She did not yet know I wanted to hear that voice, the evidence of which was so easily discarded and forgotten. I am piecing together a diary of that time from the scraps that my mother – and I – kept. I am speaking with her, and through her, rather than for her. Much like the mind and the body, my mother and I are not separate. Our illnesses have always intertwined, snaking around one another.

As a child, my body was the place where badness showed itself, and made me visible. Shame is the horror of being seen. Shame is toxic, harmful not healing, or that is what we are told. Shame is what makes you want to disappear, to become invisible in the face of others, as invisible as your illness. As attitudes towards gender, sexuality and race have shifted, we have learnt to take pride in the ways we identify, to make ourselves visible in order to deny shame its power over us. But if illness is a source of shame, and perhaps even its expression, then that feeling needs to be attended to, not counteracted with pride. Shame, in this sense, is a valuable emotion. Shame is the fact of living a disapproved life, of living a sick life, an internal experience that is measured and judged by others who say, 'You look well.'

As a teenager, I learnt to hide my illness. I had already realized that making my ill feelings visible only made me suspicious, untrustworthy. At fourteen, three and a half years into secondary school, I reflected on my experience of disbelief in my diary, remembering 'the times when the infirmary sent me away', when I needed help most and 'they have not provided'. I found out later that my housemistress had instructed the nurses at the infirmary to send me to lessons even if I had gone to them saying I was feeling too ill. 'I feel so shit because no one really believes me or cares enough to believe me or understands enough to believe me,' I wrote.

At the back of the diary – purple plastic cover, that thin kind of paper that crinkles up when you write too hard on it in biro – there

is a series of poem-like texts, different to the diary entries that list my
daily symptoms of fatigue and headaches, which attempt to expand
the vocabulary of tiredness and aching and not keeping up with
everyone else, one symptom at a time. One reads:

> I've got a strange feeling
> It's strange the way I feel
> The way feelings (occur?)
> matter
> transport signals around
> the body, telling you to
> tingle
> telling you to
> run

Aged twelve or thirteen, Elizabeth Barrett Browning, then Moulton Barrett, together with her mother, carefully edited and transcribed stories and journal entries she had written at eight or nine. According to Carolyn Steedman, this act shows her 'collecting her own archives for a later history of her childhood genius so that all her 'past days [might] appear as a bright star'. Her childhood writing served a function: creating herself. '(L)ittle girls have used written language in order to become the women they were expected to be,' writes Steedman in *The Tidy House*, on the writing of young girls. 'For nearly all children perform this task; and all children, having been made minimally competent in the written language, perform this symbolic re-ordering of their experience.'

Later, aged twenty-five, Elizabeth returned to diary writing, finding the effect on her own mind 'curious, especially where the elastic spirits and fancies work upon the fixity of character and situation'. After twelve months, it had put her in 'such a crisis of self-disgust that there was nothing for me to do but to leave off the diary'. In her introduction to *The Early Diary of Elizabeth Barrett Browning*, novelist Elizabeth Berridge asserts that the diary was 'more than a journal about feelings', as if feelings would not be adequately interesting. The diary marked the end of Elizabeth's dependence on her father, who was away for most of the year – although 'years of invalidism still lay ahead'.

It was 1831, and the family estate at Hope End in Malvern – funded by slavery – was to be sold. Elizabeth's father, who disinherited each of his children when they married as if union outside the family was a kind of betrayal, would not admit it. Elizabeth's mother had already died in 1828, after which she did not leave the house for six months and progressed with her Greek instead.

'Unwell, very unwell all the evening!' she reports on a Saturday in August; 'A strange nervous depressed feeling, as if I were both soulless & boneless!'

The following Saturday, she has to go to bed early by herself after riding her horse: 'Never mind. I enjoyed my ride. And there is no kind of enjoyment which one can have on this side of the grave,

without paying its price in pain – no flower one can pick, without nettling one's fingers! Is not this an unthankful thought of mine? Oh yes! There are heaps of flowers, which my hand, even mine, has picked, & in joy! tho' they are now lying afar, lost, & withered–'
Going to bed is the price you pay for doing what you enjoy, when you can.

Elizabeth first became ill aged twelve, along with her two younger sisters Arabel and Henrietta while the family were holidaying in Worthing on the south coast of England. Each suffered with headaches, pains in their sides and 'paroxysms' – something like spasms, convulsions or fits, but also a term used to describe a sudden and violent attack of symptoms accompanied by convulsive twitches of the muscles. She was prescribed valerian, which had been used for centuries to aid sleep, and as pain relief in the age of Pliny, to treat epilepsy in the nineteenth century, and later for 'calming nerves' during the First World War. For whatever reason, herbal or otherwise, Arabel and Henrietta recovered. Elizabeth did not.

As a teenager, Elizabeth experimented with self-presentation in letters to her mother, with *being known* as a sick child: '(M)y constitution and my appetite is as bad as ever,' she wrote from the 'Spa Hotel' in Gloucester where she was being treated, believing she suffered from 'natural ill health', despite seeming well for most of her childhood. Elizabeth referred to her illness as 'the mystery'.

EBB – as she would refer to herself later, and as I will now refer to her too – was attended to by several doctors during her teenage years. Complaining of chest pains that spread around her back to her spine, Dr Nuttall in London noted her 'wild' heartbeat, and Dr Baron in Gloucester prescribed 'great quiet and a recumbent posture', cold showers and hot baths. Cupping – a treatment during which glass cups are placed on the skin to create suction – was employed to treat her *as if* she had bronchitis, even though she didn't. It was Dr Coker to whom she first described the feeling that her spine was swollen, aged fifteen, in 1821, after several years of confounding ill health. EBB was prescribed laudanum – a suspension of opium in alcohol – to help her sleep.

According to her biographer, Margaret Forster, EBB also spent some months in a 'spine crib', being treated 'as for a diseased spine'. What is a *spine crib*? It sounds like it would be restrictive, and hard; a contraption designed for spinal deformities, the kind associated with advanced forms of tuberculosis, a condition EBB was never diagnosed with, or some kind of dislocation. It sounds like it was designed to correct a physical condition, rather than a bedridden teenager with no apparent spinal problems.

A 'spine crib' sounds related to what was known as the Utica crib in America, named after the New York asylum that introduced it from France in the 1840s, in which patients were restrained tightly by their feet, and at the waist with their hands, so that not only was their movement restricted, but also their breathing and circulation. Favoured by asylum superintendents and physicians, the cribs were denounced by neurologists, who found evidence of their misuse in autopsies on patients whose lower extremities had been paralyzed by the confinement. According to the *Encyclopaedia of Asylum Therapeutics, 1750–1950s* by Mary de Young, the '"ungracious looking" device' became so controversial during the era of moral treatment that some asylum physicians, including the superintendent at Utica, gathered them up and publicly burned them. The spine crib also recalls photographs of paralyzed children strapped into blinkers and Thomas splints, bound at the ankles, knees, hips and waist, in metal beds in polio wards in the 1950s.

I look for a spine crib in the Royal College of Surgeons online catalogue, scrolling through photographs of the 'deformed' spines of patients with rickets, taken from behind, orthopaedic corsets that look like suits of armour and spinal supports for scoliosis in the Wellcome Collection image database. I find a photograph of a woman from the St Bartholomew's Hospital Archives & Museum whose face is covered by her arms, leaving her breasts exposed – the cost of staying anonymous forever. According to the caption, her spine is straight 'when she lies on her back'. The photograph doesn't have a date. It looks like it could have been taken by the nineteenth century neurologist Jean-Martin Charcot, Surrealist photographer Lee Miller in the 1930s or Francesca Woodman in the 1970s. The

45

woman in the photograph is wearing a stiff wool skirt and something white underneath, the faint appearance of underarm hair. When I look closer, I see the bed she is lying on is just a bed, covered with a coarse blanket – closer to Bourgeois's metal bed in her *Cell* installation. I don't find anything called a spine crib, but the name makes me think it must have been infantilizing.

EBB's body – and the reasons for her staying sick – was like mine: an unsolvable puzzle. She remained at the spa hotel for her sixteenth birthday, even though, according to Forster, there was no need for her to do so. EBB refused to believe her doctors, who said there was nothing wrong with her. She didn't listen to their warnings against excessive writing and reading, even after she was told that this kind of intellectual stimulation was 'too exhausting for her debilitated condition'. EBB was treated as though she had a disease, even though Dr Coker found 'nothing obviously wrong with the spine'. In fact, there didn't seem to be anything physically wrong with her at all. 'Spinal problems' was merely the most treatable aspect of EBB's ill health.

In her thirties, Dr Chambers (one of Queen Victoria's medical men), initially found EBB to have 'no DISEASE', 'only an excitability and irritability of the chest which requires precaution'. He prescribed leeches. Her health fluctuating, EBB distracted herself with novels and prepared her poems for publication. 'I am better a great deal than I was last week, and have been allowed by Dr Chambers to come downstairs again, and occupy my old place on the sofa,' she wrote to H.S. Boyd in June 1838. 'My health remains, however, in what I cannot help considering myself, and in what, I *believe*, Dr Chambers considers, a very precarious state, and my weakness increases, of course, under the remedies which successive attacks render necessary.' Only the week before, she had been confined to her bed. Despite using a stethoscope to determine she did *not* actually have tuberculosis, Dr Chambers deemed EBB's lungs finally 'affected' by autumn, weakened by the treatment she endured. With medically unexplained illness, cause and effect start to lose all meaning. The treatment for one kind of weakness causes the deterioration of another.

When our bloods came back 'normal' ['as expected'], indicating that there is nothing wrong with our thyroids or livers, nothing alarming that could be causing our symptoms, we hear the same thing as EBB: *no disease*.

'My beloved friend,' EBB wrote in November 1840 to fellow poet and friend Mary Russell Mitford; 'You have not thought me ill or—worse still—unkind, for not writing?' '— I feel bound more than I ever remember having felt, in chains, heavy & cold enough to be iron—& which have indeed entered into the soul. But I do love you still—& am rather better than worse—likely, I do suppose to live on.'

Who has not, in times of illness, confused illness with unkindness, sickness with failure, and badness? Who has not thought: *I have brought this on myself.*

EBB had sunk into a depression. Dr Chambers had convinced her father to send her to Torquay, part of the Devonshire coast known as the English Riviera, or he would 'not answer for the consequences'. Torquay boasted an unusually warm and wet climate, creating an almost exotic landscape, which promised to be good for Elizabeth's health. Torquay had started to attract people with ill health in the early 1830s, transforming the naval port into a popular resort for the upper classes. Its population doubled in the ten years after the Browning siblings left in 1841. Torquay's mild climate, sea air, freshwater baths and southerly exposure marked its reputation as a health resort, but every spa or resort town had its own promoters. Thomas Clifford Allbutt, a distinguished physician who was at one point Commissioner for Lunacy in England and Wales (a position established by the Lunacy Act 1845 to oversee asylums and the welfare of mentally ill people), favoured the 'milder upland airs' of Malvern, or the 'dry sunny slopes' of the Sussex Downs. Some doctors prescribed merely a 'change of scene', believing the clean, fresh, rural or seaside air, but also simply leaving the family home, to be beneficial to health. Others recommended seaside communities: Brighton, the fishing village-come-Regency-health-resort; Bournemouth or Margate, and even abroad, to Tangiers – known at the time as 'the Torquay of Africa' – or the real (French) Riviera. The house the Browning siblings rented in Torquay – at the personal expense of Elizabeth alone – was situated on Beacon Hill, overlooking the harbour. She had travelled with Henrietta and her beloved brother, Bro, by boat to Plymouth. The train line wouldn't be built for another decade.

EBB knew Torquay was good for her health but found it 'hard to bear', and wanted to leave, even if she was better rather than worse, alive and not dead. Her 'kind physician' refused to let her escape before spring, convinced the move would be 'fatal'. She wanted to 'dare it & go' but her father and sisters would not hear of it. The presence of her family seemed to be more of a problem than a cure. 'I want them all to go & leave me here with my maid for the winter,' she wrote to Mary; 'I shd be far easier & happier if they wd—far easier.' She likened herself to iron chains because of her dependency on others, but I imagine she meant that her body felt cold and heavy, and also constrained, the wet air and the feeling of being constantly monitored compounding one another, so that she felt more like a metal object, observed and watched over, with no sense of time or space, than a person with a body.

EBB wrote to her correspondent to confess these wants – for her family to leave, to leave herself – because she knew Mary would understand. She too had spinal problems, and was frequently unwell. Their relationship played out through correspondence rather than one watching over the other. EBB offered her advice to Mary, which included taking up a 'recumbent – not a merely leaning position', claiming: 'It would lessen both the actual fatigue, & the evils consequent upon sedentary habits.' (She also insisted, in her lengthy experience, that taking to bed for a week was preferable to being unable to leave your room for a month.) Hearing her friend was unwell, EBB recommended Mary learn to be 'a Lollard' like her, making sure to lie down 'on a sofa instead of on a chair', and 'study the art, not a very difficult one, of writing in a recumbent position'. To adapt to one's own inexplicable illness is to learn, to be an expert when there isn't one at hand. It is to be outside: a Lollard is someone without an academic background, who cannot rely on the academy to hold them upright, and who must therefore prop up themselves. The movement was led by John Wycliffe,

48

dismissed from Oxford for criticizing the Catholic Church – a heretic. Elizabeth uses the word to criticize 'the upright masses' rather than the Church. Elizabeth possessed the language and mind of a professor of illness, with plenty of experience in the matter of spinal health and treatment, even joking to Mary: 'This is very learned, is it not? – I think I deserve a diploma.'

Mary's letters do not survive – EBB destroyed them – but EBB's letters to Mary are expressions of care from one invalid poet to another: two women living with the strain of domineering fathers as well as painful spinal problems with limited, and even damaging, treatment possibilities. By this point, Mary and EBB's friendship was already five years old, and was a meeting of 'feeble' spines as well as lively minds.

Now, we might call EBB's condition 'orthostatic intolerance', or OI: the inability to be upright without experiencing symptoms such as light-headedness, headaches, weakness and fatigue, the result of either an immediate and large increase in heart rate as the heart struggles to keep blood flowing to the brain and upper body (postural orthostatic tachycardia syndrome), or a drop in blood pressure (neurally mediated hypotension). EBB claimed to write as well or as badly lying down as she could at a desk, finding sitting upright for any length of time 'exceedingly fatiguing'. She sounds like my mother writing her own case history, unable to work because of 'orthostatic intolerance, anxiety and of course extreme fatigue'.

EBB turned her orthostatic intolerance, what would now be *managed* rather than *cured*, into an advantage. Her health did not improve during her stay in Torquay. It was colder and damper than she expected. EBB and Henrietta returned to London in 1841, without their brother, who had tragically drowned during their stay. It was then that she became infamously confined to the upstairs of her family home.

When her father first bought 50 Wimpole Street, EBB compared it to Newgate Prison, as if she was already plotting her own confinement, willing herself into isolation with purpose. EBB took to her bed instead of her domestic duties, engaging herself in her poetry, sleeping and working on a sofa – not exactly a bed, but definitely not a chair. Her room, decorated with dark green wallpaper, was on the third floor of the four-storey house. A large table was placed in the room to hold all her vanities; coronal shelves were papered with teal and crimson merino for her books, and busts of Homer and Chaucer. Scarlet runners, nasturtiums and convolvuluses ('morning glory'), and great tendrils of ivy grew up outside the window from a deep box of soil, almost covering the glass. What might be considered gloomy she found pleasure in: listening to the sound of the leaves against the pane, and even 'being sanguine'. A transparent blind gave her a landscape, which lit up when the sun shone through it: 'a castle gateway, and two walks, and several peasants, and groves of trees which rise in excellent harmony with the fall of my green damask curtains'.

According to Berridge, EBB lived in a world in which there were two paths for well-off headstrong women who actively resented their role in the Victorian household: those who 'cast off their protective colouring and stood out boldly against the background like vulnerable animals to be sniped at', and those who 'used it, took cover in illness'. 'EBB chose the second way, although unconsciously . . . It enabled her to opt out of the feminine role her age and position in the household demanded of her: now she need take no hand ordering it, for fear of overfatigue, nor in sewing or embroidery, which she hated. Music, French, Italian, a little singing, were available: she could now choose what she wanted and discard the rest.'

Here is that myth, born and sustained – that to be ill is to hide, to crouch rather than stand (up or out), which would be the better path, the braver, riskier path, even if it left you worse off; the myth that to be inexplicably ill and dependent on the care and support of others is a choice, a way of getting out of what you don't want to do, a choice that clever, deceitful young women make for themselves.

The idea that being ill means 'taking to bed', that it is a choice, that it is decadent, excessive and privileged, that it is connected with the sanguineous temperament rather than a health problem, that it is weak or lazy and therefore unworthy of help, that it is the result of giving up or doing too much, that it is a 'way out', that chronic illness is enabled by an overbearing mother – these are cultural myths that

50

confine some women inside and shut others off from legitimate illness experiences. This is what is referred to when we are told: *It must be nice to spend all day in bed*. It sounds like a choice rather than a necessity; it sounds like only something wealthy white privileged people can do.

The myth of the fragile white woman or girl who takes to her bed harms everyone with a chronic illness; those whose experience is narrativized in this way, and those who are denied access to it, namely people in minority racial and ethnic groups, who are far more likely to experience misdiagnosis and medical neglect and are also more likely to have ME/CFS.

'My diary is not meant to be read by any person except myself,' wrote EBB in her 1831 diary: 'but she deserves to be let behind the scenes. Mine are very ill painted.'

Your diary makes a space to voice your feelings, however incoherent or exaggerated; where you embroider; where you gossip; where you speak without judgement, fear or shame. When I asked my mother if I could see her diary, she said she was not ready to show me. By then, she knew I would be showing it forward, bringing it into view, because I believed there were others who deserved to be let behind the scenes too.

¶ Storm coming

I write notes on my phone, and I then forget about them – like I did with my childhood diaries. I do not use them like my lists of acceptable ways to describe my symptoms in medical contexts. They are another record for my future self.

> new note
> I am trying to visualise somewhere that doesn't hurt. Palms of my hands? Inner ears? Toenails? – or are those places near enough pain to still hurt
> Can't look at a screen or the page of a book. Can't move. The pain grips all around. It has me by the neck and pelvis and jaw and the backs of my legs
> Can't relieve it, not with heat or medication or herbs or thoughts or company
> what does it feel like to be struck by lightning
> It's like that, plus nausea.

> new note
> I cannot be anything other than horizontal, cannot go and get my laptop from the living room
> my body is so heavy, a dead weight
> darkness in the day from a storm coming is a relief, holding up my phone to make notes is too much, I can only hope I will rest and wake feeling more vertical, enough to sit up and work
> [The day after travelling to Bristol and back to meet a professor who treats children with ME/CFS]

> new note
> Hands feel swollen but they are not.

> new note
> kept awake by hips for 4 nights running, carefully push my thumb into the fleshier part and release pain

new note
the ache is low and continuous, a losing battle between sleeping in pain and waking in awareness of it. You know, those times when you wake up and you know you need to sleep. My body is rigged.

new note
Being ripped apart from the inside.

new note
'It's like a big syringe in the sky and when it hits you it puts all this stuff in your body. It turns your insides completely around.'
[This is how a retired heavy equipment operator from South Carolina who had been struck by lightning ten times described the experience on ABC News.]

new note
What felt like hours of ringing – not in my ears, in my head
Nothing you can do apart from go home before it starts.

new note
It is frightening. And sometimes it is being frightening. I am rude and angry and spiteful, and I don't hate myself for it.

new note
So folded up in myself I can barely walk.
[I think this is something my mother said to me, but I cannot be sure.]

new note
backed into a corner.
[The same with this one.]

new note
/ as if something has short circuited and cannot be felt in any other way. I have triggered the shaking fit, and in that moment, I am in control of it.

53

new note

For a long time, I have not lived as an ill person, but today I think maybe that's not true. I am living a sick life. I don't know any other.

These notes speak of violence. Rarely do they attempt to describe pain with medical lexicon. There is no *stinging*, or *burning*, or *stabbing*. Rarely is the pain located in one place in my body. The *violence* – the battle – is the experience of illness, not the illness itself. It is what seems to happen between body and mind.

Alice James described something similar to this violence, recalling the first acute attack of hysteria she remembers specifically in 1867 or '68, aged nineteen, although they had begun in her childhood. It was to be one of an infinite succession of conscious abandonments, as she wrote in her diary two decades later: 'As I lay prostrate after the storm with my mind luminous and active and susceptible of the clearest, strongest impressions, I saw so distinctly that it was a fight simply between my body and my will, a battle in which the former was to be triumphant to the end.'

'Owing to some physical weakness, excess of nervous susceptibility, the moral power *passes*, as it were for a moment, and refuses to maintain muscular sanity, worn out with the strain of its constabulary functions. As I used to sit immovable reading in the library with waves of violent inclination suddenly invading my muscles taking some one of their myriad forms such as throwing myself out of the window, or knocking off the head of the benignant pater as he sat with his silver locks, writing at his table, it used to seem to me that the only difference between me and the insane was that I had not only all the horrors and suffering of insanity but the duties of doctor, nurse, and strait-jacket imposed upon me, too.'

In this entry, dated 26 October 1890, Alice referred to a paper by her brother William, titled 'The Hidden Self', published earlier that year, in which he drew on Pierre Janet's treatments for hysteria as a way to understand the self as split or divided. Janet and William James shared the belief that hysterical women had limited perception, which made them unable to 'handle' the world. Symptoms such as paralysis were the only way for the hysteric's body to cope with its limited possibilities and restricted awareness: 'An hysteric woman abandons part of her consciousness because she is too weak nervously to hold it all together,' wrote William. 'The abandoned part, meanwhile, may solidify into a secondary or subconscious self.' William, like Janet, believed the hysteric could be cured by 'tapping the submerged consciousness', through hypnosis. 'Get at the secondary personage by hypnotisation, or in whatever way,' Janet wrote, 'and make her give up the eye, the skin, the arm, or whatever the affected part may be.'

It is as if Alice took on the theory of the nervous 'abandonment' and applied it to herself – her own brain and eyes and skin and arms. 'It may be the word commonly used by his kind. It is just the right one at any rate, altho' I have never unfortunately been able to abandon my consciousness and get five minutes' rest.' From an older age, she claimed William and Janet's version of hysteria as her experience twenty years earlier. Maybe it was a relief just to read in medical literature what she had felt in life. After all, Alice had by this time passed through an infinite number of these abandonments, always a fight between her body and her will. She wrote of having to abandon her brain, rather than her legs ('. . . violent revolt in my head overtook me so that I had to "abandon" my brain, as it were.'). She had never been without the sense that if she let herself go for a moment she must *abandon it all*: 'When all one's moral and natural stock in trade is a temperament forbidding the abandonment of an inch or the relaxation of a muscle, 'tis a never-ending fight.'

Alice was thinking of her brother, reading his work, which she appeared to have always embodied. She was still writing hers in secret. Alice wrote her diary as she was reaching the end of her life, but for many years she had been living in sick time, somehow always in parallel to the rest of the world, and yet out of step. Illness was her occupation, because illness takes up time, the time of not-doing what you want to be doing, the time of explaining why it has taken you a year to reply to a letter. It also changes the quality of time itself, slowing it down, and breaking it up.

'So, with the rest, you abandon the pit of your stomach, the palms of your hands, the soles of your feet, and refuse to keep them sane when you find in turn one moral impression after another producing despair in the one, terror in the other, anxiety in the third and so on until life becomes one long flight from remote suggestion and complicated eluding of the multifold traps set for your undoing.'

William had his own 'sort of crisis' in 1868, 'an unspeakable disgust for the dead drifting of my own life for some time past', during which he turned to psychological research. At times, he wrote like his sister's physician, conflating her personality and notions of ideal femininity with her health, or what we might call 'well-being' now: 'Let Alice cultivate a manner clinging yet self-sustained, reserved yet confidential,' he wrote, 'let her face beam with serious beauty, & glow with quiet delight at having you speak to her; let her exhibit short glimpses of a soul with wings, as it were (but very short ones) let her voice be musical and the tones of her voice full of caressing, and every movement of her full of grace, & you have no idea how lovely she will become.' If only Alice could overcome her disposition and ill health – she would become the embodiment of Victorian femininity. Instead, she refused it all, including marriageability. She couldn't refuse the doctors, who had the power to diagnose and treat her, to legitimize her ill feelings.

The same tension that brought Alice to all her pains – diagnosed by a Dr Townsend as 'gouty diathesis complicated by an abnormally sensitive nervous organization' and paralysis brought on by anxiety and strain – also produced within her a 'tide of speculation'; 'luminous waves that sweep out of my consciousness all but the living sense and overpower one with joy in the rich, throbbing complexity of life'. An 'excess of weakness' was often coupled with an equal sense of vitality, so much that she reported having to be reminded she had been sick in the first place: 'The headache had gone off in the night and I had clean forgotten it.'

Illness makes gaps. If illness has its own kind of time, it also has its own spaces: the sickroom, the bedroom, the living room, and treatment room, all at once private and public, at once confining and protecting. The diary is another kind of space. As a hysteric, a person who was an *invalid and not insane,* Alice wrote her diary to record her own case history, to document what happened, or rather didn't happen, and so that she 'may lose a little of the sense of loneliness and desolation which abides me'. Alice wrote to control her own narrative: 'I shall at least have it all my own way and it may bring relief as an outlet to that geyser of emotions, sensations, speculations and reflections which ferments perpetually within my poor carcass for its sins.' She was her own medical man as well as a sick woman – a dual life that defied notions of healthy and well.

Alice was troubling, a problem through her ill health, which could also be conceived as a feminine virtue, but her distinctly unfeminine ill-disposition to doctors, indeed all men. 'I think the difficulty is my inability to assume the receptive attitude,' she wrote to William at the beginning of 1886, 'the cardinal virtue in woman, the absence of which has always made me so uncharming to and uncharmed by the male sex.' Alice wrote through her apparent absence of charm, a refusal to adopt the appropriate feminine virtues, just as, to some extent at least, she refused to be well. As a sick woman, with no apparent organic disease, she was supposed to be receptive, not resistant, to follow a man and his treatments rather than her own desires and needs – something which can still be so easily dismissed as a bad attitude, as being *basically furious.*

¶ *Never-ending*

Every day that starts 'let's just try to have a better day than yesterday' ends in a worse one. Who gave me this shitty advice – or did I make it up? Why am I setting myself such a high standard?

My mother says, 'I'm just going to write today off.'

'It will never be *different*,' I say. 'Tomorrow will probably not be better; it might well be worse. We cannot keep *writing days off* as if our normal is anything other than this, as if we *should* be doing more with our time.' The chronic in 'chronic illness' comes from the Greek khrónos (χρόνος), meaning 'time' – an abstract, never-ending concept.

I do not say: 'That is your internalized ableism talking.'

I'm sure this tendency would be called 'chronic perfectionism' by someone who does not know her, or us.

'Normal' is different when you live on the precipice, on the edge of both wellness and illness. It is living in 'crip' time: warped, queer, endlessly *changed*.

Alison Kafer's definition of crip time is extra time. Crip – or sick – time is queer, a departure from straight time, 'whether straight time means a firm delineation between past/present/future or an expectation of linear development from dependent childhood to independent reproductive adulthood'. Crip time is different to productive kinds of time, which is really just one – narrow, *straight*, restrictive – version of time. Crip time is straight time extended, stretched out, bent, warped. Crip time is time that cannot be straightened out. Crip time is the time of being in hospital for prolonged periods, or institutionalized, or in bed in your home most of the time. You can lose a lot of time when you're ill, but you also need more time to do things. You do things slowly, in waves rather than stages.

Being crip – sick, ill, disabled – changes your experience of time. 'The present takes on more urgency as the future shrinks,' Kafer writes; 'the past becomes a mix of potential causes of one's present illness or a succession of wasted time; the future is marked in increments of treatment and survival even as "the future" becomes more tenuous.'

There aren't specific times of day, really, unless they are the times you take your medication, or even 'days of the week'. No Tuesday lunchtimes, no Saturday nights. 'Last week' and 'in a few months' time' don't really exist. All of this means the task of *having a better day than yesterday* is even more impossible. There are no *days*, or *weeks*, no *yesterday*, so what, then, is trying, what is bettering, let alone today and tomorrow. When there is no straight time there is no way of measuring these things. The days are really just mornings anyway, or what feels like a smaller and smaller window of being able to stand or sit up, which happens *sooner rather than later*.

Crip time is failed productive time – the time of not doing, and potential undoing.

Crip time reveals itself when you think about the future. Do you see a future in which you will get better, or do you see one in which things might be different, but you will never be *cured*?

Crip time is failing to make the most of your time, it is failing to fulfil normative expectations, of using your time wisely.

Crip time is time spent in and with the body-mind, described by Jinny as her 'companion' in Virginia Woolf's *The Waves*: 'always sending its signals, the rough black "No", the golden "Come", in rapid running arrows of sensation'. It is a night kind of time for Virginia too, obscuring sights and enhancing the other senses: 'We are out of doors. Night opens; night traversed by wandering moths . . . I smell roses; I smell violets; I see red and blue just hidden.' Crip time is what she describes in her diaries as 'partly mystical. Something happens in my mind.'

When you live alone as a crip, your body is your only companion, where all desires and pains are focused, and cannot be redirected. They have nowhere else to go. Your conversation with it a source of both conflict and joy.

Sickness changes time, and pace of life; and in doing so, it changes what 'health' is: not a system but a scale, not a battle but a balance, or a flow.

Louise Bourgeois started her *Insomnia Drawings* during the wet New York winter of 1994. She used paper that already looked discarded. Every morning Bourgeois's assistant Jerry Gorovoy would gather up these drawings from her bed, bin or the floor of her Chelsea brownstone, 220 in total. Cast off from sleeplessness, these pages of drawing and writing were never intended to be published. To finish a drawing – or a diary entry – and discard it, even onto the floor from your bed, is the act of a child who knows her mother (or long-term assistant) will save it, knowing that it is for other people, including a future self. Bourgeois drew watery landscapes, all lines and no shading. Rain turns to flood water. Waves are also spikes, falling water is a guillotine (either could chop off your head). Thoughts and memories ebb and flow in unstructured insomniac time: 'the drawings of the night / They all emerge from the water. Why together / water is the great unknown, the night.' Bodies of water are much like the night: dark and formless, the locus of unknown horrors. Water is dangerous; it floods and fills, destroys, drags away. The sound of rain changes your dreams – maybe it changes your waking (insomniac) thoughts too, the noise of water hitting glass and tile and tarmac and wood. It can also be soothing, regenerative. Past present and future mix up in the flood.

I still have all the notes I made at university for my final third-year BA exams on post-war American art and the work of Louise Bourgeois. It was the year of Bourgeois's retrospective at the Tate Modern, where we were lucky enough to be taught by Professor Mignon Nixon in front of the work. I slipped pages of text – some typed, some handwritten in all caps – into plastic folders with cut-out photocopies of artworks and photographs I hoped to reference: Bourgeois's 1947 folio of prints titled *He Disappeared into Complete Silence*; her needle-like 'Personages' sculptures roughly carved from wood, expressions of a mother's ambivalence towards her family (cutting and caring); her *Arch of Hysteria*, a photograph of the artist with her three sons – her living *personages*. My notes about the sculptures read like code, or secret formulas, which almost make sense to me now. I imagine they almost made sense to me then: 'appendages/packages/organs – physical economy implies psychic economy'. Much of Bourgeois's work involved silencing, a loss of voice. In *He Disappeared*, a man tells a story so fast no one could hear it. Another has his head chopped off by the ceiling. A woman dies without anyone knowing.

60

Around this time, I was often ill, meaning that I could not concentrate very well, that I was sometimes confined to my bed for a few hours in the afternoon, whole days and occasionally weeks, but not enough to miss too much university or send me home to my mother. The feminist reclaiming of the hysteric as a sign of protest against patriarchy, re-classifying centuries of marginal women as victims of patriarchy rather than of their own internal drives, did not seem to have much to do with the realities of living with unexplained or invisible illness that I had experienced. I was still being silenced, or felt that no one would want to hear me.

I recognized in Bourgeois's sculpture, drawing and printmaking a sensitivity to her body's language, which she – and then Mignon – interpreted through psychoanalysis, as 'the return of the repressed'. I felt like I understood Bourgeois, but not the child who made a model of her father out of bread and then destroyed it at his table – my father, and the oedipal in general, was always part of a separate reality. I was more interested in her fixation on the figure of her mother, often figured as a spider, the Bourgeois who pushed her sculpture of that mother – small and hard – onto the floor, and let it smash to pieces, on camera. The mother is blamed for a daughter's failure at self-love: 'Love your neighbour as yourself – It is difficult to achieve this ideal when you always feel that / something is wrong with you.' I always felt something was wrong with me too – and at this point, I still believed I had to be away from my mother to be well (enough). I was drawn to the Bourgeois who was small and hard, like me. The Bourgeois who was also a mother, a daughter, an artist, a writer, an insomniac.

Bourgeois drew a clock face with twenty-four numbers, rather than twelve – a clock for the person who spends all day and all night awake. When I look at the clock drawings on my computer screen, awake at 5 am, I think: 'Why aren't all clocks made like this?' I no longer look to clocks for precise times, only to see what kind of day it is (morning or afternoon or evening?); to ask *what have I missed?*

Nights spent awake induce many questions: 'has the day invaded the night or the night invaded the day?' she asked, in 1995. But the insomniac analyst has no answers, only more questions, which cannot be conclusively answered, infused with guilt and self-doubt:

61

why are we here? / How do we manage to appear? / for how
much time? / to what end? / is it worth our while? / have we
said thank you? / have we achieved our / potential? / have we
fulfilled our responsibilities / I . . . am lucky to have made it /
I am lucky to have made it, be alive. / thank you

Bourgeois was an analyst of insomnia. Night is time for reading secretly, for writing and, in LB's case, drawing. The *Insomnia
Drawings* are annotations, not of dreams but of waking reality, when
sleep – and structured, straight, clock time – has abandoned you,
and you can only question yourself. In the 1950s, undergoing intense
psychoanalysis, she wrote: 'I believe insomnia comes from guilt – /
Prove it – / Do not waste your time with defences – / Look behind
the defences at the wound.' Night is an even lonelier time when
you are the only one awake, your husband and sons are asleep in
the house, caught in a catch-22 of failure: 'I cannot sleep because
I / am angry / I am angry because I can / not sleep.' For Bourgeois,
insomnia, like her other bodily symptoms, signalled the return of
repressed trauma.

Spiders sometimes appear in Bourgeois's night drawings, as they
do in her sculptural work, an ode to her mother. 'I shall never tire
of representing her,' Bourgeois writes in *Ode à ma mère* (1995)
– another work from when my mother first became ill. 'The spider –
Why the spider? Because my mother was deliberate, clever, patient,
soothing, reasonable, dainty, subtle, indispensable, neat and as useful
as a spider. She could also defend herself, and me, by refusing to
answer "stupid", inquisitive, embarrassing personal questions . . .
The treatment of fear.' A spider hunts and hides. It protects and
withdraws. It makes architecture out of a body, and out of fear of
that body, fear of being that body. The spider demands to be read
as house, body and image.

In drypoint prints, Bourgeois's mother-as-spider is protective and
tough, ready to defend and attack. In *Spider*, a plate added to the
second edition of her illustrated book *He Disappeared into Complete
Silence*, she appears suspended from the ceiling of an empty room.
In *Spider Woman*, the spider's body is a human head out of which

strands of hair become its legs. Bourgeois's spider is the ideal mother, but she is also its opposite: a head and legs, with no reproductive body/womb to birth another. The spider-mother is all needles and eyes and hair.

There is tension in Bourgeois's feelings towards the spider-mother – she is both real (related to her mother who rewove antique tapestries) and mythological (as when Arachne challenged the goddess Athena to a weaving contest, who subsequently turned her into a spider in punishment). The need for attachment, however small and hard and sharp you are, comes with ambivalence: pulling and pushing, cutting and caring. This is the principle that structures the experience of being a daughter, and a mother – that it is not good or bad, but it still defines you.

As students, my friend and I loved that as a woman in her eighties, Bourgeois napped on a sofa in her studio while a seamstress sewed and stuffed her sculptures. Now I think she was probably not only elderly but exhausted from a life of sleepless nights.

Years later, when they were published, I read the writings in her 'daybook' – what you could call her journal – in which Bourgeois played both analyst and analysand. Pre-menstrual tension manifests itself as pain in her abdomen, hardly noticeable, 'like a vertigo at the hollow of the stomach', which makes her feel like there's something wrong with her, that it is her fault she is in pain. This is followed by immediate diarrhoea, 'related to unconscious material or rather showing awareness / of repressed wishes'. Post-menstrual tension, on the other hand, is 'revengeful + aggressive', a kind of physical evidence that there is something wrong with her, 'but it is / "your fault" you did it'. This outwardly aggressive pain seems to replace the anger 'in everyday situations', which she interprets as 'self-reproach at not measuring up'.

In the weeks before I finished my degree, I spoke to my mother far more frequently than I had as a child at boarding school. We shared our experiences on the phone, sometimes daily. She was suicidal, and alone. A relationship had broken down. She told me she wanted to die. For the first time, I felt that as a reality – she might die, on purpose. How could I tell her what I did not know then? That she felt there was something wrong with her – and that I felt the same. (I didn't then inhabit the knowledge of illness I have now.) Illness had been something my mother and I had already been possessed by for a long time. We saw ourselves as defective, unlovable.

Illness occupies the mind and body, like a hobby, a job, or a subject you study. It can fill you up, until your sense of self is defined by it. It makes you feel like a fake and a fraud. It shames you into difference. If chronic fatigue and pain are much like shame, they also affect how you perceive yourself, as a person with a body. Ill feelings make you both impressionable and hard. To stop yourself feeling suddenly diffuse, as if you are disintegrating, you make yourself small and solid – impenetrable. you appear self-contained because you spend most of your energy trying to hold all the parts of yourself together. Illness made me guarded, quiet, small, contained, like Bourgeois, who wrote: 'and what's the use of talking, if you already know that others don't feel what you feel?'

My hands seized up a few days before I was due to sit my final exams. I couldn't think, couldn't remember anything – names and phrases and ideas and images all mixed up together. I believed that I had not really understood much of what I was now supposed to know, and be able to interpret, and argue clearly, that I could not possibly write an exam paper. Besides, I could not hold a pen.

I asked for assistance, on my mother's instruction, something I had not done since I was a child, when I learnt to distrust anyone with authority, medical or otherwise, because they wouldn't help me, especially if I asked for exactly what I knew I needed. Even after all the failed battles my mother had fought on my behalf, she still believed in asking, or knew I had no choice. The university administrators made it seem so easy. They gave me a laptop to write on, and a room of my own. I was twenty years old, and surprised that I could have my 'access needs' met. I wouldn't have that language for ten more years.

I was able to sit my exams but it still seemed pointless. I couldn't remember anything anyway. It felt like cheating without even getting a good grade. I do not remember any of the questions, but I am sure they were predictable by the well-prepared with unfogged brains.

When it comes to illness, it sometimes seems like there is no way out of shame – you are always being left behind.

I left London the same day as my last exam – I had to be with my mother. I felt the pull of belonging and the inability to do anything else, but also the need to not have to explain how I was feeling.

If illness is 'the night side of life', as Susan Sontag put it, perhaps, then, invisible and unexplained illness is that time you wake up between night and day – too early to get up, almost light but still dark, nearing dawn. It is that time when you cannot really think or move or go back to sleep; you can only stare at the ceiling, and question yourself. If sickness is the night-side of life, insomnia is never not being awake to illness.

In the opening of her famous book *Illness as Metaphor*, Sontag uses the metaphor of two kingdoms, healthy and sick. With chronic illness, and in particular those that do not appear to have a physical cause, you might feel like an interloper, like you do not belong to either one. Or maybe that you have a fake passport, and you are hoping no one finds out in either world that you're not really supposed to be there.

Sontag's journals are full of lists: DOs and DON'Ts, books to BUY, things to read and write and remember, but also: Roman army units; Literary Agents (NYC); the four principle ideas of Hindu mythology 'embodied in 4 "persons"'; quotes by Jackson Pollock. One of the notebooks from 1961 is simply a list of films she had watched, sometimes three or four a day. When editing the journals, Sontag's son David found that some years she didn't record exact dates at all – without this information, all time becomes water. One entry from 1961 lists things 'Never to talk about', and consists of three things only: her son, her childhood and her mother.

Even if she vowed never to talk about her, Sontag's mother does occasionally appear in the journals. In August 1948, aged fifteen, dreading the misery of a life like her mother's, or any of the people who passively involved themselves in sterile relationships – 'what rotten, dreary, miserable lives they lead' – Sontag writes: 'How can I hurt her more, beaten as she is, never resisting? / How can I help me, make me cruel?' By December, preparing to leave the family home – and her mother's misery – in Los Angeles to attend Berkeley, she is 'almost on the verge of madness . . . tottering over an illimitable precipice'. Her emotional needs are overwhelming, with time so short and thoughts so changeable. 'What, I ask, drives me to disorder? How can I diagnose myself? All I feel, most immediately, is the most anguished need for physical love and mental companionship' – two things that her mother had failed to supply her with. Going home to visit for the weekend, Sontag finds herself finally free of her 'dependence on / affection for' her mother. 'She aroused nothing in me, not even pity – just boredom', she writes, relieved from the burden of her mother's feelings. 'College is safety, because it is the easy, secure thing to do . . . As for Mother, I honestly don't care.'

To remind yourself to not speak (or write) of your mother seems absurd. It is almost impossible to begin with if you are talking about yourself. You are barely separate from them, and want to please them, to be funny to them in letters, to love them and understand them – to see the future through them, and to desperately escape them, to become your own person. Then again, a mother is too present – *too much* in your sense of self – to be written or spoken about clearly. Perhaps speaking about your mother is just too revealing.

'As a child, I was a feverish little Deist,' wrote Sontag at the end of December 1956. A month later, Sontag composed two versions of a text titled 'Notes of a Childhood' in her journal, an evocation, as her son and editor calls it, 'written in a notational, almost stream-of-conscious manner . . . the closest she came to straightforward autobiographical writing'. Of course, it is a list. Of course, her mother barely appears. Sontag's 'Notes of a Childhood' is all out of order, or it reads that way. It reflects not just the awkwardness of a flow of consciousness forced into list form, but how memories get stuck to bodies: 'Daddy showing me how he folded his handkerchief. (In their bedroom. Daddy dressing.) / Telling Mother I would rather not be Jewish as she was getting into the shower.' When she does appear, her mother does not act; she is merely *there*, as witness to Sontag's thoughts and experiences – 'On the train to Florida: "Mother, how do you spell pneumonia?"'; 'Crying in the movie *For Whom the Bell Tolls* – with Mother, in a big Manhattan theatre.' – reflecting the feeling that: 'I hardly saw her. She was always away.' The notes feel more like an exorcism than an autobiography – as formal as a list of books to buy or films seen that week.

Sontag rarely writes about her mother, but she mentions writing *to* her: 'DO / Shower every other night / Write Mother every other day.'

Where are all those letters the ones she wrote to her mother?

Sontag writes of detachment from her own feelings, of looking to other people to tell her what they would like them to be, as a form of loyalty to her mother. 'I wasn't my mother's child – I was her subject

67

(subject, companion, friend, consort. I sacrificed my childhood – my honesty – to please her),' she wrote. This habit of 'holding back' made everything she did feel somewhat unreal: 'My intellectualism reinforces this – is an instrument for the detachment from my own feelings which I practice in the service of my mother.' The singular nature of her mother's feelings dominated their relationship: 'Mother was never angry with me, only hurt.'

I never felt my mother as bad. Despite her illness, and the anger I appeared to direct towards her, she was never like Sontag's mother, 'this tragic woman, a Niobe, a casualty of life'. In her journal, Sontag narrates her mother's ill feelings as a form of control, 'magical powers which my mother ascribed to me – with the understanding that if I withdrew them, she'd die'. If Sontag's mother made her feel 'Happiness is disloyalty', my grandmother made my mother feel inferior. Another kind of inheritance, which, like illness, doesn't always feel much like love.

Sontag didn't share her diaries in her lifetime and conceived of them as an act of self-creation rather than documentation of her authentic self. 'The journal is a vehicle for my sense of selfhood,' she wrote in 1957. 'It represents me as emotionally and spiritually independent. Therefore (alas) it does not simply record my actual, daily life but rather – in many cases – offers an alternative to it. In the journal I do not just express myself more openly than I could do to any person; I create myself.' Sontag barely wrote of her own experience in published work, most markedly when writing *Illness as Metaphor* after her cancer diagnosis and treatment. 'My "I" is puny,' she wrote, creating herself, 'cautious, too sane.'

Sontag drew on Alice James's diaries to write the play *Alice in Bed*. She merges with Lewis Carroll's Alice, attending a version of the Mad Hatter's tea party from her sick bed, where she is joined by other writers: Emily Dickinson, who wrote, 'I LIKE a look of agony, / Because I know it's true', and the feminist journalist Margaret Fuller, as well as Kundry from Wagner's *Parsifal* and Myrtha from *Giselle* – two angry 'ghosts', as Sontag called them. Alice's dead mother also appears at the party, uninvited. In Ivo Van Hove's staging of the play in 2000, Alice, played by Joan MacIntosh, is trapped in a transparent cast of her own body. The cast, which is a kind of costume, is a metaphor for her sick bed, but also her mind, trapped inside her body. Except Alice does travel without leaving her bed. 'I will not fall into the gulf of history,' she says, walking the streets of Rome – where Henry and Margaret Fuller lived – through layers of time. 'I will cling to the side. Because I'm in my mind, which is like a boat or a chair or a bed or a tree.'

Sontag's mother appears very infrequently in her diaries from her late teens and twenties – concerned with the relationships she chose herself: husband, ex-husband, lover, ex-lover, girlfriend, ex-girlfriend, son. It is like a map, a diagram. A diary is somewhere to be definitive, in the knowledge that not only will you change your mind, but that this version of yourself exists in an alternative reality to the one you are living in, with your son and your childhood and your mother.

'One of the main (social) functions of a journal or diary is precisely to be read furtively by other people,' wrote Sontag in 1957, 'the people (like parents + lovers) about whom one has been cruelly honest only in the journal.'

Of course my mother read my diaries. I had left them for her to find.

My mother sends me a drawing she made in therapy dated December 1998, towards the end of my first term away from her at boarding school. She is represented as an outline of a person, like the ones drawn around victims of murder in noir films, or Bourgeois's prints and drawings, except she has drawn a pink heart on her chest. She could be leaping or dancing, or lying dead, or asleep. Closest to her are little doodles of our cats: 'for me, soft hugs'. Everyone else – her children, partners, parents, friends, carer – are spread out around her, linked to her and sometimes each other with straight lines, like the arms of a clock. It is a map of her feelings about the people in her life – a *spider-diagram*. My name is underlined in yellow. Underneath she has written: 'So worried about her right now: feel her health & wellbeing is totally in my hands. Trying to do the right thing for her.'

My mother's spider-diagram is a map of disbelief and denial. The line drawn between me and my grandmother is annotated: 'Doesn't accept there is anything wrong with Alice.' One of the notes underneath my father's name, underlined in brown: 'In denial about Alice. Doesn't seem to listen.' Along the line of relation – from one corner of the page to the opposite corner, with the drawing of her in between – reads: 'Doesn't accept some of the stuff around them that came from me or is suggested by me.' Only 'L', her girl-friend, supported my mother when it came to my illness: 'Shares my belief and acceptance of Alice's illness,' she has written under her name. There is no mention of what I believed or accepted. Maybe it was just a given that my feelings were her feelings and didn't need mentioning. Maybe it was too difficult to write them down, even in therapy.

Her friends are listed under two categories: 'takers' and 'givers', one of which – my ballet teacher – 'accepts Alice's illness & supports her on it'. The shorter list of takers comprises not only those who use her energy without thinking, 'friends with whom I really try to seem normal', but whose denial is useful to my mother, in that they are also friends 'with whom I want to do normal stuff'. Her carer ('W') is responsible for both tiring her out and assisting with house-work: 'helps me/hinders me'. I remember this, how overbearing W was when she was in the house, even when cleaning and ironing, how she would talk and talk, how like a member of the family she became and how exhausted my mother would be when she left.

As for Sontag in her journals, maybe all diaries, my mother's therapy diagram was a vehicle for her sense of selfhood. With this spider-diagram my mother turns herself into the spider-mother who cannot care without feeling like she is causing harm, and the disbe-lieved daughter who cannot be cared for without being harmed. A mother's love is not so different to a daughter's: protecting and with-drawing, a needle-like love, cutting and caring.

¶ No one likes blue

As a child, my mother took me to a healer called Joan, who must have been in her seventies, or older. First, she asked me questions about how I was feeling. Then I would lie on the foldout therapy bed in the middle of her living room while she held her hands over different parts of my body, surrounded by bowls of fruit and plants that other people had exchanged for healing. Only occasionally did she touch my skin. My mother sat on a chair by the bay window. A painting of a small house in a landscape hung above the mantelpiece.

One time, Joan narrated the colours of the rainbow, guiding me and my body through the light, from red to violet. She asked me which colour was best when she was done. 'Blue,' I told her, hesitantly, not knowing which colour to choose. She said that was the worst colour, that no one likes blue. My mother agreed. I had got it wrong. I felt ashamed, scolded myself for not doing it right.

My mother also went to Joan for healing and had acupuncture while I was having osteopathy at the subsidized Natural Health clinic. She had chronic pain at the time – a symptom of hers that would wane during my childhood, when mine was waxing, to the extent that it felt we had very different illnesses. (Our symptom languages were not so similar after all.) While I waited for her session to finish, I would imagine what was happening to her, and whether she was covered in needles. She always looked serene when she came down the stairs.

The acupuncturist asks me what ME stands for in our first session. I tell her I cannot remember, and that it doesn't really matter because it was a confounding diagnosis then and now. She writes down 'History of ME' and subsequently brings it up whenever I mention feeling tired. I can't really talk, can barely keep myself upright. I can feel my muscles wanting to slack, to fall away from my bones. My mind is thick. I don't want to be touched. I think: if I lie down, I will shut down.

I'm at the acupuncturist, now in my early thirties, because I don't want to go to the doctor again. Something drew me to it, the puncturing, maybe. Finding blockages, flows obstructed, release. I thought it might be a way of engaging with the porous nature of my body – going beyond touch, and, of course, verbal language. Making proper holes. Acupuncture puts your body in the world, but it also links you up with something else – a constant notation of constellations and elements, cycles and rhythms beyond it. Going was my attempt to seek help for pain – for someone to witness it, to measure it in my body somehow. To pay attention to it.

I expected the pain to be all in my skin, but it was in more than that.

The acupuncturist tells me I have Raynaud's Syndrome. She noticed how the blood drains from my fingers sometimes. 'You didn't know it had a name, did you?' she says, and I smile weakly, knowing just because something has a name doesn't mean anyone thinks it's real.

Cold temperatures, anxiety or stress triggers Raynaud's. The condition occurs because your blood vessels go into a temporary spasm, which blocks the flow of blood. Google searches for 'blood drains from my fingers' give up fibromyalgia studies and links to autoimmune conditions (while it can be idiopathic – primary Raynaud's – it can also predict the onset of diseases like Lupus, MS, Lyme disease, and other connective tissue disorders). Apparently, Raynaud's is slightly more common in women than men. It also appears on the list of 'testable abnormalities in the absence of any single organic cause', as part of Dr Byron Hyde's definition of ME, alongside sleep dysfunction and Ehlors-Danlos Syndrome, as well as SPECT, MRI and PET brain scans, immune system tests and circulating blood volume tests. Blood vessels that go into temporary spasm are another kind of failure, a blockage, and an indicator of maybe something, maybe nothing. I am a collector of syndromes, which are in themselves collections – the process of grouping and managing. Everything seems related when you don't understand what's going on.

My grandmother once said my hands were worse than hers. I had just gone for a swim in the sea in Norfolk and they looked like a dead person's hands. This was several years after she had a stroke.

She put her hands around mine and rubbed. Trying to get the blood going again, the blood that flows down through the generations of my family.

What else have we inherited?

The acupuncturist takes my pulses, looks at my tongue, and presses her fingers into the flesh across my abdomen. She does my astrological chart without telling me anything about it, uttering words and names like 'metal' and 'rabbit', all the ways I am connected to the cosmos, noting the parts we have in common. She chooses her locations; the needles go in. A sharp pain in my toe falls off into numbness. One goes in my forehead, and some more in my leg and arm (the right side, 'because you are a woman'). She says the needles go in easy with me. I told her they never did when they were taking my blood as a child. 'I'm trying to *avoid* the veins,' she explains.

A pulse keeps time. Measuring it keeps track of your health – compared to what is considered 'healthy'. Too low and you risk not getting enough oxygen to your organs. Too high and it is *racing*. When you go to acupuncture, you have six pulses where you thought you had one. They can be thin or thready or loose. The six relate to your organs, not just your heart, the radial thud of your living body. Deeper still and your qi can be measured.

I kept going back for that deeper measurement. She would measure them all again at the end of the session – once I had lain there for twenty minutes in the dim light – to make sure her needling had worked, this white woman versed in Chinese medicine who thought my antidepressant medication was 'really strong', and was then worried when I stopped. That was a danger signal, apparently. Would I even know if my body was in danger? Would I even know what the signals meant? Would she?

When I next see the acupuncturist, my pulses are stronger. I ask her if they are always different, for everybody, every time, and she said that they are.

'It's a different day,' she says. 'You've been bleeding.'

She tells me Princess Diana died the same day nineteen years ago. The acupuncturist is still worried that I had abruptly stopped taking my medication. I said: I am better than the first time I came, remember, when I could barely keep my eyes open, or speak, even if I am feeling a bit tired today.

'Well,' she said, 'you *do* have a history of ME.'

I lie on my back on the acupuncture table and try to imagine my body from her perspective – hovering above myself. A needle goes into my right ankle to 'help with concentration', sending an electric shock into the sole of my foot.

In Virginia Woolf's 1921 story-poem 'Blue & Green', she appears to be looking at a green glass object. The light slides down it during the daytime and pools on the surface below. The effect makes her think of parakeets, and the sounds they make, and then palm trees and their needles 'glittering in the sun'. The light becomes pools of water that 'settle on the marble' as the earth turns; 'rushes edge them; weeds clog them; here and there a white blossom; the frog flops over; at night the stars are set there unbroken'. And then evening comes and green turns to blue.

The blue is darker because it is night. She sees a 'snub-nosed monster' in the water, and then on the beach, 'blunt, obtuse, shedding dry blue scales'; a wrecked rowing boat with blue ribs, and the 'blue veils of madonnas' in the waves. Her mind leads her, and us, away from the domestic space of objects and hard surfaces to water, to the sea, and then directly into the colour blue, transcending all objects and associations entirely. We can't go with her, totally, but we can go on our own journeys in our minds, lying down horizontal, or sitting up in bed.

Woolf leaves the material reality of objects and rooms behind, guided through associations and emotions by an awareness of colour and light itself, to somewhere outside of everything known – like I was guided by Joan. The same could be said for the experience of pain: a physical sensation that extends to the other senses and other realms beyond our grasp, that is nevertheless integral to ordinary life. There is no *doing it right*.

Maybe blue was the best colour after all.

All the names I know for ME/CFS are derogatory: yuppie flu, mass hysteria, shirker syndrome. Most of what you read in books and articles on ME/CFS flatly condemns the experiences of millions of people. One Norwegian study suggests that people with a diagnosis of ME had an unhealthy 'in-group' identity based on 'premorbid personality traits' or behaviours, a sentiment Edward Shorter described in 1992: 'Many patients today have acquired the unshakable belief that their symptoms represent a particular disease, a belief that remains unmarred by further medical consultation.' Ten years later, the *British Medical Journal* ran a poll, which classified ME as a 'non-disease'. We were made to think that we only had a shared belief we were ill; if we changed that belief, we would not be ill anymore.

Growing up, I did not believe I was ill. I believed that I was somehow faking illness without even meaning to, which meant that I was bad. I believed that my symptoms were not a sign there was something organically wrong with me, but that I wanted to avoid doing everything. I believed that I must not care enough. My mother and I met the criteria for nervous illness, or hysteria, visually speaking – 'We have observed that nervous diseases have generally been supposed to be particularly connected with the sanguineous temperament,' wrote Sayer Walker, a physician from Essex, in the eighteenth century, surveying the various types of nervous patients, their temperaments and appearances. 'That irritability to which they have been ascribed, is often indicated by the fine skin, the blue eye, the flaxen hair, and the large and full blood vessel.' It is as if I had not only inherited the wrong kind of illness from my mother, but the wrong gender and the wrong temperament.

More women than men are diagnosed with ME or chronic fatigue syndrome, and more women report being abducted by aliens. Both are, according to Elaine Showalter in *Hystories: Hysterical Epidemics and Modern Culture*, published in 1997, incarnations of modern hysteria, along with eating disorders, hypochondria, multiple personality disorder, and Gulf War Syndrome. When I first read Showalter's book, I thought of my home, and my family, of my mother and I cloistered together; her supposed 'hysterical' reading of her own body, and mine, of sickness spread by suggestion, imitation and (alternative) therapy; of our ill feelings as a shared language; of the doctors who read our 'circumstances' – poor, queer, female – as toxic and sick, as another symptom that needed to be relieved.

'Shannon Tiday's mother says her daughter has faced accusations that the condition is all in her head,' reads one report. At the time, Sharon was a ten-year-old girl from Plymouth with a diagnosis of ME/CFS. 'I was told maybe she is a bit of an attention seeker, maybe your daughter actually likes being ill.' The idea that someone – a child or adult – would want to be ill to get attention, have a belief they were ill when they were not or need to be ill in order to express their feelings, are all ways of making the person who feels ill responsible for their sickness. 'To tell you your child likes being ill, it's like saying your daughter doesn't really want her childhood,' said her mother. 'What child would want to be ill with an illness like this?' The well are not derided. They are not believed to be faking wellness. It is as if being well means you already have all the attention you need.

Why would you want to be ill when being ill is so much worse than being well?

The history of ME is haunted by women blamed for making their daughters ill and then caring for them too much. In 2008, Kay Gilderdale, previously a nurse, was charged and later acquitted of the attempted murder of her daughter Lynn, who had been bedridden with ME for seventeen years. Two years before Kay helped her daughter Lynn die, she was reported as saying her daughter was 'not dead, but not alive properly' due to her quality of life.

There are documents relating to Lynn's health online, because that's where sick people often share their experiences, advise others and conduct activism and advocacy. One is a letter by Kay, 'Appeal for appropriate care', which details Lynn's experience with doctors, including a psychiatric consultant who insisted on treating her as an in-patient, during which time her health rapidly declined to the point that she could do nothing for herself: 'We wanted to believe what they said so much that we held on, even when we saw her deterioration, but sixteen days after her admission, we knew we had to take her home.' Kay provides exact dates and lists her daughter's symptoms in medical language: muscle spasms, nausea and pain. For an appeal, the letter – asking that Lynn's case be considered when treating severely affected ME patients – is measured and clear, rather than 'emotional'. In her time caring for her daughter, Kay must have learnt how to speak to doctors.

Extracts of Lynn's online diary – meant to be read by a few friends – were published in the press after her death. 'This is no whim and certainly not just because of the reactive depression diagnosed a few months ago,' she wrote. 'I am no longer on anti-depressants because they weren't doing anything . . . I really, really, really want to die and have had enough of being so sick and in so much pain every second of every day and, basically, one serious health crisis after another.' 'My body and mind is broken . . . I have nothing left and I am spent.' *The Daily Mail* called it her 'diary of despair'. The article was illustrated with photographs of her doing ballet and sports, 'prior to her illness'.

Mothers who care for disabled children face significantly different demands than mothers of non-disabled children. They have more interactions with medical professionals and institutions, where they are frequently in the position of trying to get appropriate treatment and services for their children. During these interactions, the mothers' knowledge of their child will likely be ignored or discounted. The mother is expected to be completely self-sacrificing in their caregiving, and is often blamed for their children's disabilities, for the failure of treatment programmes, and for the children's inabilities to live independently – often an impossible ideal. 'In short, mothers of children with disabilities are subjected to more institutionalized control, more bureaucratic monitoring, and more social judgements of the quality of their caregiving than mothers of children without disabilities,' writes Susan Wendell in her book *The Rejected Body*. Such a society exploits mothers' caregiving, demands unlimited sacrifice from them, and then blames them for giving too much care. It is as if mother-child relationships are the real disease to be afraid of.

I tried so hard to get you help.

¶ The worst thing

In 1976, BBC Radio 4's Woman's Hour broadcast a segment on what was then termed 'Iceland disease' after an outbreak in Akureyri, Iceland in 1948. Dr Celia Wookey, a member of the Patients Association Iceland Disease Group, announced a survey she was undertaking, and invited people with experience of the condition to complete a questionnaire, requiring participants to indicate symptoms affecting them from a long list. This was not anonymous – participants were to include their name and contact details, with consent to contact their doctor wrapped in, and were asked to include stamps for replies from Wookey herself.

Wookey divided the symptoms between four columns, the first being what she thought of as 'the most useful' in diagnosing Iceland Disease: headaches, muscle pain, sensitivity to light, excessive fatigue, numbness, nausea, looking pale or 'grey', memory loss, insomnia, depression. The next three columns – presumably *not as useful* in diagnosing Iceland Disease, but common among people with the illness – contained a hodgepodge of symptoms, from abnormal bowel movements, vaginal discharge, painful joints and sore throats to more 'emotional' symptoms such as frequent crying, 'cold in head' and feelings of panic and guilt. This list of symptoms was followed by a number of questions concerning the participant's experience of illness: the time of day when symptoms were worse, how quickly they experienced the onset of symptoms, whether they had got any better, and if any other family members were affected. When Wookey first devised the questionnaire, the symptom of 'feeling awful' was included in the first column – the ones most useful in diagnosing Iceland Disease – but this was subsequently removed. Although it was 'too non-specific', it was surprising, Wookey later remarked, 'how many patients volunteered the information that they had never felt so awful in their lives.' Eighty-nine per cent of participants ticked this symptom, second only to 'excessive fatigue', which was reported by ninety per cent of respondents.

Wookey published the data collected in these questionnaires, and more detailed case studies, in 1986. The length of illness reported ranged wildly, from one to forty-four years. Thirty-one per cent of respondents reported having become ill suddenly, with sixty-one experiencing a more gradual onset. The longer they had it, the worse the prognosis, with the longer-affected reporting less improvement. Seventeen per cent had another family member who was affected. My mother and I would have been in that seventeen per cent, and we were not the only ones for whom this commonality was considered a sign of hysteria. In one of Wookey's case histories, a woman referred to as J.C. ('Case History 10') listed symptoms that were anything but 'non-specific'. They are, unless you have felt them yourself, too specific to make sense. Each one a question that was still unanswered after many years of illness: 'Why are certain parts of my arms so bruised and tender to touch with no bruising to show, and why if they are gently rubbed does the pain disappear for a short while? Why am I so much more emotional now than before the illness and why does my temperature rise every few weeks and chest pains last so long always on the left side and always when I'm still? Why is simply sitting perfectly still the recipe for the slow build-up of the ill head feeling that can become torture in its intensity.'

I have underlined this section in my copy of Wookey's book because some of these symptoms are like my symptoms, and some are like my mother's symptoms, and because, like 'Case Study 10', every one of our symptoms is a question, a chaos of cause and effect. Like my mother, J.C. was accused of teaching her children how to seem sick.

I too have that *ill head feeling*, the sensation of being punished, slowly.

J.C.'s illness began when she was thirty-five years old. As a child, she had hardly missed a day at school, and seemed to have 'boundless energy' as she got older. In the summer of 1972, both of her children became ill with infections and convulsions, but not with anything doctors could diagnose. After several months, the older son seemed not to recover, remaining languid, dreamy and pale, and becoming irritable, petulant and tearful. She spent her nights rubbing the back of his head, where it was tender. For many years, my mother – and whoever came to our flat to help her – did the same for me. Our experiences, two decades apart, overlap in more ways than this.

Her sons had been ill for a few months before J.C.'s strange symptoms began – pain that would not go away, tenderness at the back of the head, in the same place as her son's, aching, tiredness and tearfulness, high temperatures. She was 'indefinably unwell', unable to pinpoint how. When she was cleared of cancer, and her sons found not to have epilepsy, she started to feel her GP thought she was exaggerating not only about her children but also about herself. The day she says her illness began, after several weeks of decline, she was in Devon with her family. 'I lay there, wondering what had hit me; I felt as though I couldn't move.'

J.C. was diagnosed with what was called 'masked depression' and prescribed antidepressants by a psychiatrist, but her temperature was still erratic, and she was sent to Guy's Hospital for more testing. 'I didn't feel depressed,' she said, 'only frustrated and ill.' She 'wasn't used to being disbelieved'. But what would she have been disbelieved about before?

At the hospital, she was not allowed to sleep as much as she needed to, and was made to take walks, and eat sitting up. The psychologist was certain it was a medical problem, and the medical doctor was sure it was psychological. J.C.'s mother and husband convinced the psychologist she was not mentally unwell. If not for the care of her mother and husband, she was sure she would have been forced into psychological treatment, and 'chivvied', causing her to be bed bound like this for life. Upon exertion, she felt excruciating pains and sudden exhaustion, 'as though the cork from my energy bottle had been removed and life was draining away'.

Later, when she was eventually referred to a neurologist, they told her that she looked perfectly healthy and to 'not let imaginary illnesses get you down'. The doctor playfully slapped her on the arm, which hurt, and accelerated her anger. She blindly struck out sideways, sending the neurologist reeling: 'the culmination of anger that had been built up over the years of disbelief'.

Back at home and 'surrounded by love', but still with no diagnosis, J.C. slept for most of the day, the curtains drawn – just as my mother did. Her two children were intermittently ill, and the younger child collapsed at school. When their family GP examined him, complaining of leg and back aches, and abdominal pain, he commented that 'of course, a child would pick up symptoms if there was illness around him'. It was suggested that J.C., as a mother, was making them ill, and the boys would be 'better off' at boarding school. J.C.'s account was included in the broadcast on *Woman's Hour* with Dr Wookey. Exhausted and in pain, she was only able to participate having lain flat on the floor of Broadcasting House beforehand.

My mother has stories of disbelief like these, and not just from doctors – from women she knew who came to help her at home when she was bedbound early on, and my brother and I were still at primary school, women who had their own ideas about the reasons for her debilitation. A friend who cooked her dinner and then forced her to eat it sitting up at the table. The mother of a child at my school who would do my mother's shopping and then tell her she only believed she was ill. My mother did not have a husband, or a doting mother, to care for her, to convince people she was not mentally unwell – my mother had to do that herself. These were the people she relied on, with two young children. They were almost strangers: the other parents who took me back to their houses after school; the carers who did our laundry and cooking. Like J.C., our family life was affected by illness. Despite the economic disparity between our families, J.C. was still financially hit by her inability to work; she had to sell her car, her only means of travel, and so became effectively housebound.

Once my mother was confined to her bed most days, like J.C., it was normal for me to spend most of my time at other peoples' houses. I never had to accompany my mother to the supermarket because she couldn't go herself. She relied on friends to do her shopping and pick her children up from school. A friend would make her dinner and then tell her to get out of bed in order to eat it. She remembers a woman who was a psychiatrist and mother of a child at my school, who was one of the most helpful people to my mother when it came to the school run and food shopping but would tell my mother that she didn't think she was really ill, and that she just needed to 'get up and go for a run'.

'That would have been the worst thing for me to do,' she says.

¶ Fresh and gorgeous

'That was the day I couldn't walk,' she says.

Over breakfast, I had noticed a photo of my mother and brother that I hadn't seen before, newly displayed in a frame on the dining table. I told her she looked nice, not thinking about what year it must have been. My brother looks about five years old. She tells me it was taken by my godmother – her oldest friend – on my brother's birthday. We were all in Stanmer Park, an estate on the outskirts of Brighton. She thinks we played rounders – these are things I don't remember at all, they are the things she has to tell me.

'I ran,' she says, 'and then I couldn't move.'

Back at our flat, she went to bed while my godmother rang her GP. 'It was early on,' she says. What she means is: *I didn't know how ill I was. I didn't know I was going to be ill – on and off – for the next twenty-five years.*

It is just the two of us and the dogs for Christmas. Even without my brother – who for the last eighteen months has been dropping in to see my mother twice a week, and driving her to memorial services at the care home where my grandfather lived the last months of his life, and going to all events where her LGBT choir is singing at the weekends – we are squeezed in her house amongst too much furniture on which too many things are precariously perched, and not enough working radiators. At first, I can't bear her doing things, my patience is too limited. She won't be helped and won't listen when I tell her to stop and sit down. And I frustrate her. She doesn't want to be told what to do and acts like I am telling her off. I do the same to her: I have brought my stress with me and refuse to eat enough food. It always goes like this. We have both become too used to living alone, and too riled by each other's habits. I am too lazy, and she is not lazy enough. But after a few days, we settle. Her chest infection is clearing, but she keeps saying her legs hurt – 'You know, in *that way.*' *That way* means: 'I am too tired to try and explain what I mean.' I am too tired to explain what she means.

'But don't I look fresh and gorgeous,' my mother says, looking at the photograph of herself in her early thirties, with my brother on her lap. She does look young, and gorgeous, because she is. She is tanned, her face set with a calm, smiling expression. She doesn't look like a sick woman – at least, how they are depicted in paintings, or films, or stock images: slumped over, head in hands.

In the photograph in the park with my brother, she looks so composed. This composure was the product of innocence, of not knowing the severity of her illness, or the effects it would have on her life, but also of maintaining an appearance of wellness for her children and friend, of *keeping it together*. This composure masked an interior turmoil.

'I was unravelling,' says my mother.

This metaphor is structural more than visual. Unravelling refers to a textile that was once complete, woven and neat, until it starts to fray. Fabric can fall into nothing if a single thread is pulled for long enough.

To unravel is also to solve something complicated. It applies when the mysterious becomes *known*, when the case is solved. It is how EBB described her illness, which no doctor could explain: 'Time', she wrote, 'seems to have no effect in unravelling it.'

I know what it is to unravel. I cannot imagine what it would feel like to fall apart with two children to take care of.

My mother always looked well, and that, I am sure, worked against her. She did not look as ill as so-and-so, a woman my grandparents knew, who, they told my mother, *really* had ME. My mother did not look as unwell as the woman on her third or fourth round of cancer treatment who we would visit quietly in her single bed in the afternoons. When she was not bedridden, she always got dressed, every day. When she was able to work, my mother was never seen to be anything other than well, as the carer rather than the cared for, as if you can only be one or the other. In the mid-1990s, when that photograph in the park was taken, she might have looked well but she was anything but.

Stays at my grandparents' house when we were children were 'like a test'. They would watch my mother to make sure she was doing as much as everyone else. 'When they left me alone in the house,' my mother tells me, 'they would say: "don't just sit here and call all your

83

friends," like I was a grumpy teenager.' What made them think she wasn't as ill as she claimed to be? She already had a diagnosis, from a renowned Immunologist in London, but her GP still told her 'we were crazy' – even though they never referred us to a psychiatrist. Did they think she didn't *look* sick enough?

I, on the other hand, look sickly and pallid, and thin, dark circles, limp limbs, can't keep head up, in photographs. I tried to do dance lessons, but they would put me in bed.

'There was always a drama with your mother,' my grandmother said to me once. By 'drama' I think she was referring to my mother's illness, which seemed to have infected me, her child; 'the daily drama of the body', as Woolf put it. She was not believed, by doctors or her ex-husband, her own mother – or rather, she was believed to be 'making a drama' out of our situation, and ill feelings – hers and mine. She was a trained performer after all – a dancer, and a singer.

It was unfortunate that my mother has always known how to pose for photographs, to perform. When I was young, I used to come across her headshots in our family photo albums. Once she was ill, this training worked the other way. She answered the phone as if she had just woken up exhausted, whether she had or not. When able to work she posed as well, refusing to be seen to be as sick as she was. Posing as ill made her no less ill, just aware of other people's expectations of her as either sick and therefore unable to do very much at all, like answer the phone, or well enough to work, or clean the house, or look after her children on her own – which she could not. This is how I learnt that ill feelings are a kind of protection.

As a child, I lived within the boundaries my mother built, both safe and sick. These were the circumstances I found myself in: the wall I helped to build.

There was no doubt that the drama of our illness, which actually played out in bed, at home, in the dark, rather than in public, but was suddenly visible when encountered by anyone else, was specifically female in nature. Only women get called *hysterical*, especially mothers, or children. The assumption being they are less able to control themselves.

The names for ME/CFS are weapons used to blame sufferers,

to call them lazy, not really sick, but also not well enough to work: *invalid*. We were *visibly* able to do better but refusing to do so. We were stubborn, resistant scroungers. There was nothing really wrong with us: we *wanted* to be ill. I knew more about the stigma around my diagnosis than the history of it. I knew it was not what you wanted to be diagnosed with. The 'difficulty' of diagnosing it transfers onto the person being diagnosed – they too are labelled difficult.

What *does* a sick woman look like anyway?

EBB's portrait hangs next to her husband Robert Browning's in the National Portrait Gallery 'Early Victorians' room. Their bulky gilt frames tilt towards each other, slightly away from everyone else: the three Brontë sisters looking decidedly unimpressed, their brother having erased himself from the group portrait; George Eliot; Charles Dickens; the leader of the Gothic movement in architecture, Augustus Pugin; and Queen Victoria's favourite painter, Edwin Landseer. On the other side of the wood-panelled room is a bronze cast of the Browning couple's clasped hands in a glass cabinet. It's hard not to be immediately sceptical of such an object. They look too small to be life-size. How would you make a cast of two hands clasped together? Surely you would have to cast the two hands separately, in which case they were not holding hands at all.

The Brownings are seated in each of their portraits. Quick, messy strokes of paint describe the white lace around EBB's sleeve cuffs and the buttons down the front of her high-neck black dress. You can't see her hands. Her head drops slightly forward. The expression on her face says she is not at all surprised to see you. It says she has agreed to receive you, and that she would like you to leave again at some point soon, so she can rest, and work. She has puffy circles around her eyes, as if she told the painter, Michele Gordigiani, 'Don't bother painting them out,' or, perhaps, 'Try adding them in.'

Robert leans forward, his weight on his right elbow, resting on a table, or perhaps the arm of a sofa. His pose is immediately active. When I look at his face, I see hers: similar, as if they are related by blood rather than marriage. EBB also leans on her left arm, but her whole pose is stiffer, less chosen somehow, more difficult to hold, and there is something about the chair, which is as wide as it is high-backed, made of dark wood covered in an ochre fabric, and decorated with two rounded *oreilles*, or ears, at the top. The chair makes her look grand, like she's sitting on a throne. It is as if her body is boxed into the furniture, propped up by the back and arm of the chair, because she's unable to sit up for very long. When I walk around the rest of the gallery, I see that no one else has a chair like it in their portrait. The strange chair, the tired skin around her eyes, the sloping position: standing in front of the Browning portraits, I read her as sick and him as well. I am convinced this is a portrait of an ill woman, even though there is no mention of her condition in the wall text. Her profession is listed as Poet, not Invalid. Would you know she was housebound for most of her life from her portrait, if you did not know already? Maybe the chair was painted in afterwards, or it wasn't a chair at all. Perhaps it was a bed.

How is a sick woman *seen*?

Harriet Hosmer, the sculptor who cast *Clasped Hands of Robert and Elizabeth Barrett Browning*, described EBB as well as any portrait painter: 'The same abundant curls framing a face, plain in feature, but redeemed by wonderful dark eyes, large and loving and luminous as stars. The nose slightly disposed to upturn; the mouth, well, perhaps in this feature we discover the key to some of Mrs Browning's less delicate verse, large, full-lipped, yet harbouring always a sweet compensating smile. Her voice, slow and with the somewhat laboured enunciation peculiar to delicate health. The manner ever gracious, with a touch of shyness at times. Small in stature and in form so fragile that the gentlest zephyr might have borne her away.'

Hosmer thought Robert stood 'on a higher plane', 'fulfilling in every sense the ideal we have formed of a poet'. If Robert was energised and present, EBB was barely there at all. She was too delicate, too slow and contained, too unknowable, to be described as *the ideal we have formed of a poet*, and therefore more fascinating to Harriet, as a sculptor whose self-presentation and success relied on being energetic, a friend, and a woman who loved women. In 1857, at the end of a four-page letter from Robert about sick houseguests and winter weather forecasts pre-empting Harriet's arrival in Florence for another visit, EBB added her own note to the sculptor, written in the third person, using her nickname Ba, as if to confirm the tenuousness of her physical presence in the world: 'Ba's best love and as Robert won't wait, dearest Hattie, at Florence now, and Rome afterwards. E.B.B.'

It is said that Hosmer did not carve into the hands but left them precisely as they were cast: authentically *theirs*. Hosmer would know the difference, being welcomed first into their circle to spend time with the Brownings, and then into the intimate and time-consuming act of moulding their clasped hands herself.

At first, I thought it impossibly small, and too difficult to create the cast, to be real: a refusal on my own part, perhaps because of the general stuffiness of some of the pictures on the walls, and the power dynamic represented in such an uncommanding object. It is not just the cuffs around each of their wrists – Elizabeth's in lace, like that around her neck in her painted portrait; Robert's plain – that distinguish one from the other. Robert's hand is active; his fingers clasp hers, passively laid on top of his, as if someone had just put it there. If you turned the object around in your own hands, you would not see hers at all. The body from which her hand was cast could be asleep, or dead. That hand would slip out of hers if he only loosened his grip.

How does a sick woman *see herself*?

Unlike her predecessor, George Sand, 'Thou large-brained woman and large-hearted man', Elizabeth would write as a woman. Influenced by those who came before her, she would be a poet of her own making: *EBB*. In 1844, after many years of suspicious treatments for her confounding ill health, there were to be no more doctors. She prescribed her own treatment of poetry, rest, warmth, sensible eating and her beloved laudanum to help her sleep.

EBB thought herself 'little & black like Sappho' – who, like Hosmer, loved women – with 'a mouth suitable to a larger personality' and 'a very little voice'. She described herself as a 'blind poet' who knew little of 'life and man', for which she would gladly exchange her ponderous, helpless knowledge of books for some 'experience of life and man, for some . . .' Her painted likeness at the National Portrait Gallery captures her entirely: uncapturable, there and not there. The personality Harriet described, EBB's contradictions expressed in her physicality – upturned and loving, mouthy and sweet – are painted in with the dark circles around her eyes and the ornate carvings of her chair, its scale, I see now, used to show her small stature, rather than the grandness of her lodgings. I recognise myself in Harriet: invited into EBB's life and kept at a distance; unable to completely identify, or even fully encounter her – Elizabeth Barrett Browning, Ba, E.B.B. – as anything other than the elusive presence she created for herself.

¶ Danger signals

Several months after my mother's relapse following my grandmother's death, my mother asks for an MRI scan. It reveals nothing, except her similarity with other people who have imaginary illnesses.

'They didn't find the lesion,' she tells me, on the phone from the neurologist's. If my mother is still seeking a physical cause for her ill feelings, despite being told repeatedly by doctors there is nothing physically wrong with her, it is not because she is convinced she has a lesion in the brain, but because she has new – and terrifying – symptoms all the time. A lesion sounds like a relief because someone might then take her seriously.

'If I had a lesion then everyone would believe me,' she says. 'They wouldn't think I was mad.' I have to oppose her, or I will think I am mad too. I would rather she did not have a lesion.

Later, I will read the letter reporting the results of the MRI scan to her GP, for which the neurologist felt the need to state she was 'very emotional', and that she had cried during the appointment. She is sometimes too articulate, which is another kind of untrustworthiness. It is as if not-being-sick is the real curse. After all, isn't a test supposed to result in a diagnosis, and then potential treatments? Aren't tests the first step on the path to cure and recovery? Ours have only ever come back either 'negative or normal' and have therefore dictated the diagnoses and treatments we have received: chronic fatigue syndrome, ME, fibromyalgia, *hysteria*. Woolf knew, without knowing what was really wrong with her, that you can name a problem – influenza, tired heart – any number of ways, and still not know how to solve it. 'What is a "murmur"?' she asked in 1922. 'I don't know – but I gather it's not a thing that matters in the least.'

In the absence of any meaningful referrals – we had one session of family therapy, several years after she had pleaded for help from the local service – my mother took me to a clinic that provided heavily subsidized alternative treatments for families on benefits. At the homeopath's I would try to describe how my body felt, which parts were hurting and how. My mother sat next to me, urging me to speak, because, as with most treatment for physically unexplained illness, you need to be able to say what you are feeling: there is no other test. My mother would remind me of something I told her on the phone; that some pain had got worse, or better; that I had more energy, or less. But I didn't have a verbal language, the kind that pain destroys and that the body remembers. It was as if my body had its own rules for feeling, thinking and remembering. Every few weeks the homeopath altered my chemistry with varying doses of zinc – the only thing that seemed to have any effect, to the extent that it made me visibly spaced out – from her cabinet of powdering white pills, indistinguishable apart from their labels. She always asked me to keep a diary, to write down how I was feeling, otherwise she would not know if it was working, but I never did. When I looked up the uses of zinc many years later, I read: '*Zincum met* is often considered where there is restlessness of feet or legs. This remedy type also exhibits a poor memory, mental exhaustion, sleeping difficulties, weakness, headache felt in the occiput or temples, poor sleep and a sore throat.' *Weak, restless, difficult* – it is as if the language of the illness I was diagnosed with, and the remedies used to treat it, was written into my nature.

How we felt did not match up to what could be recorded externally. We didn't look as sick as we said we were. Our testimony was the only proof.

'I'm sinking down, and down,' my mother says.

We are lying in two separate beds against opposite walls in her bedroom, facing each other, a dog curled up with each of us. She has not moved yet. 'It's as if I won't be able to get up.'

She sounds like she is quoting Woolf's diary – 'Directly I stop working I feel that I am sinking down, down. And as usual, I feel that if I sink further I shall reach the truth' – or Emily Dickinson in her poem, 'I Felt a Funeral, in my Brain', one of 360 poems she wrote in 1862:

And then a Plank in Reason, broke,
And I dropped down, and down –
And hit a World, at every plunge,
And Finished knowing – then –

'– and my ears, obviously,' my mother says.

'Your ears?' I ask, feigning confusion so she would explain what she means. I know my mother knows this feeling well.

'You know,' she says, 'that white noise surging through your ears.'

'Yes,' I say. 'I know exactly what you mean.'

I am sure she has said this to me before, but I have never really *heard* her say it. It is as if I have tuned her ill feelings out, and mine along with them. I know what she means because I have felt that same sensation myself. I have felt that plank break too.

According to Leonard Woolf in his autobiography *Beginning Again*, physical symptoms often preceded a breakdown in Virginia's mental state. Headaches, insomnia and physical strain were what he called 'serious danger signals', which could send her back to the nursing home for treatment. The first symptoms were a peculiar headache low down at the back of the head, insomnia and a tendency for the thoughts to race. 'If she went to bed and lay doing nothing in a darkened room, drinking large quantities of milk and eating well, the symptoms would slowly disappear and in a week or ten days she would be well again.' Leonard encouraged Virginia to *go to bed* to save her physical symptoms turning into mental strain, which was 'far more dangerous', and harder to treat, because, unfortunately, you can tell a woman like Virginia to rest but 'you cannot tell her not to think, work or write'. Leonard could only read her behaviours as a series of signs, having no access to the real pulses she was feeling in her own body, the ones that told her 'No', that forced her to refuse food and rest.

Leonard found her refusal to eat one of her most troubling 'danger signals'. During these periods, she would maintain that she was not ill, 'that her mental condition was due to her own fault – laziness, inanition, gluttony'. If she lived 'a quiet, vegetative life, she was well and sane', he maintained, 'but to tell her, as doctors always did and I often had to tell her, that she must live a quiet, vegetative life, was absurd, terribly ironical'. Virginia believed illness was her punishment. And who wouldn't, after several rounds of treatment by doctors who consistently prescribed rest at the nursing home, 'stuffing', and three glasses of milk a day, who insisted you were neurasthenic, that there was something wrong with your nervous system, that it couldn't be 'beaten for extreme eccentricity', that you were perhaps 'insane'. Leonard interpreted Virginia's hostility to treatment, and the nurses and doctors around her, as one such danger signal: 'She would argue as if she had never been ill – that the whole treatment had been wrong, that she ate too much and lived a life too lethargic and quiet. Below the surface of her mind and of her argument there was, I felt, some strange, irrational sense of guilt.' Guilt is the horror of seeing oneself as others see you. It is perfectly normal, until it is 'irrational', when it becomes so immobilising it sends you to your bed, or through a window.

My mother speaks of feeling as if she has been poisoned, or run over, of being knocked sideways, or *hit by a truck and left at the side of the road.* Or *sinking down, and down.* My mother's language for ill feelings is incomprehensible to doctors. She is not really sinking. This is how she is feeling, both physically and emotionally, because they are very much related. The feeling of *sinking down, and down,* or *white noise surging in your ears,* are what most people would probably just call feelings. To my mother, they are symptoms of illness. I still cannot see why they have to be one or the other. In the absence of understanding about what is causing the pain that we feel, we imagine what our illnesses look like.

In her 1982 book *The Mile-High Staircase,* Toni Jeffreys tells the story of a woman who tried to tell her doctor that there was a crab inside her, 'tearing at her with its claws, eating her'. No physical evidence was found at the time, because the technology available was not capable of detecting the problem, and she was placed in a mental hospital. Years later, when another doctor (the doctor who told Jeffreys the story) was called upon to perform emergency surgery on the same woman, he discovered that she had a stomach ulcer greater in diameter than a grapefruit, which is very large for a stomach ulcer. She was right, there was a mass in her body – not crabs, exactly, but not nothing either. It was as if she had had too much flair for metaphor. It was impossible – just like being injected by a huge syringe from the sky or being in a microwave.

My mother says: 'The antidepressants are still making me feel like a mung bean.' It sounds like a hex, a witch's curse: 'One eye is on top of the other and my brain is full of slop.' Does sinking further down and down mean you reach the truth? What if the truth is: there is nothing wrong with you? What if it is: this is your fault? How far down would you have to go?

The author Susan Wendell once told a specialist that relapses of her disease could happen so suddenly that it felt like being injected with strong poison. Decades later, the metaphor still seemed like a good one, and one that most people would be able to grasp, but from the look on the specialist's face, she knew she was 'in danger of being sent to a psychiatrist forthwith'. Others with an ME diagnosis agreed with the description, but she never used it again to describe her ill feelings to medical professionals. 'Yet who knows, at this early stage of investigation, that my metaphor might not provide a valuable clue to the nature of the disease?' It is certainly one my mother has used. It is a metaphor I too feel in my body.

'The more I have learned about medicine, the more nervous and careful I have become about describing my own symptoms,' wrote Wendell in *The Rejected Body: Feminist Philosophical Reflections on Disability*, published in 1996. As someone with a diagnosis of ME/CFS, her use of the word *nervous* is striking.

One weekend in 1985, Wendell, a professor of Women's Studies, came down with what she describes as the worst flu she had ever experienced. She went to bed with a high fever, coughing, nausea, light-sensitivity, perceptual distortions and intense pain in her joints and muscles. Her fever subsided after a week, but she kept getting weaker, and many of her symptoms persisted. She became virtually bedridden and could not walk to the end of her street. After about nine months of illness, a specialist she was seeing regularly told her there was nothing more she could do. It took her two years of gradual exercise to return to work part time. Her constant muscle pain, weakness and periods of profound fatigue with dizziness and/or nausea and/or depression, headaches lasting for several days and intermittent problems with short-term memory, especially verbal recall, persisted for many years. To function well she needed ten hours of sleep a night, and to rest lying down for several hours a day. She eventually managed to work three-quarter time as a professor, but otherwise lived 'a quiet, rather careful life'.

At the time she became ill, in the 1980s, doctors in the UK were familiar with her illness, but ME was virtually unknown in North America: 'The history of my own illness has coincided with the gradual discovery of ME/CFIDS [CFS] by the rest of the world.' As time went on, Wendell's struggles were not with the disease and its somewhat unpredictable limitation around which she could plan as best she could. Her struggles became primarily social, and what she termed 'psycho-ethical': 'I live in the world of the healthy (or fairly healthy),' she wrote. 'I do not "look sick" or "sound sick" as people tell me all the time, and I think only those who know me well can see when I am having a hard time with fatigue, nausea, or pain.' The disability caused by her chronic illness was not readily apparent to most of the people around her.

Wendell articulates the alienation, including that felt between patients and their own experience, that can occur when the language of scientific medicine dominates encounters between doctors and patients. Language like *malaise*, or even *fatigue*, which is not necessarily an accurate description of someone's experience. A doctor with ME tells Wendell she calls fatigue 'cellular exhaustion' – a description that draws on scientific language, but not scientific fact. 'Cellular exhaustion' is closer to how she feels in her body, which is mediated by scientific understanding. It is not that she is experiencing her body as cellular, but that she experiences exhaustion that is so deep and pervasive, that it feels as though something is wrong at a cellular level. 'Fatigue' is misleading, in that it suggests a normal condition experienced by healthy people, which can be corrected by rest, food or other strategies of renewal. 'Cellular exhaustion', on the other hand, writes Wendell, 'suggests an abnormal condition, of a quality, severity, or persistence not experienced by healthy people, that is not responsive to normal strategies. The latter is much closer to the experience of ME patients.'

Wendell speaks so candidly about the complex relationship between chronic illness and disability, and the assumptions people make about you when for all intents and purposes you are visibly

94

well and undeniably sick. Her book provides relief in that it is not concerned with searching for cures.

When I email her, Wendell replies to tell me she doesn't talk to anyone about ME anymore. She does not say why, but she does not need to explain. I can of course cite her book, she says, which is in the public domain. Her email is kind but formal, and legal. She has done the work she is able to do. She has already written her experience, already told me everything I need to know. She argued for a feminist disability theory in 1989, only a few years into her illness:

'People without disabilities tend to assume that a person with a disability is unable to participate in most of the life activities they consider important,' she wrote. 'Thus they infer that someone who can work at all cannot be significantly disabled.'

Wendell was speaking to mine and my mother's experience of common assumptions about disability, about how difficult it was to accept our own limitations, and even more so to convince others to accommodate them. She writes candidly about her struggles with guilt towards people at work, her community, and friends and family: 'I need other people to accept my physical limitations, to take my word for it that I cannot do more than I am already committed to, or that when I say I need to rest, I do, or that I had to spend the previous day in bed.' *Is that so much to ask?*

How do we ask for acceptance without risking the accusation that we simply do not want to do something, to carry our share of the load? How are we supposed to be good when, like good people everywhere, we are supposed to give everything we have until it hurts? 'Everyone is supposed to feel exhausted and overworked,' writes Wendell, 'so why should I be the exception? We don't have time to be ill, to coddle ourselves.' In Wendell's time, there was no place for self-care and wellness, which have been politicized and de-politicized over the last four decades. It is hard to shake the feeling that if you are not exhausted and overworked, that must mean you are not really pulling your weight.

'I don't want to be scared,' says my mother, sounding like J.C., whose worst symptom she reported as the 'frightening indescribable malaise' that deprived her of her true personality. 'Scared' is not on the list of Wookey's symptoms – but appears in the case histories of the participants she interviewed. My mother is fearful of how her body feels because she has pushed herself too hard, because she has not rested regularly enough to do anything but stay alive, because she has crashed too fast, and can feel herself *sinking down and down*.

I too feel myself sinking, and am often frightened, and scared. It takes someone to make a space – a questionnaire, a radio programme, a book – to be able to speak or write your own case history of ill feelings, to build a language of your own, to describe them to one another. I have only just begun to speak about my experience of ill feelings. Will the time come when I say: I don't want to talk about it anymore?

'But I have had restlessness till it made me almost mad,' EBB wrote in 1845 of an earlier time: 'I lost the power of sleeping quite – and even in the day, the continual aching sense of weakness has been intolerable – besides palpitation – as if one's life, instead of giving movement to the body, were imprisoned undiminished within it, and beating and fluttering impotently to get out, at all the doors and windows.' The words 'almost' and 'quite' in this letter are so politely feminine, at once dramatized and restrained. She doesn't scream like the hysteric, which is, presumably, along with her race, gender, class and independent wealth, how she got access to the healthcare she required.

This hysteric does not wail and scream. They beat and flutter.

In her letters, I read the effort of being practical and rational – nothing close to hysterical, or addicted. 'It might strike you as strange that I who have had no pain – no acute suffering to keep down from its angles – should need opium in any shape.' The symptoms she writes of at this time are so familiar to me, and my mother: weakness, sleeplessness and insomnia, the feeling of being imprisoned by a living body, overwhelmed by its sensations, and wanting to escape it all together. I want to reach into her metaphors and find my own buried within.

EBB writes of a web of pain that would be smoothly unravelled in death. In the sonnet 'Pain in Pleasure', she animates thoughts, imagining them as flowers and bees, pleasing forms of life, each with the power to cause pain.

96

A THOUGHT lay like a flower upon mine heart,
And drew around it other thoughts like bees . . .
The thought I called a flower, grew nettle-rough –
The thoughts called bees, stung me to festering.
Oh, entertain (cried Reason, as she woke,)
Your best and gladdest thoughts but long enough.
And they will all prove sad enough to sting.

Pain lends itself to metaphor, welcomes it, even – like illness in general. If pain is a web that holds me inside it, it also unravels me. It is possible, sometimes, to unravel *it* – the mysteries of my nervous body – in turn.

Sometimes there is no reason for our ill feelings, just like there isn't enough language: it is too arbitrary. When my mother is feeling very ill, she says: 'My ME is really bad.' It's another way of saying 'awful' – not specific enough for a questionnaire.

I say: 'I feel like shit.' If my ill feelings are a part of me, there is pain that cannot be completely relieved.

'I feel like a hard-boiled egg being pushed through a slicer,' my mother says to me on the phone, another attempt to describe how she is feeling in her body-mind. I have only ever seen an egg slicer at my grandmother's house, used for cutting eggs into mayonnaise and pressed between slices of buttered white bread. I have never known my mother to have an egg slicer, so, I think, she must feel like she is being pushed through the one my grandmother owned. I imagine the egg slicer as the opposite of a medical device – separating indefinitely rather than containing, an object of torture, or imprisonment; a cruel punishment. You can't put a sliced egg back together.

Five years after my grandmother died, my mother still talks about her ears: 'You know, that whooshing sound when it clicks in; and then an eeeeeeeeee.'

I imagine my pain much like the map of my peripheral nervous system, spreading out like flames through my body from its centre, like flowers over the back of someone struck by lightning.

¶ Examine me

The reception is empty when I arrive at the specialist outpatients clinic. I have passed through the busy ENT department and reached a dead end: a waiting room with blue painted walls and large windows, heated by the February sun. I stand there for five minutes before someone enters, asking when my appointment is. I think she is the receptionist, but she is actually the psychologist I will speak to in around forty-five minutes time, once I have seen the consultant rheumatologist, and a physiotherapist. She hands me a patient health questionnaire to fill out while I wait.

The format of the questionnaire will be familiar to anyone who has presented with depression or anxiety. I have to rate how often I have been 'bothered' by a number of 'problems', divided up between two categories labelled only A) and B), over the last two weeks: 0 ('not at all') to 3 ('nearly every day'). I take the piece of paper and sit on a lilac plastic chair, peeling my winter coat halfway down my back to cool down. A sign on the empty reception booth reads 'Be amazing!' in pink.

The GAD-7 is a seven-question anxiety screening test, developed in 2006. The PHQ-9 is a self-administered patient health questionnaire, a version of the Primary Care Evaluation of Mental Disorders developed by Dr Robert Spitzer and his team for the American pharmaceutical company Pfizer in the 1990s. The PHQ-9 measures against the nine DSM-IV criteria for Major Depressive Disorder, which have more or less carried over to the DSM-V, and include depressed mood or loss of interest or pleasure in daily activities, impaired social functions, fatigue, diminished ability to concentrate, feelings of worthlessness, insomnia or hypersomnia, and suicidal thoughts. Once a patient has been screened for conditions that may mimic or coexist with Major Depressive Disorder, such as substance abuse, medical illness, other psychiatric disorders or bereavement, the diagnosis of Major Depressive Disorder can be confirmed. For scores over ten (10–14: moderate depression), pharmacotherapy is advised. Pfizer also happens to be the company that introduced the SSRI Zoloft (sertraline) to the market in 1991, and makes Lyrica (pregabalin) for neuropathic pain, which is also FDA-approved for the treatment of fibromyalgia in the US. In 2009, Pfizer, which merged with UK company GlaxoSmithKline in 2018, was forced to pay $2.3 billion in criminal penalties and settlements for marketing Lyrica and three other drugs for non-approved uses. Despite owning the copyright for the PHQ-9, it licenses the test for free.

I circle the numbers I think reflect *how often I have been bothered* by my tiredness, inability to concentrate and disturbed sleep – symptoms of depression but also fibromyalgia and ME/CFS – while a man wearing what looks like a hazmat plastic suit moves several lines of chairs out of the way to access the electrics in the ceiling. Another outpatient – a man in his sixties – emerges from his initial consultation and sits down on a chair behind me. He checks his phone, having already filled in his questionnaire.

The lowest you can score is zero, and the highest is twenty-seven. Despite taking antidepressant medication and attending weekly talking therapy, mine is clearly in the twenties: *severe*. None of the specialists I see that day at the outpatient clinic use the diagnosis 'Severe Depression' or 'Major Depressive Disorder' but each of them points at the piece of paper with the circles around the number threes, and tell me I have scored very highly, which almost feels like winning but is very much losing. Where do all these pieces of paper that record my mental health as I have judged it on a specific day go? I think about this alternative health archive of which I do not have a copy: does anyone look at them? Are they digitized? In any case, I was not referred here for a diagnosis of depression, so why am I taking this test?

In the consulting room, the rheumatologist asks me questions about my mood, whether pain or fatigue 'affects' me more, or whether they are equal, which they are. I tell her the pain I was in a month ago has relieved somewhat since I started taking an antidepressant (SNRI) called Venlafaxine, which I had to ask my GP for, having read that it has been shown to reduce neuropathic pain – the kind of pain you get after shingles or a spinal cord injury – but also pain associated with fibromyalgia, the kind of pain that doesn't appear to have any cause at all.

99

'Is that because your mood has improved?' the rheumatologist asks with a smile.

'That's the thing,' I say, gesturing to the questionnaire with all the threes ringed: 'It hasn't.'

I narrate my experience of pain, cognitive problems and fatigue over the last twenty years, the way these symptoms have waxed in periods of stress or distress – when I had started a new school at eleven, when I was approaching my final BA exams at twenty, when a relationship slowly broke down and then broke at thirty-one – and waned in others. This narrative makes sense to an extent, until it doesn't. (Some days I am in more pain than others, and there is no apparent reason why. I am never not in pain.) This narrative shows willing. It demonstrates thought, and reason: that the doctors know best. But as I speak, I hear someone else talking – the story I am telling does not sound right at all. It sounds neat, and structured. And it does not sound like my voice. It does not sound like angry silence.

She asks to examine me. I hold out my arms as she pinches the tips of my fingers, working over my hands and then up my arms in one quick motion, triggering what I know to be unreasonable shocks of pain. My face screws up, and my mouth makes short intakes of breath as I speak:

Yes.

Yes.

Yes.

I feel each of her fingertips as a sharp object as she continues to press all the way up my legs. By this point I am holding my breath, silenced by what feels more like a procedure than a test, unable to say Yes in the agony. Every time I say Yes, my body is screaming No. When she holds my foot and lightly twists my leg, pain explodes in my hip.

'I touched you very lightly,' she says afterwards.

'Liar,' I want to say. 'If I were to look down, I would see stab marks on my skin.' The rheumatologist explains that I definitely have fibromyalgia: all my blood tests were either negative or normal, but I am still fatigued and in a lot of pain.

'Fibromyalgia is just a name that stuck,' she says; 'it just means

100

you have pain.' She does not refute that I am in pain, just that there is a physical cause for it. 'The likelihood is that this will not go away, but the main thing to remember is that you cannot be disabled by it.'

What she means is: there is nothing physically wrong with me. I am not injured or inflamed, my connective tissue and muscles are not damaged, therefore I cannot be physically – medically speaking – *incapacitated*, even if that is, on occasion, my everyday experience. For some reason my body hasn't learnt how to switch out of 'crisis mode', and is sending pain signals to my brain without proper cause. *The Name That Stuck* is defined as 'a distinct pathophysiology involving central amplification of peripheral sensory signals'.

'We could call it pain symptom syndrome,' she says.

That's a shitty name for a syndrome, I think, having not actually spoken in a long time. The experience of illness and the diagnosed syndrome itself suddenly feel very distinct, as if one were not related to the other at all. I have always hated the word *syndrome*. A syndrome is vague by definition: 'A group of symptoms of a disease to which some particular name is given.' There are hundreds of syndromes, and many are named after places (Stockholm syndrome) or the doctors who first described it in detail (Prader–Willi syndrome). Unlike a disease, a syndrome can be a *suggestion*.

I have questions but not the kind I can ask. What would have happened if I had circled all the zeros instead of all the threes on my patient mental health questionnaire? Would you diagnose me differently or assume I was lying? Why is my body misfiring and not someone else's? What if there is something else going wrong, but it's happening where no one is looking? What if there is something wrong with my central nervous system? Has my blood been tested for elevated cytokines? Has it been tested for Lyme?

She might have meant physically incapacitated, but she said *disabled*. Medicalisation presents a view of the disabled individual as tragic. You can of course have a chronic illness and be able to do some tasks one day and none the next but *disabled* – that is considered a dirty word. Either way, disability is a construct, an ideological one determined by capitalism and individualism, but it is also a social construct. 'Despite the objective reality, what becomes

101

a disability is determined by the social meanings individuals attach to particular physical and mental impairments,' wrote sociologists Albrecht and Levy in 1981. 'Certain disabilities become defined as social problems through the successful efforts of powerful groups to market their own self interests.' Disability is, in part, produced by the social policies concerning it. When the rheumatologist says, 'I cannot be disabled by it', she is also saying 'the state does not consider this a disability', i.e. I cannot be disabled in the eyes of policy; I am not eligible for disability benefits. She means: I am on my own.

My appointment at the specialist outpatient clinic confirmed I didn't have osteoarthritis, or rheumatoid arthritis – but blood test results had already ruled these diagnoses out. My pain was not localised, meaning it was both specific (to me) and general (the whole of my body), and I was not inflamed. This is why I received my diagnosis, on the basis that it is not a diagnosis, just a *name that stuck*.

For several centuries, muscle pains were known as rheumatism, or muscular rheumatism. 'Suffering is diagnosed relentlessly as personal,' Adrienne Rich wrote in 1996. And, 'we lack a vocabulary for thinking about pain as communal and public.' Rich had rheumatoid arthritis, and underwent numerous operations, but she mostly avoided associating the pain she wrote about with her own body. She didn't want that writing to be reduced to her illness, or herself. Her writing on pain becomes a gift to all of us – already beyond herself and her body, it is free to release us too:

> The problem is
> to connect, without hysteria, the pain
> of any one's body with the pain of the body's world
> For it is the body's world
> they are trying to destroy forever
> The best world is the body's world
> filled with creatures   filled with dread
> misshapen so   yet the best we have
> our raft among the abstract worlds

A different, specific pain – her pain – is *inside* her body, and she is signified by it, not the other way around:

Dear Adrienne,
  I feel signified by pain
from my breastbone through my left shoulder down
through my elbow into my wrist is a thread of pain
I am typing this instead of writing by hand
because my wrist on the right side
blooms and rushes with pain
like a neon bulb
You ask me how I'm going to live
the rest of my life
Well, nothing is predictable with pain
Did the old poets write of this?
– in its odd spaces, free,
many have sung and battled –
But I'm already living the rest of my life
not under conditions of my choosing
wired into pain
                    rider on the slow train
                    Yours, Adrienne

But I am not writing about pain – the feeling of it, anyway. I am writing about the naming of that pain as more than a sign of a possible – diagnosable – disease, even when that pain has 'an Element of Blank', as Dickinson wrote. *So the pain not be wasted.*

That morning at the specialist outpatient clinic, I also see a psychiatrist and a physiotherapist. In every appointment, I notice how compliant I am being. I don't speak back, or query anything said to me. I nod. I don't even ask questions, apart from one: 'Are you going to write all of this in a letter because I won't be able to remember what you are telling me?' When I mention this to my mother a few days later, she will say that in the doctor's office she is 'a good girl'; she is well behaved and resists the urge to ask questions: 'It happens every six months, I ask for another test because my

103

heart is beating irregularly, but then I quieten down again. I don't want to get into trouble.'

The psychiatrist decides that the scenes of violence to my own body I often imagine reflect a more general sense of bodily susceptibility rather than the desire or habit of self-harm, which can induce relief in some people with mental health difficulties. I feel like I'm under physical threat when I'm in public, which she seems to think reasonable.

'That is fair enough,' she says, in relation to this sense, and these images, which often involve my skin being sliced open. 'You feel pain and tiredness in your body. Of course you feel vulnerable.' Now I don't ask questions because I don't have the energy. Are they still suicidal thoughts if I'm not the one inflicting pain but I'm the one having them? Is that a different kind of fantasy?

I don't know what she writes down. She seems strangely satisfied. I get the sense I should be achieving more and doing more. I am not *disabled*, after all.

The physiotherapist offers me hydrotherapy and physiotherapy, explaining they don't offer massage – 'and anyway, *everyone* likes massage' – because the NHS guidelines state that exercise is more effective as a treatment. I can sense her picking over her words carefully. Pain and fatigue are messages: they signal for you to stop moving, to rest after injury or infection, 'but in people with fibromyalgia that only makes the problem much worse', she says. I think she means: I could cause myself *real* damage if I listened to my body, if I stopped to rest when it was screaming in pain.

'How old are you, thirty-one?' she says, looking down at her notes. 'You're still young; you should be able to do what you want to do.' She means: *don't write yourself off yet*. I almost agree with her. I accept her offers. What does she say to the women in their fifties, or the man in his sixties who she saw before me? I do not verbally question why someone with pain associated with depression can't have massage as well as hydrotherapy. I don't say: 'I don't think anyone is faking crippling pain to get a free back rub.'

At the specialist outpatient clinic, I do not say: But I *am* disabled. Or: The thing is, I should not have to do what I don't want to do.

No one says: 'It could be that fibromyalgia is actually nerve pain, and that's why your medication is working.'

'You need to build up how much you exercise,' the physio advises. 'So, if you walk for thirty minutes a day, start increasing it by ten per cent, which isn't really that much.'

In a few months' time, before a hydrotherapy session, the same woman will say: 'Getting up in the morning and going to work might not seem like a goal, because it's not something we even think about really.' A woman in the group will respond, calmly: 'You would if you had fibromyalgia.' I will stop myself from laughing. I will want to push the physiotherapist in the pool and tell her to get back out into the cold basement room and feel the pain shooting up her spine.

Why am I asking for a medical diagnosis, for this name that has stuck to refer to my meaningless sack of symptoms? I know this clinic is here to relieve me, to tell me I can be as abled or disabled as I want, that I have not been granted a real disease that would require invasive treatment, and that, to a great extent, is indeed a relief. I need this name, this syndrome, so I can get treatment beyond the SNRI I have asked for, even if that treatment is not really what I want. I know that patients report improved satisfaction with their health, fewer symptoms and reduced healthcare costs, once they have a diagnosis of fibromyalgia. They are telling me I am okay because I am. It is me telling them I am not. At the confirmation of my diagnosis, I feel relief and panic at the same time: *what happens now?*

Diagnosis is rarely affirmative. It can introduce you to new information, possible treatments and even a supportive community, a group of people, a forum, a place to share your experiences, the feeling you are not alone. And it can shut you in a category. Diagnosis is, in the words of Eli Clare, a queer disabled academic and writer, 'a tool and a weapon shaped by particular belief systems, useful and dangerous by turns'. You have to question if this naming works in your favour, and how will it be used against you.

That day I walk for thirty minutes, thinking that is one way to start, to act on an instruction, any kind of advice. When I get home, I sleep for hours and hours, waking up at 6.30pm thinking it must be past ten. What *now*?

105

¶ Intolerable bursting

The term 'fibrositis' was coined by British neurologist Sir William Gowers in 1904. Originally covering acute lumbago, brachial neuritis (a form of peripheral neuropathy) and similar conditions, for which Gower said that there was no indication of the formation of inflammatory fibres but that this was not enough to justify a denial of its inflammatory nature, it was much more loosely applied as the century progressed. Pain associated with fibrositis usually varied from 'a vague stiffness' to an 'agonizing burning or stabbing pain, and in all cases the pain is made worse by movement of the affected part and by cold and damp'. J.B. Harman identified two types of fibrositis pain: a 'sharp' quality 'such as is found with painful lesions of the superficial structures of the body' and a 'dull' quality, ranging from 'a mere ache to an intolerable bursting or cramp, such as may arise from the viscera; and, more important still, the pain is so poorly localized that its greatest intensity may be felt at some distance from its point of origin'. The name 'fibromyalgia' emerged much later, when Harvey Moldofsky and Hugh Smythe, working with ideas developed by J.H. Kellgren on referred pain, described widespread pain and 'tender points', pain when pressed via digital palpation on eighteen points across the body, in the 1970s. The first American College of Rheumatology criteria were developed by Frederick Wolfe and published in 1990. At the time, Wolfe thought fibromyalgia was a disease. He now sees fibromyalgia as a 'continuum', a physical response to stress, depression and economic and social anxiety. 'Some of us in those days thought that we had actually identified a disease, which this clearly is not,' Wolfe told the *New York Times* in 2008. 'To make people ill, to give them an illness, was the wrong thing.'

Only identifiable diseases get names. Being in a lot of pain is not an identifiable disease – it is a symptom, in this case, without an apparent cause. Pain is almost beyond medicine, beyond the body; Kellgren said that the phenomena of pain belonged to 'that borderland between the body and the soul'. This is the power of diagnosis. It is more than a name. It can be a curse, a *wrong thing*.

106

If my ill feelings are a symptom of the human condition, why do I feel them more, or have a lower tolerance of them? Isn't *everyone* in pain? Isn't that what makes us *human*? Except, of course, I am not *human*, I am also *gendered*.

Between eighty to ninety per cent of people diagnosed with fibromyalgia are women. (Male, as far as I can tell) specialists and researchers have speculated that this is because women have 'less muscle'. Studies have reported that women have a 'lower tolerance of pain'.

There is a hierarchy of pain, and women's pain is *the worst* – not objectively worse, they just *feel* it more. Pain, when it is relayed by women – in a medical context, in any context – is inevitable, insurmountable, and indexes only their gender. Their bodies are speaking out of term, amplifying sensations others find bearable, maybe even negligible. If only these women would *stop listening* to the pain. They might be able to do *what they want to do*.

I am not a tender person. I am small, and hard.

Does being in pain make me a woman? Even if I don't actually feel like one?

Wolfe's original American College of Rheumatology diagnostic criteria for fibromyalgia relied on a diagram of tender points as well as widespread chronic pain. The idea being that if you had eleven or more out of eighteen tender points, you would receive a diagnosis of fibromyalgia.

Both occiputs –

Yes

and the second ribs

Yes

and the lateral epicondyles

Yes

and knee (medial fat pad proximal to the joint line) and the upper outer quadrants of buttocks

Yes

and the posterior to the trochanteric prominence

Yes

These are the sites where tension is more likely to occur, in any body. For people with fibromyalgia, they hurt all the time. It's the feeling of your body holding itself together – except it is also pain that defies the physiology of the body itself. It is the sensation of *pulling yourself together* but, unsurprisingly, not being able to.

Without a blood test, physicians rely on self-reporting – testimony gathered in conversation with the patient, and questionnaires about the frequency and severity of their symptoms, such as the ones I was asked to complete at the specialist outpatient clinic. 'Self-reporting is important,' Wolfe has said in an interview. 'When I wake up in the morning with a headache, no one else knows I have a headache or how severe it is. Whether I choose to go to work or not go to work, it is based on the severity which is only known to me.'

What is it with these people comparing disabled peoples' everyday experiences with their own – non-disabled – one?

Except Wolfe also said, in the same interview: 'Self-reporting is inherently problematic. Inherently it has a degree of validity problems.' Self-reporting is inherently problematic for science, as it is a subjective outcome with implicit bias. Tender points might seem like a more objective criteria for diagnosing the condition, but that didn't work either. In 2005, Wolfe conducted a study that showed that the ACR tender point requirement actually hindered the fibromyalgia diagnosis in general practice, as many patients with clinical fibromyalgia had fewer positive tender points on their assessment day than the required cut-off for a classification. The new 2010 criteria employed a 'widespread pain index' that evaluates nineteen areas of the body for pain, and a 'symptom severity score' that analyses the severity of fatigue, waking unrefreshed and cognitive symptoms, which 'may be helpful' in diagnosing fibromyalgia. (Depression is not considered a useful indicator.)

In naming my condition, what Wolfe terms my 'constellation of problems', I am reminded: *this is not a disease*. Every treatment offered therefore addressed my belief that I needed to do less, and the effects doing less have had on my physical body, mood and emotional state. After all, how can you effectively treat someone who isn't sick in the first place?

In the days and weeks that follow my appointment at the clinic, I feel more confused than before, as if the clinic had been established to tell people like me that there isn't really anything to be done for me. I have to change my beliefs about what I can do, stop listening to my body. I feel more and more like I am doing this to myself.

I have a body that is not to be trusted. I can't remember if anyone said it wasn't my fault, just that they know that 'it's hard', and that 'it hurts'. When I get the letter in the post – a copy also sent to my GP – it says that even though I scored Severe on the self-report questionnaire there is 'no cause for action'. My diagnosis has explained the score and is to be expected. Does fibromyalgia explain my depression or the other way around?

These are the things I begin with: uncertainty, and new information that seems to conflict with itself and what I am actually feeling in my body – my *ill feelings*.

I try and draw the spectrum the consultant told me about – *pain on one side, fatigue on the other* – but it doesn't make any sense. The straight line she drew in the air with her hands bends round on the page, looping back on itself. I need another line to describe how close to illness I have been at different times in my life; sometimes intimate, sometimes estranged. I have never heard chronic fatigue and chronic pain syndromes being described as a spectrum. Neither has my mother.

Other diagrams I find online include 'the fibro cycle', which attempts to describe how pain relates to muscle tension: daily stress causes you to limit your activity, which causes fatigue, and then depression, which in turn causes muscle stiffness and pain. But this cyclical diagram doesn't feel entirely accurate either; it should look more like a web, or a vortex. One thing doesn't necessarily lead to the next. What if all these things – stress, fatigue, depression, stiffness and pain – all just have the same physiologic triggers? What if the diagram was more like a detonation, would it look more like how a 'flare-up' feels?

Pain puts all of us on the same spectrum. There is no real difference between us, only more or less, liveable or not. Still, I am trapped in a bind: the doctors claim that if I weren't so depressed, my other symptoms would be relieved; if my other symptoms were relieved, I would not be so depressed. They are the same thing and they are not. All anyone can say is that they are related, like siblings, or a mother and daughter.

'Such a nervous system I have – so irritable naturally, and so shattered by various causes,' EBB wrote to Robert; 'the tranquilising power has been wonderful.' Opium – what EBB called 'my amreeta draught, my elixir' – could calm her disposition, 'keep the pulse from fluttering and fainting', and 'give the right composure and point of balance to the nervous system', rather than the 'spirits' 'in the usual sense'. Her most specific diagnosis seems to warrant such a treatment: 'derangement in some highly important organ', whatever that means.

There is a reason EBB wrote to her future husband about her opium use. EBB was shamed for her addiction, despite her relatively fashionable diagnosis. In a poem published in 1857, social reformer Julia Ward Howe accused EBB of relying on opium as the primary source of her poetic imagination, writing: 'I shrink before the nameless draught / That help to such unearthly things, / And if a drug could lift so high, I would not trust its treacherous wings.'

EBB and Robert romanticized her opium 'habit' during their courtship: 'Can I be as good for you as morphine is for me, I wonder,' she wrote to Robert during their courtship, 'even at the cost of being as bad also? – Can't you leave me off without risking your life, – nor go on with me without running all the hazards of poison – ?'

'May I call you my morphine?' he replied. How could he survive without the 'proper quantity' of his 'metaphorical drug'? She was his addiction, without the actual prescription. His body was not ill, not 'affected', like hers. He did not need the same kind of treatment: a brisk walk was enough to rouse him. To Robert, during their courtship, EBB will eventually insist that she had never raised the initial prescribed dose, but since he cared so much she would 'get to do with less', slowly and gradually, just as her London adviser, a mysterious 'Mr Jago', had told her.

Laudanum was first concocted by sixteenth century Swiss alchemist Paracelsus, who wrote: 'All things are poison, and nothing is without poison.' Contrary to the ideas passed down from Hippocrates and Galen, who believed that a balance of four humours (blood, yellow bile, black bile and phlegm) influenced physical health, behaviours and emotions, Paracelsus believed that diseases were caused by external agents to the body, which could then be countered by alchemical materials. He treated syphilis with sulphur and mercury, believing the dosage made a substance either poison or remedy. He also claimed to possess 'a secret remedy' called laudanum, 'superior to all other heroic remedies'. Laudanum could be produced by dissolving lumps of opium into brandy, adding to the opium a host of bizarre ingredients, including 'half a scruple of must and a half scruple each of corals and a magistery [in alchemy, a substance to which healing powers were transmuted] of true pearls'. This he fermented in dung for a month, adding 'a scruple and a half of the quintessence of gold'.

During the nineteenth century, opiates, as either opium, morphine, laudanum or codeine, featured alongside cocaine and cannabis in numerous nerve tonics. Daffy's Elixir, Godfrey's Cordial and Dover's Powder, patent medicines with secret ingredients, were sold at druggists well into the twentieth century, even after the UK Pharmacy Acts of 1868 and 1908 restricted the use of unlisted ingredients in medicines. Throughout the Victorian era, doctors typically treated their patients with some form of the drug in conjunction with other prescriptions, such as bed rest and stays at health resorts. The opiate habit became rampant among the affluent and poor alike, who could buy patent medicines cheaply. And it was given to children. Godfrey's Cordial, also called 'Mother's friend', was the leading children's drug, containing opium, treacle, water and spices such as ginger or sassafras. Three quarters of all deaths that took place from opium occurred in children under five years of age. Four drops killed a nine-month old child in nine hours. Another who was two days old was killed after consuming just a drop and a half. Druggists sold 'syrup of poppies' of varying strengths as a soothing medication for children, which was also potentially lethal. Laudanum was nevertheless suggested for morning sickness, alongside horse-riding and a diet including chicken, game, mutton or roast beef.

EBB's self-medication was unpalatable to many, whereas her diagnosis was perfectly acceptable. I keep thinking: why are the treatments suggested to my mother and me – cognitive behavioural therapy, mindfulness, antidepressants, diets used to curb body fat and induce a state of wellness even in the healthy – all seemingly acceptable, everyday, or even fashionable, when our diagnosis is anything but? – when it is shameful, or plain embarrassing, as if it is something we should just *keep to ourselves*.

Despite her beloved elixir being both indispensable remedy and ruinous, shameful poison, EBB drank that dark reddish-brown liquid. It tasted bitter, like poison should, even when perfumed with herbs and spices. She must have known she was meant to feel ashamed, to see herself as bad.

The pharmacological treatment available to me as someone living in the UK with a diagnosis of ME/CFS and now fibromyalgia includes antidepressant medication, which can be prescribed 'off label', pain relief (NSAIDS such as ibuprofen) and muscle relaxants. I take an SNRI, which targets both serotonin and norepinephrine transporters blocking the re-uptake of both neurotransmitters. It makes my body numb where there was tension and pain. I still ache, still have pain, and I know the full force of it is there, underneath, waiting – I know it would seize me upon its return if I stopped taking my twice-daily pills – but it is less overall.

Drugs do not necessarily make me well, but they can sometimes take the hard edge off feeling ill. I am always hesitant to go back on medication. I don't want to be compliant, to have my mood stabilized for the sake of productivity and the feelings of other people around me with drugs sold by big pharma. I am not sorry for my anger. I have lived with it my whole life. Just like the chronic fatigue or severe menstrual cramps, joint and muscle pain, insomnia and anxiety. This is the body I live in, the one I write from, and I read from, and sometimes it is angry. I don't want to be without it, that anger. Sometimes I think I have the right to be angry all the time, the literal expression of the feeling that I want to escape my body, but it is exhausting.

A letter in my mother's health archive from the early 2000s lists her history of prescription medication, which includes three different

113

antidepressants, even though, as is stated in the same letter, she had expressly told them she did not feel depressed. According to the NHS website, 'antidepressants can be useful for people with CFS/ME who are in pain or having trouble sleeping'. Antidepressants are commonly prescribed within the general population, without the need for a specific diagnosis – in 2016, 64.7 million antidepressant items were dispensed in England, more than double the number in 2006. And it is not just ME/CFS and fibromyalgia patients that are prescribed antidepressants for their physical symptoms – they are prescribed for chronic migraine, complex regional pain syndrome, sciatica, chronic back pain and MS.

The first time I was prescribed medication, it was a relief. I went from feeling terrible, with no words for feelings, and only the pain that I was told was not real, to being depressed, maybe even having Depression: what I thought of as a treatable condition. Medication seems to offer not only a treatment, but a diagnosis. SSRIs – selective serotonin re-uptake inhibitors – relieve the symptoms of depression and anxiety, such as mood swings and disordered sleep, as long as you can stand the side effects. Unlike in the seventeenth century, when it was thought that bile in the liver caused sadness, we have learnt to affect our brains with chemistry, slowing down the re-uptake of neurotransmitters to stabilize our moods.

The first SSRI I took changed the way my body smelled so extremely it made my tendency to depersonalization worse. This was 2015. I had been sleeping too much, not going to work enough. I had no energy. The GP wanted reassurance that I wasn't only relying on medication to 'get better', that I was going to therapy. She told me the drug was just like any other medication: 'If you had a problem with your heart, you would take medication for that, wouldn't you?' My body and mind had never felt more detached from one another, as if my ancient ME/CFS diagnosis had realized its potential to eradicate the connection. It didn't work. I tried three more.

Another GP casually printed me a new prescription for Prozac (fluoxetine), the wonder-drug developed in the 1970s as a treatment for high blood pressure, made famous by Elizabeth Wurtzel's 1994 memoir *Prozac Nation*, saying: 'I will give you a repeat prescription but if you're struggling to go to work you need to address why that might be.' I still wasn't going to work, and was often unable to get out of bed. I could manage my mood with medication, but I still had the same problems, and those were mine to deal with. It didn't occur to me I could be something other than depressed, that these symptoms – decreased energy, sleep disturbance, weight loss – could be biological markers of another chronic illness. He made it sound like cheating.

'I trust you not to take them all at once,' he continued, laughing to himself. This repeat prescription was a bargaining tool, and a weapon I could potentially use on myself. My skin burned. I wanted to leave, or shout at him, or hurt him, but I had no energy to respond in any way. I smiled weakly, probably. I wanted to tell him to never say that to anyone ever again, but my body remembered not to act agitated in a doctor's surgery because they will not take you seriously. And anyway, I already knew I could harm myself with the medication that was designed to 'help' me, and that diagnosis and treatment can be both a relief and a source of shame. Sertraline stopped my panic attacks, but it also might have increased the constant pain across my body, the tension in my hips, the shocks of electricity and digestive problems. And then my body rejected it. Around half an hour after taking it, my mouth would fill with bubbly liquid, not acidic, like it was made in my stomach, but strangely neutral and odourless, an intense pain in my abdomen. This is not romantic, or ideal, I thought, with my head over the toilet. This is not making me excitable and productive. What if my physical symptoms get worse – do I have to choose between mind and body? Are they not one and the same thing?

When I swallow my prescription, that pill is ingested, absorbed, transmogrified and transported via my bloodstream to my liver, where it is metabolized and dispersed through my entire body – fat, muscles, skin and the blood-brain barrier, where it arrives at the cerebral synapse that modulates the re-uptake of neurotransmitters serotonin and norepinephrine in my brain. Only once it has been dispersed throughout my whole body – gut and liver, circulatory system and synapse – does it become psychopharmaceutical: a drug with an effect on the mental state of the user, me.

Each time I start a new course of medication, and once the initial effects – good and bad, or 'adverse' – wane, I feel better. These effects make me think it is working, and then that working stops, which only induces more shame: the shame of being untreatable, of being somehow 'resistant' to medication, or, paradoxically, it doesn't work because there is nothing wrong with me, that maybe even when I am doing the therapy and taking the medication, I will never feel any better because I am actually totally fine and I just think I could feel better. Do they not work because I have enough serotonin, but am lacking something else? Should I be making myself get up at 7am and do exercise every day like the sleep expert says, even if I have only been asleep for one hour, and a thirty-minute walk means I won't be able to leave the house for two days?

Coming off sertraline caused 'brain zaps', which feel like electrical currents coursing through my brain, and sometimes my body, just underneath the skin. I felt the physical effects of anxiety, even without anxiety: the physical sensation of electricity inside me did not correspond to any emotional upset; it was not triggered by anything other than a chemical reaction, a rapid depletion of medication. I felt *insane*. When it happened, I had to stand still and look at the sky until it passed.

Antidepressants, like all pharmaceuticals, are not wholly beneficial or damaging: this ambivalence is a necessary part of treatment. A *pharmakon*, from the Greek φάρμακον, meaning drug, poison, philter (potion), charm, spell or enchantment, is at the same time poison and remedy: it is not possible to distinguish between its character as harmful and its ability to heal. To ask for treatment – remedy, healing, cure – is to invite harm, damage, injury. And anyway, it is impossible to tell whether a behaviour or sensation – agitation, aggression, suicidal ideation – is an 'adverse' effect of a drug, or some other event, and that includes depression. When I take my medication, I can visualize this ambivalence, this ambiguity, this non-agreement between good and bad, healing and harm, knowing

116

how this drug interacts with every system in my body, that there is no real distinction between the pill and the world. My current medication has such a short half-life that I get the same zaps after a delay in taking my next dose. Each zap is a reminder, that by taking my medication twice a day, I am staving off the effects of its withdrawal as much as my own chronic pain and depression.

¶ Three good teeth

I have often wondered why I regularly score so highly on the depression scale (Instruction: 'make an appointment with your GP to discuss treatment') even when I don't necessarily feel particularly depressed. Perhaps it is because many of the statements refer to bodily sensations, including pain, tiredness and sleep disturbance, and their frequency – in my case 'almost every day' – in order to gauge your mental health. Depression is a symptom, a state, not a cause.

In her diaries, Woolf described physical symptoms during periods of mental illness. Recurrent fever, flu-like aches. High temperatures and a 'jumping pulse' were diagnosed by doctors as the symptoms of influenza, pneumonia and a heart murmur, but for Woolf, at least, her state of mind and her pulse seem to be one and the same: 'My eccentric pulse had passed the limits of reason,' she wrote in 1922, 'and was insane.' These physical symptoms are intertwined with her emotional and mental symptoms; neither is more important or more valid than another.

In May 1922, Virginia's doctor extracted 'three good teeth' to bring down her temperature – teeth-pulling being a treatment for influenza but also neurasthenia. Her heart, this 'damnable organ', was 'invalided' by the infection, which condemned her to lie in bed for several weeks. During this extended recovery, and eventually 'furious, speechless, beyond words indignant with this miserable puling existence', Virginia was taking visitors, 'but you know what frauds they are', she wrote to Vanessa. 'They come in and sit down and produce a bunch of violets, and then say how nice it is to be in bed, and how they wish they could be in bed, and how well I look – which as you know always makes me furious.'

I feel her resistance in my body: 'I get the jumping pulse and pain if I do anything . . .' she wrote in the summer of 1927. 'It's so easy with this damned disease, to start a succession of little illnesses, and finally be sent to bed for 6 weeks.' For Virginia, the 'disease' was damned but so was she: damned to her bed, like a child being punished. 'This melancholy,' she wrote in 1929, 'it comes with headache, of course.'

118

These physical symptoms of illness seem to be brought on in times of stress, of expectations and of deadlines. In notes to herself, Woolf wrote of losing language during periods of illness, of becoming familiar with how the body responds to stress and exertion. Saturday, 11 February 1928: 'I am so cold I can hardly hold a pen . . . Hardy and Meredith together sent me torpid to bed with headache. I know the feeling now, when I can't spin a sentence and sit mumbling and turning; and nothing flits by my brain, which is as blank as a window.' Her loss of language is a symptom of illness, but also a signal, a message, a command: *Rest*. 'So I shut my studio door and go to bed, stuffing my ears with rubber; and there I lie a day or two. And what leagues I travel in, the time!' Woolf's body-mind is the site where anguish shows itself. She feels time physically as it loops and lapses: 'Such "sensations" spread over my spine and head directly I give them the chance; such an exaggerated tiredness; such anguishes and despairs; and heavenly relief and rest; and then misery again.' Time in her body-mind is also water, which drags her under and crashes over her in waves: 'Never was anyone so tossed up and down by the body as I am, I think. But it is over; and put away . . .' She is 'hacking rather listlessly' at the last chapter of *Orlando* and has 'got bored', clearly exhausted her reserves of energy as well as enthusiasm, still hoping for 'a fresh wind'. Her pulse doesn't keep time so much as have its own torturous agenda. Her sentences are filled with resentment, and exhaustion, the difference between what she can do and what she *could* be doing, and all lost time spent not thinking or doing – her punishment for illness.

The Woolfs had bought Monk's House in Sussex in 1919. Virginia's writing room, her studio, which she could lock and leave to *go to bed*, was not in the house – it was in the garden, where Leonard learnt how to grow plants, passionately, and where she sometimes also slept. She also wrote and read in her bedroom. It seems like everywhere in the house and garden held all the potential for horizontality. There's a chair in Virginia's bedroom, covered with a shawl gifted by Lady Ottoline Morrell, and a board she could place over her lap to steady her notebook. Bookshelves in place of a headboard. I can imagine her reading in bed, the way she would have done as a girl, for that is what children do: read in the most covert and hidden place, at night, when the house is quiet, when movement is restricted, or necessary, because reading under covers is by nature quiet, immobile, private and free. This is what I think she meant when she wrote, 'literature is no one's private ground; literature is common ground'.

I think of my mother's nightly refrain: 'Go. To. Bed. Now. Please. Alice,' spoken as if she was exhausted by me, kept up by the idea that I was awake, rather than the actual light from my bedroom. As if she did not know I was already in bed, creeping around and inside it.

Bed isn't just the place you are confined to when you are ill, when you feel those sensations spread over your body, struck down with a series of 'little illnesses'. Bed rest is freeing. Illness allows you time away from 'the army of the upright' and the 'ideologies of the healthy'. In horizontality, and domestic confinement, Woolf found a new point of view, a way to travel. With horizontality comes knowledge that what she knows about words has entered her body through her senses, and eventually there will be no such thing as work: 'Nature is at no pains to conceal that she in the end will conquer,' she wrote in 'On Being Ill'; 'heat will leave the world; stiff with frost we shall cease to drag ourselves about the fields; ice will be thick upon factory and engine; the sun will go out.' Poetry is not the same to the ill, the clouds look different, and so too does the rest of nature – she knew Leonard's garden would be reclaimed along with industry, and the rest of the world that that army strives to master. Sick time is time to resist.

At age twelve I didn't know any of this. I didn't pretend to belong to the 'upright masses', who Woolf pitied. I was angry, and I let that feeling show. I resisted. I refused to keep my feelings contained, even though externalizing – sharing – could only ever be misunderstood.

'Literature does its best to maintain that its concern is with the mind; that the body is a sheet of plain glass through which the soul looks straight and clear.' 'On the contrary,' Woolf asserted, 'the very opposite is true.' We think through our bodies. She called for a literature of the 'daily drama of the body'. We need a 'new language' for pain, she wrote, from her sick bed, one that is 'primitive, subtle, sensual, obscene'. I read Woolf's essay for a seminar while I was doing my MA. At the time, in my early twenties, I could not identify with her experience. Had she written from convalescence, when she was really ill?

'That has never happened to me,' I had said to my seminar group, thinking of my childhood, my experience with illness, my mother in bed in the dark at home. I had never associated illness with productivity, only inability and failure. 'I was ill when I was younger,' I admitted, without any more information, as if this offered enough validation for my comment.

At the time, I could sit through a seminar or a lecture without struggling to keep myself upright, overcome with a headache, which could easily spread down my arms and legs, a sensation I had often experienced at school and the first time I went to university. I could keep up, for the most part, I thought, because I had told myself there was nothing wrong with me – and it had worked. I appeared to be well. As if I had cast a spell. Maybe I was just feeling better, but I was waiting to be ill again. I never said its name. To name it would be to make it real, rather than deny it. To name it would have felt shameful, because I had been trained to think it was not real in the first place.

But it is not living in perpetual failure, it is belonging to a different – failed – kind of time. My mother finished her BA, with a first – it just took her ten years. She did an MA, and a PhD. She succeeded. It was others who reminded her she could not keep up at work, and chastised her for not taking on more duties, for others having to pick up her slack. The able-bodied world is cruel. It fears crip time (bended, warped), access (intimacy) and crip success.

I do not remember anyone responding to my comment about illness and productivity in that seminar. It was too much to ask others to identify with these vague and unqualified statements on an unexplainable childhood illness. Now I realize that to assert that 'you can write when ill', was never Woolf's intention anyway.

So much has been written about and through illness since Woolf wrote 'On Being Ill', in and through sick time. At your most ill, there is no writing to produce – the gaps get too big. That's when time stretches and spirals. And there is already too much literature of illness – too much *fucking paperwork*. All the details and letters and questionnaires and doctors' notes. All the symptom diaries and questionnaires answered, the product of all the work of being ill. And none of it is accurate enough. Because sometimes it is too angry. It is brutal, and brutalizing to the person living with it.

The occupational health woman tells my mother she needs to 'go back to zero'.

'She says I have a limited amount of energy,' my mother explains to me on the phone, 'and I need it to make my lungs breathe and my heart pump.' She's 'heard it all before' but it is making some kind of sense to her this time. Not that that means she can easily *go back to zero*. What would that even look like when lying down is just as hard as standing up? The 'bad thoughts' take over when you do as you're told and *rest*.

'I don't know about this theory,' I say to her. 'Donald Trump doesn't exercise because he thinks we are all born with a finite amount of energy and he doesn't want to use all his up.'

Unable to walk, sleep, stand, sit or talk for very long, her body nevertheless resists, refuses to rest. She knows this means that she will 'pay the price' of exhaustion, the sensation that she's *been hit by a truck*. She knows she will use all her energy reserves up and empty her account, that her engine will stop running.

This energy limit – or 'envelope' – sounded like the 'bank account' theory of illness Alice and the James siblings subscribed to, believing that not only was suffering contagious, but that it could also be 'paid for' by another's well-being. The James logic didn't just account for the paralysis of one member, but the whole family: 'I have invented for my comfort a theory that this degenerescence of mine is the result of Alice and Willy getting better and locating some of their diseases on me,' wrote Henry in a letter home from Europe in 1869, 'so as to propitiate the fates by not turning the poor homeless infirmities out of the family. Isn't it so? I forgive them and bless them.' Why is an impenetrable breeze to some a devastating hurricane for others? Are some people really born with less energy, fewer reserves, or are they just worse at managing their accounts?

If energy is money, should I ignore the signals my body is sending? Are those signals misreporting the amount of energy in my bank account? Am I running on credit I will need to pay back? Should I ignore the text messages from my bank saying I have reached my overdraft limit, and build up how much I am doing regardless of how I am feeling, what I did the day before, and what I will need to do tomorrow?

The idea that we all have a finite amount of energy, and merely need to manage our accounts more responsibly, was developed in the twentieth century, in relation specifically to women. In 1958, Dr Marion Hilliard – instrumental in developing a simplified method for detecting cervical cancer in 1947 – wrote that fatigue was women's 'greatest enemy'. An obstetrician based in Toronto, Hilliard's advice to women was to: 'Keep remembering that a short rest at the time you need it is like money in the bank, only it will pay more than dividends.' All these economic metaphors seem even more cruel considering being sick meant growing up poor, mum having to prove her incapacity – her inability to walk up a set of stairs, or sit up for very long, her inability to work – so we could eat.

Hilliard wrote the book during her retirement, in bad health herself, because she had so often been asked: 'But, Doctor, why am I so tired?' One woman, a mother with two children, needed a daytime rest, and to cut down on household chores that weren't necessary. Hilliard's prescription: this woman's mother needed to come over once a week, so she could go out to dinner with her husband. Another woman, also a mother, thought she must have a terrible disease, but Hilliard had seen it all before, 'the same old thing': *fatigue*. Hilliard told this woman that she had to settle with having too much to do and then budget her 'income' of both time and energy accordingly. She had to budget sufficient day rest, which to me sounds like just another task to add to an already long agenda of duties. Hilliard advised women to categorize their activities, and shift some from 'priority to non-priority', cut down time spent on others, rest before they get completely tired each day, and not to delude themselves into thinking they could make up at night for the rest they didn't get in the day. Women have too much to do and only a finite amount of energy to do it. She would not have called it 'treatment' because these women were not ill at all: they were afflicted by their own femininity.

Hilliard was greatly influenced by Hans Selye, an endocrinologist who studied the effect of stress on the human body and developed a theory of 'general adaption syndrome'. A century after Henry James claimed that one sibling's good health could cause the others pain, Selye argued that the body's adaptability, or 'adaption energy', was finite, and should be used wisely and sparingly rather than recklessly squandered by 'burning the candle at both ends'. 'Our reserves of adaption energy could be compared to an inherited fortune from which we can make withdrawals,' wrote Selye in *Stress Without Distress* (1974), after several decades of research into stress, 'but to which there is no evidence that we can make additional deposits. After exhaustion by extremely stressful activity, sleep and rest can restore resistance and adaptability very close to previous levels, but complete restoration is probably impossible.'

Selye was looking for a new female hormone and had written extensively on his theory about the stages of energy, adaption, resistance and finally exhaustion, that plague the body. Hilliard interpreted this to mean that fatigue isn't itself bad but could accumulate when a woman's social or work schedule was too full, if she was living with uncertainty, for example, or 'nursing an invalid or caring for a family of small children'. Learning how to change pace, speed up and down, was the key to vanquishing the 'fatigue problem'.

Hilliard inherited Selye's ideas about stress, but also earlier Victorian beliefs about the way the body produces and stores energy, as well as notions of femininity, propriety and the duties of women – ideals that Alice James's siblings wished she embodied. Hilliard came to understand that there was something about women that made them more tired than men. Between menstrual cycles, hormonal changes in adolescence, pregnancy and menopause, and women's roles at home, at work and within community, which resulted in loneliness, frustration and missing out on a sense of achievement, fatigue was 'inevitable' for women. She still saw fatigue as the responsibility of women, and that it could be easily avoided, advising women to allow doctors to help them find their limits and what caused their stress. She also wrote that women needed to realize that sometimes they encouraged in their doctors 'a take-it-or-leave-it attitude' if they didn't 'take their treatment seriously'.

125

As a woman in her thirties living on her own with two young children, and pneumonia, my mother was perceived by doctors as exhausted, as doing too much, as needing to slow down. When her Immunology specialist in the 1990s suggested that helping me to get better might in turn help her, it was as if he meant that the best form of treatment would be to not have the stress of a seemingly sick child to deal with, on top of everything else. She is still regarded as 'too emotional' when she asks doctors for new tests or treatments, as if her general distress might explain why she feels so ill.

What about the credit cards you can't pay back? Savings accounts and student loans. Payday loans. What if the financial metaphors extended to stock and shares, and unregulated markets . . .? Sage advice is generally to be responsible with your money, but capitalism wants us to spend beyond our means. This is another reason why chronic fatigue syndrome is a metaphor for our times: the end times of capital.

I have always known you need energy in the bank to relax in the first place – metaphorically and actually.

The whole of the last chapter of Hilliard's *Women and Fatigue* is dedicated to loving God and keeping his commandments. Hilliard advised women to learn about their 'metabolic pattern'. After all, every human being is, to start with, one small cell, which develops a nervous system and an endocrine system, different metabolic patterns and rhythms of energy, all inherited from their parents: 'You and I must learn what our pattern is . . . look at your mother, father, aunts, uncles, grandparents, because you inherited your pattern from them. Find out what those inheritances are.'

Find out what those inheritances are. How far back does our bank account of energy go? What did I inherit from Aunt Vera, who took her middle name because her first name was Alice, her mother's name, and who, it turns out, 'never got out of bed'. Vera wasn't allowed to marry her suitor because 'he was found to be a bounder, darling'. My mother wore Aunt Vera's unused wedding dress from 1910 to her own wedding eighty-five years later. She has deemed herself the only one responsible enough to look after all the family photographs – only she can remember all their names. Only my

126

mother would remember she *never got out of bed*. Perhaps the rate my cells use energy matches up to Vera's, and my mother's. I have inherited their metabolic patterns, and their energy rhythms.

What else have my mother and I inherited? In my mother's health records, I read of treatment by doctors, who saw us as Alice's doctors did: our symptoms at once baffling and mundane, our personalities unmanageable and 'uncharming', our mood swings and emotional states noted down, the circumstances of our illness out of our control and yet our responsibility alone, too unstable during procedural tests, told we have less energy but could feel less fatigued by doing more, told to listen to our bodies even though they are speaking a senseless language, unable to recover beyond 'fifty per cent' – making each of us half a person. The whole time, we are sceptical and desperate, unable to listen to our bodies through the mass of sensations that run through them, so that sometimes we have to go to bed. This is what we inherited from Alice. From her, maybe we can learn that energy – or not having enough of it – is something so abstract and intimate that it can be shared between siblings, between mother and daughter, but also between companions, lovers, kin.

What if you don't know your ancestry? That is a privilege of the white, the upper class, rich not poor, the colonizer not the colonized.

The bank account theory of health and energy – the one Henry James could invent 'for (his) comfort', adopted by the rest of the James family, including Alice, and later by Selye and Hilliard – is resilient. I can't help thinking of the friend who had been told by doctors she exhibited a 'classic case of burnout' when she told them she often lost sensation on one side of her body and felt burning in her mouth. She had written to me about all the ways she has tried to articulate pain to her doctor. The word *burnout* means: you are not sick. It means you have used up all your resources, and now you need to make changes to your daily routine, re-prioritize your tasks, take care of everyone but still do less – you must take responsibility for your own energy reserves. It means: your brain is a computer and it needs to be reprogrammed. It means: your symptoms are not my problem to treat. Of course, our bodies feel less like a computer or a car than a *little rubbish heap*. Now I get tailored online ads for

'help with the brain fog and physical pain caused by Fibromyalgia':
'Reset Yourself from £295.00.'

My mother is always sending me messages saying, 'Don't overdo it', or 'don't do too much' or 'don't burn the candle at both ends', as if she is quoting Hilliard or Selye. She is always telling herself off, like Alice James, because she knows she's supposed to rest for ten minutes after each task, is supposed to pace herself, but she doesn't. She will just keep going until she crashes. Like my mother, I should be using my energy wisely, sparingly, carefully, in order to conserve it. And sometimes, I just don't. I push through to the other side, which always ends in more time in bed, more time to recover. Exhaustion leaves the boundary between the normal and pathological unstable: it is, to some extent, normal to feel exhausted after activity, and so is the fear of exhaustion turning chronic, becoming a puzzling and untreatable illness. Some would say that fear is itself a kind of sickness. But, I have always been like her – I would rather wear myself down, use myself up, empty myself out, blow my energy pay cheque like I never earned it in the first place, as if having energy – the kind that comes from rest and 'listening to your body' and 'going back to zero' – is untrustworthy, or vulgar, but mainly impossible. I used to think that maybe 'burning ourselves out' is a way to depart from the expectations of the upright masses entirely, becoming thoroughly incapacitated rather than *fatigued*. We are already always on the brink of stalling, breaking, crashing.

Sometimes resting more enables us to keep up, to do almost as much as we are expected to do, that we expect of ourselves, but the terms of our contract with the bank of energy is being re-written every day. You slow down when you feel ill, but that doesn't mean you can speed up again when you're feeling up to it. The bank account analogy is useless when how well you feel depends on your medication working or changing, and how badly it affected your sleep the night before, on whether you walked too far or not far enough, or you feel hurt, or confused, by something someone said to you.

Maybe my mother and I share an energy envelope. And maybe we share an energy envelope with all the others who have borne their ill feelings before us, and all those to come.

Sometimes it is too tempting to abandon it all, in the words of Alice James, 'let the dykes break and the flood sweep in, acknowledging yourself abjectly impotent before the immutable laws'. It is almost impossible to listen to your body if it's screaming.

¶ Wandering nerve

After the death of both her mother and father in 1882, Alice James's health deteriorated, and she spent three months at the Adams Nervine Asylum, Boston for 'residents of the state who are not insane'. Built with money bequeathed by Seth Adams, who had made his fortune running a sugar refinery, the Asylum opened in 1880. Adams stipulated that the architecture 'be plain, substantial and simple and great attention shall be paid to convenience, comfort, good-sized rooms and good air'. Its resident physician followed the theories of Thomas Kirkbride, a Philadelphia psychiatrist who advocated for small hospitals that felt more like hostels, homes-away-from-homes where women, and eventually men, could stay temporarily, while still enjoying the freedom of movement and sociality they were used to. The Asylum also followed the example of other 'Villa style' institutions, which imitated small villages, with residencies, restaurant-style dining rooms, shops and vocational buildings, organized around sidewalks and village greens. The wooden structure for the Asylum's female patients was built in the asymmetrical Queen Anne Revival style, with a complex array of sloping roofs, an assortment of balconies that looked out onto picturesque views, and a porch that wrapped around two sides of the building. Inside, it felt like a house rather than a hospital, albeit a grand one. The living areas were decorated with engravings and etchings, and rugs were scattered over polished hardwood floor.

There were no pictures on the walls or rugs on the floor in the battery room, in which a large glass case contained large brass battery discs. Various pieces of electrical equipment hung from the walls and ceiling over a therapy bed on four carved wooden legs, placed in the centre of the room – 'queer apparatus for driving the lazy blood into new life, and giving the flesh and that it implies a gentle fillip to remind it that it is forgetting its functions'. Electricity was used across Europe in the nineteenth century to treat symptoms of nervous illness. Golding Bird had established the Department of Electricity and Galvanism at Guy's Hospital in London in the 1830s. 'Paralyses, epilepsy, and the different types of manias have

130

been quite resistant to electricity when these disorders resulted from an organic lesion of the brain or the spinal marrow,' said anatomist Jean-Baptiste Sarlandiere, in 1825. For his treatment to be successful, the patient's paralysis had to be functional. By 1875, when George Miller Beard and A.D. Rockwell's *The Medical and Surgical Uses of Electricity* was published, local treatment of specific hysterical symptoms was dismissed as 'unphilosophical and usually unsuccessful' except in hysterical aphonia, or the loss of speech, in which 'any form of irritation, external or internal, electric or otherwise, may cause instantaneous cure'.

In a *Boston Globe* article from 1887, Dr Webber, who replaced Page at the Adams Nervine Asylum, is quoted as saying he was 'not sure that of all the cases treated during the year, a single one (had) been caused by inactivity and ennui'. By this time, they were mostly treating unmarried women who appeared to have worn themselves out working and waiting on others – teaching and homemaking. The journalist ends their article with a warning: 'So, take care of your nerves, good people, not only for your own sake, but that of future generations. Don't run the machine quite so fast. Slow up a little, or we shall have to turn the whole continent into a vast nerve asylum, and the chances are you wouldn't have such a good time or good treatment as the patients do out at Jamaica Plain.'

Anyone could be struck down with a nervous disorder, not least because heredity was thought to play a part, but the treatment needn't be as severe as Silas Weir Mitchell's punishing rest cure, for those who could afford it. The Adams Nervine Asylum provided hot and cold bathing, and massage, because everyone likes massage.

Alice next consulted Dr William Basil Neftel in New York, who worked from a building on 5th Avenue. Dr Neftel was a Russian-born specialist in female nervous diseases that he treated with electrotherapy, of whom she had heard great things. The experience did her some good, she admitted, 'either in spite or because of his quackish quality'. She initially reported feeling a wonderful change, thinking she was 'the lowest of organism with absolutely no insides but a stomach', but ten days later her health had shifted again, either on account of the atrocious weather or 'the misconduct of the doctor'.

131

Alice once again felt she belonged to 'the highest order', meaning she felt indigestion, or maybe the workings of her digestion, her insides working, or not working as it should. Of Dr Neftel she had no complaints, and scolded herself for allowing her hopes for recovery to rise so quickly. She blamed her symptoms – always vague, always unpredictable – on her having been made to walk too much when she first arrived in New York.

In December 1884, Dr Alfred Baring Garrod of 10 Harley Street employed galvanism, or electricity, to the affected parts of Alice's body. It was during one of these treatment sessions that he induced 'something like a paralytic stroke' attempting to relieve one of her sick headaches. At first, Alice thought the paralysis must have been a result of her nervousness. Garrod, on the other hand, claimed he had struck the pneumogastric nerve, now known as the vagus nerve, the tenth of twelve cranial nerves. Alice disagreed; it must have been the hemp, which had affected her heart. Whatever the cause, her brother Henry reported to her Aunt Kate that her legs would not move at all.

The American neurologist George Miller Beard defined neurasthenia, or nervous exhaustion, as 'a part of the price we pay for civilization', expressed as insomnia, headache and vertigo when affecting the brain, and when affecting the spinal cord: pain in the back, weakness of the lower limbs, and sometimes of the arms; 'flatulence; feeling of oppression on the chest; gastralgia, intercostal and abdominal; neuralgia of the bladder and sexual disturbance; numbness of the extremities, etc.' Beard treated one woman in 1872 much the same way as Dr Garrod had treated Alice. Her most distressing sensation was that of 'crawling and creeping in the back, arms and legs'. One month of galvanization and general faradization alternately, achieved good results. 'The sensations were most marked after fatigue, and were very annoying; these sensations were referred to the tender points in the dorsal and lumbar vertebrae. Turkish baths had given some relief.'

Tender points make our kind of pain sound pleasant.

As far as I can tell, damage to the vagus nerve does not cause paralysis in the legs, but it can inhibit speech, as it provides movement to muscles in the neck and mouth via the recurrent laryngeal nerve. Vasovagal syncope – if that is what Alice experienced – is a condition that can occur when the nerve is excessively activated during emotional stress due to a sudden drop in cardiac output, a para-sympathetic overcompensation for a strong sympathetic nervous system response. It affects young children and women more than other groups.

Alice and Katharine's move to London in November had been reported in a local Boston paper six months previously, despite having told her friend Sara that she felt she could make a home for herself in New York. In a letter to William and her aunt from an address on Piccadilly, where she was staying in a 'pleasantish' little parlour with a dark 'tomb-like closet' for a bedroom, she wrote that she had 'not "passed away" yet'. 'Excellent service, and an innocuous doctor who unmurmuringly obeyed all Kath's behests,' she reported of the boat trip, despite her seasickness and violent indigestion, which had only begun to subside. 'I feel as if I had been there all my life & it is just the place to spend the day in bed with a head-ache.' Come December, an intense attack of 'gout in the stomach', and steady pain in her legs, head and stomach, kept her in bed for nine days.

Alice consulted with Garrod 'against my conscience and my purse' and described meeting the doctor as 'the most affable hour of my life'. Garrod was a man 'rounded & smoothed by tradition', who appeared to listen with interest to Alice's 'oft-repeated tale', which, she joked, she was going to have printed in a small pamphlet 'to save breath & general exhaustion'. According to Alice, he understood without question or explanation all her symptoms, 'especially the emotional ones'. Despite Garrod's attentiveness, Alice expected nothing very satisfactory regarding treatment, and rightly predicted him to be as ineffectual as every other medical man she had already encountered, with their treatises and cures and pamphlets. He gave her 'some hints as to diet', which she insisted didn't sound 'the least bit curative'.

Her present collapse was not a mystery to her, and many months coming. 'We read his book two years ago,' she wrote to William's wife, also called Alice, '& Beach said that he was the only man in the world who knew any thing about suppressed gout. I have since heard he is the supreme authority.'

Perhaps the book Alice – and Katharine? – read was Garrod's *A Treatise on Gout and Rheumatic Gout (Rheumatoid Arthritis)*, first published in 1860, and expanded several times. In his treatise, Garrod recounts the history of gout, 'one of the earliest diseases to which flesh became heir when man began to participate in the luxuries of civilised life'.

Garrod's story of gout begins with Thomas Sydenham, 'the English Hippocrates'; a purveyor of laudanum and 'martyr of gout' himself, who was comforted by the knowledge that 'unlike any other disease, (gout) kills more rich men than poor, more wise than simple'. As an affliction, Garrod describes gout as both curative and injurious: 'It is quite true that a patient often feels much relieved by a fit of gout, for the system by this means has rid itself of much which was previously causing distressing symptoms', even though 'deposition invariably occurs in the affected joints, which henceforth acts as foreign matter and frequently causes further mischief'. Nevertheless, the condition was thought to be as curable and controllable as any other inflammatory affliction, relieved and even prevented by limiting the diet to diluents and starchy food, and forbidding stimulating or alcoholic beverages. Such a diet would include bread, arrowroot, sago, tapioca and the like, with milk, thin gruel, barley or toast and water and weak tea. Opium was not advised as it could cause the gout to return with greater violence. Instead, it was advisable to 'promote the action of the skin by hot air or vapour bath, or by tepid sponging with water or vinegar and water'. Aretaeus treated it with hellebore, but only in the early attacks, and the local application of fresh-shorn sheep's wool bathed in rose oil and wine. According to Garrod, further 'ancient' approaches to its treatment, 'which would certainly ill-suit the present generation', included bleeding, purgatives and emetics, often combined with the employment of hermodactylus (iris), abstinence in diet, as well as local appliances, scarification, fomentations and emollient ointments.

It is hard to see what about reading this book convinced Alice her condition would be relieved, let alone the fact that Garrod doesn't even indicate a treatment for her diagnosis of 'suppressed gout'. Tellingly, the prescription for 'an ordinary attack of gout' sounds like the precise advice he gave Alice: a low-alcohol and light diet, and 'the administration of some simple alkaline saline, combined with a very moderate dose of colchicum'.

He thought she was *ordinary*. It was up to her to prove she was not.

The vagus nerve is actually a pair of nerves, the longest in the body. They are comprised of eighty to ninety per cent afferent nerves, which send information from your organs to the brain, rather than the other way around. The name 'vagus' derives from the Latin 'to wander', which this nerve does. It circumvents the spinal cord and several organs, reaching down from the cranium to the abdomen. As a parasympathetic nerve, it is responsible for the bodily functions at rest, such as heart rate, breathing, sweating, blood pressure, blood glucose, appetite, kidney function and fertility, but also gut movements and inflammatory responses. Information about what you touch, the pain you feel and your body chemistry, metabolism and hormones is transmitted via the vagus nerve to the brain. I know this because of an article on 'Health Rising', a website that provides 'the latest treatment and research information for fibromyalgia and chronic fatigue syndrome (ME/CFS)': 'The last ten or twenty years have revealed that the vagus nerve (VN) is a significant immune system regulator. The cholinergic anti-inflammatory immune response it regulates mostly takes place in the spleen.'

In the mid 1990s, scientists started exploring the possible neural connections between the immune system and the brain. A researcher called Linda Watkins, now a Distinguished Professor of Behavioural Neuroscience, found that when she cut the vagus nerves of rats after injecting them with cytokines — molecules that contribute to inflammation – they didn't get a fever, suggesting that vagus nerves were the conduit through which the immune system signals to the brain to respond to infection. A bioelectronic medicine researcher called Kevin Tracey then began giving mice a toxin known to cause inflammation, before dosing them with an anti-inflammatory drug

135

he had been testing. 'We injected it into their brains in teeny amounts, too small to get into their bloodstream,' he told the *New York Times* for an article titled 'Can the Nervous System Be Hacked?' The drug halted the inflammation in the brain, but also in the rest of the body, until he cut the vagus nerve, the channel of communication between immune system and brain. 'That was the eureka moment,' he said. The signal generated by the drug had to be travelling from the brain through the nerve because cutting it blocked the signal. 'There could be no other explanation.'

After that first surgery on the rat in 1998, Tracey spent the next eleven years mapping the neural pathways of tumour-necrosis-factor inflammation, charting a route from the vagus nerve to the spleen to the bloodstream and eventually to the mitochondria inside cells. Tracey wondered if he could eliminate the drug altogether and use the nerve as a means of speaking directly to the immune system. 'But there was nothing in the scientific thinking that said electricity would do anything. It was anathema to logic. Nobody thought it would work.' What he had demonstrated was that the nervous system was like a computer terminal through which you could deliver commands to stop acute inflammation before it started or repair a body after it got sick. 'All the information is coming and going as electrical signals,' Tracey said.

When I am told my communication system has gone 'haywire', that my pain signals are 'misfiring' – what does this actually mean? These things are said to help me to understand how my body functions, but they are also metaphors that rely on technology for understanding. There isn't actual electricity running around my body to my brain and back, passing amplified pain messages back and forth – or is there? Tracey seemed to be saying that electricity delivered to the vagus nerve in just the right intensity and at precise intervals could reproduce a drug's therapeutic — in this case, anti-inflammatory — reaction. Electricity was no longer a metaphor, a comparison, an idea; it was real.

Luigi Galvani, Professor of Obstetrics in Bologna, provided the first widely publicized evidence that the nerves and muscles of animals

136

used their own intrinsic electricity in 1791. It had been the product of experiments conducted with his wife, Lucia Galeazzi, the daughter of an anatomist, who was actually the first to make a frog's leg kick when her scalpel touched its exposed sciatic nerve.

The Galvanis could produce lively movements in the legs of frogs, when an electrical machine was attached to their nerves. The vivid image of Galvani's frog legs twitching together strung along an iron railing during a thunderstorm on a roof top was widely disseminated in popular culture. Galvani's own descriptions of the event flash and burst: 'as often as the lightning broke out . . . all the muscles fell into violent and multiple contractions'. Based on his results, Galvani proposed that all animals contained something resembling electrical fluid, which flowed between muscles and nerves, responsible for all motions and sensations. (The Galvanis also demonstrated that opium could block pain by suppressing the body's animal electricity.)

Sayer Walker figured the nervous system as a material extension of the brain. He believed nerves to be composed of a familiar substance, 'so that they may be considered as continuations of that organ'. This was an observable reality, described by anatomists as 'medullary fibres or filaments', which divide into smaller and smaller bundles, 'almost infinitely'. These anatomists, he reports, speculated that each nerve also maintains its distinct structure beyond what the eye could see. This limitation – that the nervous system functioned beyond observable reality – gave rise to imaginative representation: 'By some, they have been represented as hollow tubes,' writes Walker, 'adapted to the conveyance of a fluid; by others, they have been described as solid fibres, more adapted to act by tremor or vibration. Fontana, at one time, considered these fibres as composed of cylinders, with bands, twined around them, in a spiral direction . . .'

There was much anatomists and physiologists still did not know. If nerves derived their origin and influence from the brain, how were they produced? How did they function? They started speculating how the nervous system worked and turned to newly invented electrical networks. In a public lecture in 1851, German Emil DuBois-Reymond proposed that electrical telegraphy was modelled 'in the animal machine'. The nervous system and the telegraph system appeared to have the same function: transmitting information, conveyed as alterations in electrical signals. By calling the nervous system a 'model' for the telegraph, DuBois-Reymond suggested that organic communications systems offered solutions to problems encountered by technological ones: 'just as little as telegraph-wires, do the nerves betray by any external symptom that any or what news is speeding along them', he said in 1868; 'and, like those wires, in order to be fit for service, they must be entire. But, unlike those wires, they do not, once cut, recover their conducting power when their ends are caused to meet again.'

The source and type of electricity flowing in our bodies is not the same as the electricity in telegraph wires, but an understanding of the human nervous system affected how communication systems developed, and they in turn changed how medical men understood the nervous system. Nineteenth-century media for writing and communication, such as the telegraph, typewriter and telephone, influenced not just the way people wrote and communicated, but the way they perceived their own minds and bodies, as Friedrich Kittler argues in *Discourse Networks*. Physiologists and physicists drew upon each other's representations of communications networks, participating in a 'feedback loop' of their own. As early as the mid-eighteenth century, people linked the shocks transmitted in parlour games to the fast-moving 'fluid' in the nerves. It was a metaphor that lit imaginations and made two opaque systems more comprehensible not only to each other but the general public.

According to Laura Otis in her book on bodies and machines in the nineteenth century, DuBois-Reymond, a chronic migraine sufferer, used electrical networks as a metaphor to envision how nerves and muscles communicated impulses at the molecular level: 'By comparing the electrical activity in muscles, nerves, batteries, and coils of wire, he was better able to understand the "network of interconnections".' She quotes DuBois-Reymond, who piles up metaphors, so that inanimate object and human are not just comparable but the same: 'For just as the central station of the electrical telegraph in the Post Office in Königsstrasse is in communication with the outermost borders of the monarchy through its gigantic web of copper wire, just so the soul in its office, the brain, endlessly receives dispatches from the outermost limits of its empire through its telegraph wires, the nerves, and sends out its orders in all directions to its civil servants, the muscles.'

Calling a brain an office or a computer or nerves telephone wires or muscles civil servants masks other realities. A telephone line is designed for smooth communication. Each part of the machine needs the others to do their job, except some parts can malfunction, be damaged or worn out. Likewise, technologies that were once used to explain what physiology could not might have reached the extent of their usefulness and end up holding them back. Technologies change, and, unlike bodies, they are designed by people. An office is a hierarchy as well as a network. The office is a site of invisible labour, of politics. What if you had never worked in an office, but in a factory or in a field or a home – there would be no way to understand your body in this way.

DuBois-Reymond also described his own migraine, albeit incorrectly, suggesting that tetanus took place in the muscular coats of vessels in the affected part of the head, causing pain. His sick headache – still a violent attack – had an electrical source. His pain 'responds to each beat of the temporal artery. The latter feels on the affected side, like a hard cord, while the left is in normal condition. The countenance is pale and sunken, the right eye small and reddened . . .'

The notion of animal electricity – fluid possessed by animals, including us humans, through which electricity could pass, influencing the actions of the body – had consequences for how we understand the nervous system. 'Fear will produce different actions in the heart and arteries,' writes Walker; 'if it be suddenly produced, it will be followed by a hurried and irregular circulation, and by palpitations of the heart.' 'Epilepsies have been induced by sudden terror, and these often prove the most difficult to cure.'

In September 2011, SetPoint Medical began the world's first clinical trial to treat rheumatoid-arthritis patients with an implantable nerve stimulator based on Tracey's discoveries. According to Ralph Zitnik, SetPoint's chief medical officer, of the eighteen patients

139

currently enrolled in the ongoing trial, two-thirds have improved. And some of them were feeling little or no pain just weeks after receiving the implant; the swelling in their joints has disappeared. Women with complete spinal injuries have experienced cervix orgasms via vagus nerve stimulation, I read. Maybe one day we will all be able to have our nervous systems hooked up to actual – rather than metaphorical – computers.

There are articles online about how to 'hack' your own wandering nerve, via VNS, or vagus nerve stimulation, without one of these remote controls. One says singing, which has been found to increase oxytocin – a hormone released in large amounts during childbirth now believed to be involved in sexual activity, penile erection, ejaculation, pregnancy, uterine contraction, milk ejection, maternal behaviour, social bonding and stress – and especially singing in unison, increases Heart Rate Variability (HRV) and vagus function. I think this is why my mother benefits from singing in her choir. Deep and slow breathing also stimulates the vagus nerve, and yoga. One exercise is to breathe out as hard as you can until it's really uncomfortable and until you notice how awake you are. I haven't seen studies on this, but I suspect it will help with your vagus nerve. Zinc increases vagus stimulation in rats fed a zinc-deficient diet for three days. Acupuncture is so powerful that a man died after vagus nerve stimulation from too low of a heart rate. I don't know what is true.

As of 2018, vagus nerve stimulation is being studied as a possible treatment for migraine and fibromyalgia, but this is still at a 'proof of concept' stage. During one study in New Jersey, of five patients who could tolerate stimulation, two no longer met widespread pain or tenderness criteria for the diagnosis of FM after three months. A pilot study to assess the possibility – suggested by Michael Van Elzakker – that small infections in or around the vagus nerve could be triggering it to tell the brain to produce flu-like symptoms in people with ME/CFS is underway, based on the principle that the vagus nerve boosts the activity of the parasympathetic nervous system (rest and digest) and reduces the sympathetic nervous system (fight or flight) system.

Vagus nerve stimulation is promising because it may reduce 'temporal summation', a process that causes the nervous system to become more and more sensitive to pain. That opioids do not inhibit pain in people with fibromyalgia could actually signal vagus nerve problems, as it turns out that good responses to opioids only take place in people with healthy vagal nerve activity.

Imagine receiving this doctor's orders: that your spine be sponged with salt water, that you swallow pills containing Indian hemp. He tells you your 'disease' has no organic basis, that the disturbances in your legs and stomach are entirely functional, and the weakness in your legs would not lead to paralysis, 'a grim spectre' which has been staring you in the face for a long time.

'I should have thought he would therefore have liked to do something for me,' Alice had written to Aunt Kate, even before she was paralyzed by Garrod's electricity, 'but it was only my folly in going to a great man – their interest being in diagnosis & having absolutely no conscience in their way of dealing with one.' She could get nothing out of him and expressed her disappointment comically: 'he slipped thro' my cramped & clinging grasp as skilfully as if his physical conformation had been that of an eel instead of a Dutch cheese'. Garrod's suggestions for treatment 'as to climate, baths or diet' were non-existent. 'The truth was that he was entirely puzzled about me and had not the manliness to say so,' she explains. 'I got from him however a very thorough examination . . .' The use of the phrase 'thorough examination' is disturbing, but maybe less so in light of the Dutch cheese joke, as both of them are on Dr Garrod.

Despite his exhaustive tests and diagnoses, his published treatise and experience and reputation, Alice casts Dr Garrod as a typical charlatan figure, confirming that he is, like all the others, 'a fiasco, an unprincipled one too'.

There is both pain and pleasure in not being curable, in being entirely puzzling to a doctor, especially one who causes harm, in presenting as very ill even though he believes you have no 'organic trouble', and in that doctor being entirely *usual* in his useless and injurious behaviour and prescriptions.

Were my mother and I also pleased by our being incurable, to be able to call a doctor ineffectual, rather than trying their best?

Alice was only incurable because she could afford treatment in the first place. Money turned out to be the only thing medical men were willing and able to relieve her of.

Many of the doctors who backed a biological cause for ME are now dead, including Ramsay, but also Celia Wookey, and most recently, Gordon Parish. Many of those who became ill in earlier outbreaks are ageing too. Ramsay's account of ME has existed as long as I have been alive. In that time, the biopsychosocial approach has dominated treatment for ME/CFS patients, driven by private interest and neoliberal politics. ME/CFS – and chronic fatigue associated with other conditions, including HIV/AIDS and cancer – is still allied to erroneous illness beliefs and symptom-focusing. It is still conflated with 'medically unexplained symptoms'. It is still an impossible diagnosis – too severe to be fake, too subjective to be real.

By the 1980s, the initial search for an organic aetiology had seemingly failed, despite protestations by doctors with first-hand experience of the disease, which McEvedy and Beard put down to 'altered medical perception in the community', a kind of mass hysteria amongst the medical community. A more psychosocial understanding of the illness, which stressed the mental, emotional, social and spiritual effects of a disease, rather than any potential root cause, emerged in its place. Funding for research and treatment was channelled into cognitive behavioural therapy, unlearning and graded exercise, despite patients presenting with post-exertional malaise for decades. A new name was used in clinical practice, distinguishing the widespread appearance of cases from those seen at the Royal Free that appeared to be related to the polio epidemics: chronic fatigue syndrome.

The first case definition of 'chronic fatigue syndrome' by the CDC in America concentrated on 'fatigue persisting for at least six months', but the diagnosis was contested from the outset. In 1988, a panel of eighteen medical scientists and clinicians were charged with formulating a new case definition and new name, but they could not agree. Two doctors, Alexis Shelokov from the US and Gordon Parish from the UK, refused to sign the final document and withdrew from the panel because the proposed definition and name were too different from the cases of ME they had witnessed in practice. Since then, between twenty and thirty case definitions of ME/CFS have been put forward.

In 1991, Professor Michael Sharpe, and a number of other psychiatrists, developed the Oxford definition of CFS, which is generally still used in biopsychosocial research in the UK. The Oxford Criteria requires severe, disabling fatigue of new origin as the primary symptom. This fatigue must have both cognitive and physical effects and not be due to any other fatiguing disease or disorder, such as anaemia. The fatigue must be present for at least six months and must have been present for at least fifty per cent of the time. Myalgias (muscle pain), mood disturbances and sleep disturbances may be present, but these are not required for diagnosis. When an initial infection is known and proven, a patient's case may be designated as 'post-infectious fatigue syndrome'.

In 1994, Fukuda and colleagues published a case definition for CFS and idiopathic chronic fatigue that was intended to guide research in adult populations. The Fukuda definition defines chronic fatigue as 'self-reported persistent or relapsing fatigue lasting six or more consecutive months', the absence of exclusionary conditions (including severe mental illness such as schizophrenia or bipolar disorder), severe chronic fatigue, and at least four out of the eight symptoms listed. The Fukuda definition includes but does not require what some consider core symptoms of ME/CFS, such as post-exertional malaise (PEM) and neurocognitive symptoms. The definition has been criticized for being overly inclusive, particularly of patients whose symptoms may be caused by a psychiatric disorder.

In 2003, a clinical case definition was developed utilising the term ME/CFS, which became known as the 2003 Clinical Canadian ME/CFS case definition, or CCC. Unlike the polythetic approach of the 1994 Fukuda criteria, it required the occurrence of specific ME/CFS symptoms, specifically post-exertional malaise – rapid muscle or cognitive fatigability, usually taking twenty-four hours or longer to recover – and the presence of neurocognitive dysfunction. The International Consensus Criteria (ICC) has one required symptom: post-exertional neuroimmune exhaustion, defined as the inability to 'produce sufficient energy on demand', with symptoms 'primarily in the neuroimmune regions', and points out that the response may be immediately after activity or delayed.

The 2015 NAM, or IOM, criteria was conceptualized as a way of enabling general practitioners in the US to more swiftly identify people with ME to refer to specialist care, and requires three symptoms: fatigue that is persistent and profound, of new and definite onset, that is not the result of ongoing exertion and not alleviated by rest that impairs the ability to engage in pre-illness activity; post-exertional malaise, an 'exacerbation of some or all of an individual's ME/CFS symptoms after physical or cognitive exertion, or orthostatic stress that leads to a reduction in functional ability'; and unrefreshing sleep. In addition to these required symptoms, people diagnosed with the NAM criteria must present with either cognitive impairment or orthostatic intolerance. Patients must experience these symptoms at least half the time. The intensity of the symptoms must be substantial – moderate or severe – and last six months or more.

These case criteria exist alongside each other, and many others. There is no single definition of ME/CFS, beyond it being 'a genuine and disabling condition'. David Tuller, a journalist and academic, reported in the *New York Times* that competing case definitions have led to 'an epidemiologic "Rashomon" – what you see depends on who's doing the looking – and has stoked a fierce debate among researchers and patient advocates on both sides of the Atlantic'. This lack of consensus over definitions and scales disrupts research, as well as diagnosis and treatment. As Charles Shepherd, who is still the Medical Director of the ME Association, wrote in the *British Medical Journal* in 1997 in response to the Royal Colleges of Physicians, Psychiatrists and General Practitioners' unequivocal conclusion that the chronic fatigue syndrome was a genuine and disabling condition: 'labels are important to patients as well as doctors, and support groups throughout the world are unanimous in their view that "chronic fatigue syndrome" is a totally inadequate way of describing the symptomology and associated disability. The chronic fatigue syndrome may well become a dustbin diagnosis for anyone with chronic fatigue, and a new name that is acceptable to both doctors and patients clearly needs to be found.' Twenty years later, things are much the same. 'Our main disagreement with the report concerns its undue bias towards psychological explanations and treatments. Considering the fact that some studies have failed to concentrate on a strict definition of the chronic fatigue syndrome and that others have used questionnaires that "perform poorly as screeners for psychiatric morbidity in chronic fatigue syndrome", we cannot agree that the published literature can be used to justify the conclusion that about three quarters of patients have a co-existent psychiatric illness. Equally, we are surprised that no mention is made of the view that when depression co-exists it is possibly a combination of neurobiological changes and the psychological distress that so commonly affects these patients.'

A criterion is only useful for diagnosis, treatment, research and medical education if it is unique enough to separate it from others, includes as many people who have the disease as possible while still excluding those who do not, and accurately conveys how the disease may present in a clinical setting. The means of categorizing and defining ME/CFS – more often than not regarded only as a person's subjective experience of their symptoms (illness), rather than their objective bodily pathology (disease) – is an ongoing drama, as if the diagnosis has a sickness personality. The lack of consensus is reason enough to consider the illness a 'controversial' diagnosis – never mind its unknown aetiology, and that the history of hysteria explains most of the symptoms.

Some insist on a distinction between ME/CFS, in that ME is a clearly defined disease process with a history of outbreaks relating to an as-yet unknown aetiology, while CFS by definition has always been a syndrome, loosely defined any number of ways. Some case definitions for CFS which use broader criteria, such as the Oxford Criteria, which only requires six months of fatigue, result in inflated numbers. There is also the issue that 'ME' has never been used as a diagnosis by the CDC in the United States, despite significant outbreaks in LA and Lake Tahoe. (The CDC estimates there are one million people with the illness, and acknowledges many have not been diagnosed, particularly among racial and ethnic minority groups.) Others believe separating the two impedes the action needed to advance research into possible causes and treatments. The estimate that ME/CFS affects between 0.2 and 0.4 per cent of the population would mean around 250,000 people have ME/CFS in the UK, and between 17 and 34 million people globally.

Stigma around the name *chronic fatigue syndrome* is real, even measurable. In one study, medical trainees were found to be far more likely to attribute patient's illness to medical causes if the name given was ME (thirty-nine per cent) rather than CFS (twenty-two per cent), even though they were given the same case study. When asked how they would treat the patient, sixty-seven per cent of trainees said they would use some form of psychiatric intervention when they were told the patient had CFS, compared with forty-eight per cent of trainees who were told the patient had ME. Even the trainees who were told the patient had 'Florence Nightingale Disease' were less likely to treat the patient with psychotherapy or psycho tropic medication than the group who were told they had CFS.

What is it about *chronic fatigue syndrome* that is so unbelievable, less believable than a disease named after a mythic woman? Is it because fatigue is a symptom not a cause? Is it that a *syndrome* is not a *disease*? Or that it is *chronic*, and therefore potentially unending – and therefore unbelievable, incomprehensible? Eli Clare names white Western medical diagnosis for what it is: a system of categorization. 'I want to read diagnosis as a source of knowledge, sometimes trustworthy and other times suspect,' he writes in *Brilliant Imperfection*. 'As a furious storm, exerting pressure in many directions.'

Clare asks the question we rarely dare to ask: *'Diagnosis is useful, but for whom and to what ends?'*

Diagnosis – a 'tool and a weapon' – legitimizes some pain as real and others as psychosomatic, the choice of a privileged woman. It draws borders and boundaries between the mind and the body and has political and cultural power. Maybe this is the storm that I, as a child, was *basically furious* at.

¶ *Thumb-screw*

'It is a sad irony that Florence Nightingale, the founder of modern nursing, who made such important contributions to public health through her advocacy of sanitation, statistics, and common sense,' wrote AJ Young in the *British Medical Journal* in 1995, 'should also be remembered as history's most famous invalid and possibly as its most successful malingerer.'

Florence was not the only sick woman in the family. While still a teenager, Florence's sister Parthenope was formally diagnosed by Queen Victoria's doctor Sir James Clark with 'absolutely no disease but a marked irritability of the brain'. She possessed 'a fine intellect' but needed exercise to combat her 'state of debility'. Parthenope was staying with him in Scotland at the time. Concerned that 'the extreme irritability of her nervous system, the total absorption of self, with, at times, chronic delirium' might lead to imbecility if left untreated, Clark suggested she stay with a relative. Florence's presence at home seemed to aggravate Parthenope's condition, increasing her excitement and fostering her 'monomania'. According to Florence's biographer, Parthenope 'believed herself unable to walk even the short distance downstairs', while her 'fancies are more in number than the sands of the sea'. She dictated letters every day, requesting new gowns from Aberdeen, and possessed an apparently insatiable appetite for pears. She bases some of this assertion on a line from a letter Parthenope wrote to a friend: 'The floor whirls about my head.' I have certainly felt the floor whirl about my head. Does that mean I too have only *believed* myself unable to walk; that my symptoms have always been *fancies*?

Before departing for Crimea, Florence absented herself from the family home to let her sister recover, and spent a year working in a nursing home on Harley Street. Her father William Nightingale had eventually given her an allowance of £500 a year (£30,000), which meant she could work at the nursing home without pay. News of the poor conditions at Scutari soon reached England when the Crimean War broke out. 'Want, neglect, confusion, misery – in every shape and in every degree of intensity – filled the endless corridors and the vast apartments of the gigantic barrack-house,' she wrote, 'which, without forethought or preparation, had been hurriedly set aside as the chief shelter for the victims of the war.' Her skills in account management and passion for statistics greatly reduced the number dying within six months, and the legend was born.

Florence fell ill while at Balaclava in May 1855, having just turned thirty-five. Brucellosis, the disease known as Malta or 'Crimean fever', could cause shaking chills, and extreme physical and mental exhaustion. Patients experienced generalized pain, insomnia, palpitations, depression and loss of appetite, exhibiting only minor physical abnormalities upon examination. Her convalescence was inevitably long, and she was re-admitted to hospital with severe sciatica in October, and then earache, chronic laryngitis, dysentery, rheumatism and insomnia. 'I see her at times when she seems hardly able to walk across the room from fatigue & deeply depressed in spirits,' wrote Aunt Main to the Nightingales in June 1856, as the army were preparing to leave Scutari.

Florence's 'non-specific' form of brucellosis turned chronic, characterized by recurrent attacks of the illness, sometimes years apart. Her symptoms sound like those of the nurses at the Royal Free, ME/CFS, and now long-Covid: nervous instability, restlessness, profound exhaustion, insomnia, breathlessness, nausea, fatigue, which mirrored those experienced during the acute and convalescent phases of 'Malta Fever' long after that original fever had abated. Her family were shocked at her gaunt appearance and depression. Upon returning to London, she was agitated and obsessive. Her biographers insisted she was not really ill, that she used illness for her own ends. In 1995, as an attempt to disrupt this entrenched narrative, A. B. Young wrote: 'The dreadful change in her which was apparent on her return to England in 1856 suggests that she had contracted a serious and debilitating chronic disease in the course of her service in the east.' The longer the disease was active, it seemed, the more entrenched it can become, affecting mood and personality. She has been called *heartless*, *cruel*, *tyrannical* and *reproachful*.

Her symptoms were especially intense in five attacks, presumably bacteraemic episodes (bacterial infection in the blood), when

149

Florence and others thought she might die. In December 1861 she became so seriously ill she was unable to walk and had to be carried to and from her bed. Her doctors diagnosed 'congestion of the spine, which leads straight to paralysis'. She was bedridden for the next six years. In, 1862, severe spinal pain left her 'impatient for death'.

'She arrived in England in a shattered state of health', wrote Lytton Strachey in his biography of Florence Nightingale in *Eminent Victorians*, published in 1918. 'The hardships and the ceaseless effort of the last two years had undermined her nervous system; her heart was pronounced to be affected; she suffered constantly from fainting-fits and terrible attacks of utter physical prostration. The doctors declared that one thing alone would save her—a complete and prolonged rest.'

Upon leaving the Burlington Hotel, Florence moved from place to place – Hampstead, Highgate, Derbyshire, taking the water cure at Malvern – before eventually settling on South Street, Mayfair, where she lived in her later life with her companion Fanny Gibbs. There Florence remained an invalid, 'but an invalid of a curious character – an invalid who was too weak to walk downstairs and who worked far harder than most Cabinet Ministers'. Florence lived in the house, which her father bought her in 1865, alongside other characters including courtesan Catherine Walters, also known as 'Skittles', for forty-five years until her death in 1910.

'Lying on her sofa in the little upper room in South Street, she combined the intense vitality of a dominating woman of the world with the mysterious and romantic quality of a myth,' wrote Strachey in his biography, famously written using only secondary sources. 'She was a legend in her lifetime, and she knew it.' In staying small and productive – her sofa in a little room – Florence combines all the ideal qualities of the invalid, mysterious and vital, putting her own health aside for the greater good. 'Her desire for work could now scarcely be distinguished from mania.' In every biography, it is constantly asserted that she made that myth herself.

After her death, medical opinion favoured the diagnosis of neurasthenia, otherwise known as psychosomatic illness, which seemed reasonable considering her symptom language – weakness, headache, nausea at the sight of food, breathlessness, tachycardia, palpitations and precordial pain – and her supposed neurotic disposition. In an address of the Royal Society of Medicine in 1956 on 'Miss Florence Nightingale and the doctors', Sir Zachary Cope explicitly stated that Florence had no organic disease to account for her illness. He was convinced she used her seclusion and invalidity to protect her secrecy: 'No one so carefully concealed the part she played.'

As a woman, Nightingale possessed 'an unusual power of influencing the minds of certain types of men by her intellectual brilliance, her clear logic, and her indomitable will'. These gendered characteristics were seemingly reflected in the nature of her invalidity: 'She was not paralyzed; she certainly had no serious organic disease; she lived to a ripe old age and saw most of her younger friends die before her . . . there is no doubt that Miss Nightingale's invalidity was a neurosis.' Her (mis)use of her own domestic space as a retreat from the world, in which she could be cared for, was particularly suspicious, especially since she had refused to be married, along with the type and timeliness of her symptoms, which were read as signs not of a chronic and fluctuating illness but reasons to mistrust such a wilful and secretive woman who worked in the background, ate her meals alone 'cooped up' in one room, and only received visitors by appointment.

That Florence worked *despite* her pain, fatigue and restlessness is not impressive, but rather evidence that she was not truly – organically – ill at all. 'For some time any extra exertion, any unexpected hindrance or annoying opposition, any unpleasant visitor, was likely to induce palpitations, rapid breathing, perhaps faintness, and complaint of pain,' said Sir Cope in his address. 'Like so many neurotics Miss Nightingale after a time frequently referred to the severe pain she suffered, while pooh-poohing the pains and complaints of others. In spite of all her complaints she was always able to work at anything which interested her.' She kept herself in bed out of convenience, protected from the 'active opposition of some who did not agree with her views'. In bed, unmarried, she could 'think without interruption and write to her heart's content', supported by 'a most able and devoted doctor colleague' – Dr

Sutherland – who 'did all the work which demanded visits to be made or work to be done outside'. Cope ends his President's Address to the Royal Society of Medicine by drawing a close parallel between Florence and 'Miss Barrett the poetess', whose invalidity 'quickly got better when Robert Browning appeared'. Presumably Florence thought marriage another instrument of torture, a constraining rather than enabling.

Burcella melitensis, the bacterium responsible for Crimean or Malta Fever, was isolated in 1887. Not until the twentieth century did biologist Alice Evans (1881–1975) prove the bacterium was transmitted to humans via unpasteurized goat milk or cheese, establishing the close relation between the causal agents of Malta fever in humans and abortion fever in cattle. Alice became unknowingly infected with *B melitensis* while working with the bacterium. Based on her symptoms she was diagnosed with neurasthenia, until the organism was cultured from her blood six years later. Recurrent episodes of chronic brucellosis occurred for a further seventeen years.

Alice C. Evans also noted that some patients with proved chronic brucellosis reported long delays before the correct diagnosis was made, and that the interim diagnosis was almost invariably neurasthenia. 'Florence Nightingale's case has been the same, although a delay of 140 years seems excessive,' wrote A. B. Young in 1995. 'Alice Evans's case shows how hazardous this argument is.'

Beyond the suggested eponym, Florence Nightingale Disease, Nightingale's birthday on 12 May is promoted as International ME/CFS Awareness Day. The two hundredth anniversary of Nightingale's birth was celebrated during the first UK lockdown, without any mention that she is the 'patron saint' of ME/CFS. (Conveniently, it is the same day for fibromyalgia – two for one.) In the UK, temporary hospitals named after her had already been set up for Covid patients. This was a woman who, according to Strachey, 'moved under the stress of an impetus which finds no place in the popular imagination', whose productivity during invalidity was mythologised as beyond human, to the extent that she is overcome, or crazed: 'A Demon possessed her.' It was as if she made herself ill – made herself

152

out to be ill – out of convenience, as if it was a choice, like the act of manifesting a myth out of your own life.

Florence was certainly a productive invalid; working, reading and publishing from bed. A group of assistants gathered around her, to which she dictated several treaties: 'Notes affecting the Health, Efficiency, and Hospital Administration of the British Army' and 'Notes on Hospitals', published in 1858 and 1859. The first woman to be admitted to the Royal Statistical Society, she designed 'coxcomb' diagrams to communicate how infectious diseases were causing unnecessary deaths in the Army in the East and at home. The Nightingale Training School for Nurses at St Thomas's Hospital opened in 1860. Like a woman with ME/CFS, Florence appeared to choose illness – taking to bed – as an option available to her, the suggestion being that she could easily will herself better, if it weren't for her resistance to Victorian family values.

Florence called family 'a thumb-screw, a Procrustes' bed, an instrument either of torture or deterioration, a disabilities office' – an 'unloving love'. Privileged and 'extremely well to do', Florence 'escaped' first the family home and then Victorian marriage. A profession – 'a necessary occupation, something to fill and employ all my faculties', as she wrote in her diary – was something she claimed to have longed for from the age of six.

In the Greek legend, Procrustes invited travellers along the sacred way between Athens and Eleusis to stay the night at his home. He then tortured and murdered his victims using an iron bed, by either racking their body to fit the bed if they were too short, or cutting off their legs if they were too tall – an arbitrary choice of punishments, imposing uniformity regardless of individuality. Procrustes died when he was fitted to the bed by Theseus. A thumb-screw is an early modern torture instrument used to extract information. Thumb-screws were used on painter Artemisia Gentileschi during the trial to establish whether or not her virginity was forcibly taken by Agostino Tassi. (He had raped her, said he would marry her, and then rescinded his promise; she was put on trial. As the thumb-screw tightened around her fingers she reportedly said: 'This is the ring you give me, and these are your promises.') The devices are referenced in abolitionist Olaudah Equiano's 1789 memoir of enslavement and subsequent freedom, stating that the manufacturers of 'neck-yokes, collars, chains, hand-cuffs, leg-bolts, drags, thumb-screws, iron muzzles, and coffins' are the only group that won't benefit from the abolition of slavery. 'Tortures, murder, and every other imaginable barbarity and iniquity, are practised upon the poor slaves with impunity. I hope the slave trade will be abolished. I pray it may be an event at hand.'

According to her most recent biographer, Florence's bitterness against the institution of the family 'became in time a festering wound', a feeling that was only exacerbated by her protracted illness following the Crimean War, 'a steady decline in her health which she sometimes believed had its roots in the strains imposed on her by family tensions in the years before she went away.' Her family feud was to blame for her wounded immune system, extending to the edges of her body and reaching out to meet the world.

The extent to which Florence 'took to her bed' out of some kind of living mythmaking, to eschew the strains of family and (heterosexual) marriage and give her space to work *as if a demon possessed her*, in order to gain influence and credibility, or was in fact bedbound from chronic illness, will never be known. In any case, criticism of her was enabled by the already-established imagery of the savvy upper-middle class invalid, as was her ruthless working life on the sofa. Rather than a living legend, perhaps she was actually living proof of what can be achieved by a disabled person when they have access to wealth, care and opportunity.

'There are no specific diseases; there are special disease conditions,' Nightingale wrote in 1866, believing disease was spread via miasma or 'bad air'. 'It is that which is bringing the profession to grief, and will in time work a great reform – to wit, to make them make the public care for its own health and not rely on doctrine. It is a great thing for weak minds – the doctrine of contagion.' In her old age she was under the care of Dr May Thorne of Harley Street, and came around to germ theory.

Nightingale undertook the water cure in Malvern under the care of Dr Walter Johnson. Florence thought the lifestyle she adopted while taking the water cure saved her life. She was under no illusions that water had the power to cure her, and insisted that the diet, quietness, exercise and fresh air, as well as different kinds of bathing, which she first took in 1848 and a further nine times after her return from Crimea, vastly improved her health. 'In incipient tuberculosis the water-treatment, not as a charm (as English women take medicine) but as part of a treatment, I have seen to be effectual,' she wrote to Edwin Chadwick, 'the rest of the treatment being open-air during the greater part of the day (riding or otherwise according to the patient's strength) bedroom ventilation at night, diet founded upon improved digestion, the result of the open air exercise – sometimes gentle gymnastics, mild cold-water sponging and little wet-sheet packing.'

Charles Darwin and Alfred Tennyson, and even Henry James, were famous advocates of the cure, and visited the hydropathic (water cure) doctors at Malvern: Dr James Wilson and Dr James Gully, who, like Florence, distrusted orthodox medicine. At Malvern, you would be called at 5 am, stripped by your bath attendant and wrapped tightly in a cold wet sheet and packed in blankets where you would stay for an hour. Your coldness would ease as your body adapted to your new environment. Water was administered via drinking from the hills and blasted at your frail body through a pipe. Dinner was always boiled mutton (no rich or spiced food, no alcohol or tobacco.) Ironically, 'the water cure' was also later used to refer to a form of torture.

I hear this a lot, and I think it's true: movement eases pain, especially in water, if you have the energy to do it. So, we move together in the water, twelve or so women in a pool in the basement of a hospital, anticipating the sting of cold when we eventually get out. NHS hydrotherapy – even though I am grateful for it – provides none of the hospitality and comfort of the Adams Nervine Asylum.

I feel shame being there almost naked in the water, awkwardly smiling at the other women, mostly older than me but not older than sixty, concentrating on their own movement rather than their pain.

A young white man leads the sessions, after the middle-aged white woman has spoken to us about 'setting goals' and 'trying to get back to doing the things we like doing', like dancing, and getting up in the morning. The man ticks off exercises on a spreadsheet. I don't feel inside my body, I feel administered. We are all going through the motions.

I want to ask what the other women feel too, but there is no conversation before or after the session in the pool, which lasts about twenty minutes. There is only silence, and being spoken to.

'Has this been helpful for you?' I ask a woman in her fifties, quietly, by the lockers, like a rubbish undercover agent. She says: 'Sort of, but you only get four sessions, and it's not like you can keep doing it when you get home unless you have your own swimming pool.'

Afterwards, I am exhausted. With the travel there and back, and the rest I have to do afterwards, it takes a whole day to do 45 minutes of therapy.

In my second session, a man who I can only guess was a trainee – and who was not introduced to anyone enrolled in the session, that I saw – was taking up space in the pool. He was joking and messing around, and I had to tell him to move away from me. He was shocked, like he had only just realized we were all there. I was also shocked: Why was there a random able-bodied white man in their twenties sploshing around in a small pool full of women with chronic pain, women in swimsuits, women with trauma, at least half of which are women of colour?

'You tell him!' the other trainee said, as if I was exercising some kind of 'girl power', as if I was a child who had just spoken up for the first time and needed someone to back me up. No one else said anything. He kept his movements small after that, looking sheepish, more from being told off than doing something wrong.

I didn't go back. Having only completed two of my four hydrotherapy sessions, I did not get the other physiotherapy initially offered. I did not ask for it and I still do not know what that involves, but I did not want to put myself in a situation like that again. I try and go the local pool to swim and stretch like I have been taught at the hydrotherapy sessions, but it is too cloudy for the children to do their swimming lessons. They all stand at the side hoping their parents aren't too far away to come back and get them. No one tells me to get out. Why is it too cloudy for children and not for me? Am I already doomed?

Have I chosen not to get better, to distrust the man who taught us techniques to use our bodies more? Have I chosen to take back control – to choose permanence, to choose my body over someone else's thoughts about what I should or shouldn't do to myself?

Why does it not feel like a choice?

Of convalescence in Cambridge, Massachusetts, rather than Europe, Alice wrote: 'When one can only take a passive part in life, the bare, crude, blankness of nature here with nothing to call one out of one's self preys upon the soul, and makes the process of getting well a task and not a pleasure.' Part of her treatment – self-prescribed – was reading the trashiest of novels, such as *Cousins* by 'Mr Smith'.

I stop working as much as I can, and start resting more, as best I can. I start *managing my account*. I make the process of getting well a pleasure not a task.

'I can appear to keep up with everyone else but I will suffer the consequences later and no one will see that,' I write in my phone.

I sound like my mother.

¶ The same thing

'They are saying the same thing they were saying thirty years ago,' says my mother.

She has been reading about some research in America that has shown people with ME have compromised immune systems, which was what immunologist Anthony Pinching suspected in the 1990s. 'That was when he treated patients with ME, and patients with HIV and AIDS,' my mother explains. 'In the waiting room there would be all the women with ME with their heads slumped to one side, and a lot of very sick men.'

For years I kept asking myself *Why*? Why haven't things changed in twenty, fifty, a hundred and fifty years? Why has the medical understanding of ME/CFS not moved on since the 1970s, with small-scale studies and no agreed-upon diagnostic criteria or biomarker? Why is this illness with too many names still considered psychological despite having a WHO status as neurological decades ago, as if that confirmed its identity as neither, as *invalid*.

The simple answer is that in the 1990s and early 2000s, a group of psychiatrists helped change the idea of illness, which was taken up by politicians desperate to reduce the number of people on incapacity benefit. Illness as a concept proved too easily corruptible, too accommodating of shifting borders and boundaries, too susceptible to political influence.

Medical diagnoses reflect societal ideas of what causes ill feelings, which is to say that, as a 'physically unexplained' syndrome, ME/CFS came to be considered, in the words of Simon Wessely, Professor of psychological medicine at King's College, London, 'not simply an illness, but a cultural phenomenon and metaphor for our times'. Wessely was one of a number of scientists who not only influenced public health guidelines for treating ME/CFS, but also helped to 'develop the thinking' that would inform the revision of disability benefits in the UK, which would lead to the PACE trial (Pacing, graded Activity, and Cognitive behaviour therapy; a randomised Evaluation), part-funded by the DWP, which has been called 'flawed' and 'not reliable', but also: 'one of the greatest medical scandals of 21st century'.

158

In the late 1980s, Wessely and his colleagues developed the cognitive behavioural model (CBM) of chronic fatigue syndrome, defined as: 'an acute illness giving way to a chronic fatigue state in which symptoms are perpetuated by a cycle of inactivity, deterioration in exercise tolerance and further symptoms', compounded by depressive illness, resulting in a 'self-perpetuating cycle of exercise avoidance'. With Trudie Chalder and others, he proposed a series of 'simple rehabilitation strategies', including cognitive therapy to help the patient understand how genuine symptoms arise from the frequent combination of physical inactivity and depression, rather than continuing infection, and a gradual return to normal physical activity, or graded exercise therapy (GET). Wessely's treatment programme focused on altering patients' belief that 'physical symptoms always imply tissue damage', otherwise known as 'catastrophizing', symptom focusing or 'bodywatching', and 'behavioural factors such as persistent avoidance of activities associated with an increase in symptoms', otherwise known as 'maladaptive avoidance behaviour', which involved a gradual increase in exercise such as walking or swimming. He has continually highlighted the resemblances of CFS with neurasthenia, the diagnosis given to upper-class hysteric patients at the turn of the twentieth century that was believed to be an effect of the speeding up of modern life. Both diagnoses are, according to Wessely, 'culturally sanctioned expressions of distress'.

In 1994, Wessely set up the first NHS programme dedicated to CFS treatment at King's College, and later, the Centre for Military Health Research to investigate Gulf War Syndrome. His work showed that chronic fatigue syndrome was an important public health issue, but he also stressed that the psychological treatment of symptoms was more beneficial to patients than research into a possible biological cause. As one of the most influential figures in the debate surrounding ME/CFS for around twenty years, from the early 1990s to the early 2010s, he believed CFS to be a 'mirror of society', inasmuch as it is a 'general disorder of perception, perhaps of both symptoms and disability'.

We were called *hysterical* for a reason. Sydenham's definition transformed how hysterical patients were treated in England from the seventeenth century onwards. Mood swings led family members to resent the hysterics whom they cared for: the irregular timing of the changes in behaviour meant knowing the triggers of emotions was impossible. The lack of a clear diagnosis, and the range of vague and changeable symptoms they exhibited, point to the challenges in caring for a hysteric as well, the fear that came from a lack of knowledge. Hysterics were deemed 'unsavable'; no cure engendered a refusal of in-depth care.

In November 2001, five years before New Labour's 2006 Welfare Reform Bill, thirty-nine people, including Wessely, convened for a conference at Woodstock, near Oxford, titled 'Malingering and Illness Deception'. The conference was supported by Chief Medical Officer Professor Mansel Aylward and funded by the newly renamed Department for Work and Pensions. New Labour had committed itself to halving the 2.6 million people who were claiming Incapacity Benefit (IB), turning long-term sickness and chronic illness into a political issue. It was decided that Incapacity Benefit should be treated like the ME/CFS diagnosis had been for the last twenty years: as a cultural phenomenon rather than a health problem, as a metaphor in and of itself.

Professor Gordon Waddell was also in attendance, who, together with Aylward, would write 'The Scientific & Conceptual Basis of Incapacity Benefits', which provided the 'scientific evidence-base' for the 2006 Welfare Reform Bill. In their report for the DWP, Waddell and Aylward defined *illness* as an 'internal, personal experience', and *sickness* as a 'social status accorded to the ill person by society', as distinguished from *disease*: 'a disorder of structure or function of the human organism that deviates from the biological norm'. The biopsychosocial model of illness gave the DWP an out: it was not that these people were incapacitated because they were sick, and therefore deserving of state support; they only believed themselves to be incapacitated. They redefined incapacity as a psychological and social phenomenon, which could be cured by getting back to work.

Out-of-work long-term disability benefit was changed from Incapacity Benefit (IB) to the Employment and Support Allowance (ESA) in October 2008 as an attempt by the New Labour government to limit claimant numbers by half. Outsourced to the private sector, all claimants of the new ESA would be subjected to the Work

160

Capability – or 'fitness for work' – Assessment, exclusively conducted first by Atos Healthcare and then Maximus. The WCA uses the Waddell and Aylward biopsychosocial (BPS) assessment model to determine whether claimants are eligible for long-term sickness benefits or had to look for work. Anyone applying for ESA was deemed to be playing a 'sick role', a term borrowed from American medical sociologist Talcott Parsons, who argued that when someone becomes sick they enter a role of 'sanctioned deviance' in the eyes of society. Illness is a state of mind, not a biological reality. According to Waddell and Aylward, the sick role can become a 'trap', in which 'the patient continues (futile) attempts to find a medical solution and remains passively in the sick role awaiting "cure", even when there is no medical reason for permanent incapacity'. The social status of a person as sick, they argued, should have nothing to do with the medical model of illness, which assumes medical treatment is the solution to incapacity, especially seeing as many health problems don't have a good medical answer. Instead, their solution was getting better, or, more importantly, getting back to work. The sick role, they insisted, was always meant to be a temporary social contract.

Sanctioned deviance. I am reminded of my being a witness to my mother's collapse, and of her and me being accused of causing harm to one another, rather than relief; of our punishments – which often meant seclusion or separation, and others knowing best, and making decisions for us; of being sent to bed by your own headaches. And Woolf being sent to bed with her damned disease. And EBB, who always resented the implication that her illness was imaginary and longed for a precise (organic) diagnosis to explain her physical symptoms, and was therefore, eventually, in (her biographer) Forster's words, 'largely responsible for her own incarceration in Wimpole Street'. In another version of the story, it was her father who kept her there. Mr Barrett was from a long line of West Indian slave owners that stretched back to the seventeenth century. Tyrannical, egoist, selfish are the words used to describe him most often, but I have also read 'deeply rooted psychological disease'. Why avoid passing judgement on Elizabeth, who, having given birth to a healthy child in 1849 after three miscarriages, wrote of being blamed had her child been 'a puny, sickly infant', and when one of 'the great

161

London physicians' had even 'predicted evil' because of the lauda-num Elizabeth was prescribed as a teenager and took for the rest of her life? It is as if she was the only person who could ever really be responsible for the ill feelings that really confined her. EBB's desire is the root of her downfall, makes her deserve incarceration, whereas EBB's father's greed is an inherited disease – not his fault.

I remember when my mother had to be reassessed for 'fitness to work', having previously received John Major's Incapacity Benefits (replacing Invalidity Benefits in 1995). She was made to demon-strate how many stairs she could walk up and asked if she could lift an empty box. If she was to earn over £140 a week, it was legal to strip her of her entire 'allowance' – another infantilizing word, borrowed from nuclear family life, which suggests that if you don't behave yourself, you lose the privilege of pocket money rather than income support.

A socially produced problem became the responsibility of the incapacitated individual, who was accused of shirking and malin-gering to avoid contributing to the needs of the market. The medical diagnosis and prognosis of the claimants – including existing claim-ants – were completely disregarded. Work, abstracted from the realities of paid employment, became a health outcome, and even a form of therapy: 'work itself is therapeutic, aids recovery and is the best form of rehabilitation', reads the report by Waddell and Aylward. Not working – which was previously supported by incapacity bene-fits – was now perceived as 'one of the greatest known risks to public health', more than working in the North Sea, or 'smoking 10 pack-ets of cigarettes per day', even, according to Wessely, increasing your likelihood of suicide forty-fold after six months. If only incapacitated people could get back to work, even if that work was mundane and dissatisfying and rife with inequality, maybe they wouldn't be so inca-pacitated after all. It was decided that no one who was ill should have a 'straightforward right to Incapacity Benefit'. Reform of the system was presented as 'a matter of social justice as well as expenditure'. To say that the inability to work is comparable to smoking is to say it is a lifestyle choice; a wilful neglect of your health.

Once the reform bill had been introduced, austerity measures

162

installed by David Cameron's government created a climate of fear for chronically sick and disabled welfare-dependent claimants, causing preventable harm and unnecessary deaths, including suicides, and a huge increase in antidepressant prescriptions, as reported by journalist Frances Ryan. 'Death has become part of Britain's benefit system,' she writes. (One of her case studies in her 2019 book *Crippled*, is a man with ME/CFS who had spent the last decade sleeping rough in London. Another is a woman with fibromyalgia and other health conditions, who did not understand what fibromyalgia was – when she was assessed she was given 'zero points' and told 'if Stephen Hawking can work, so can you'.) Ryan also reported that, by 2017, it had been calculated that the outsourced 'fit to work' assessments were costing more than it was saving in reductions to the benefits bill. These are structural inequalities: 'The acceleration of the benefit sanction system is emblematic of a wider shift in this country towards a perception of disabled people as "work-shy" scroungers – boiled down and packaged as major government policy.'

Chronic illness – and all other forms of disability that inhibits your ability to work – was recast as a form of malingering, a choice, originally of a soldier to shirk his responsibility to risk his life in battle. (Wessely actually told the history of the practice – his enthusiasm – at the *Malingering and Illness Deception* conference in Oxford.) As if *going into battle* was ever a reasonable expectation of a human being. It is these views – and the trial results reported by the PACE authors – that justified government policy on disability, chronic illness and 'fitness' to work, while, at the same time, as Ryan points out, disabled people who *could* work were routinely shut out of employment.

My mother's illness was deemed a short-lived experience, a temporary struggle she could overcome *if she really wanted to*, not the cause of a legitimate need for long-term welfare. This was the case for everyone, regardless of their condition. It was as if medical diagnosis was irrelevant. As Sontag wrote in *Illness as Metaphor*: 'Psychological theories of illness are a powerful means of placing the blame on the ill. Patients who are instructed that they have, unwittingly, caused their disease are also being made to feel that they have deserved it . . . Nothing is more punitive than to give a disease a meaning – that meaning invariably being a moral one.'

No diagnosis exists without power, without borders and boundaries. ME/CFS destabilizes the categories of illness. That no one can agree if it is a disease of the mind, body or a combination of the two only compounds the narrative of ME/CFS as a 'mystery illness' without a real cause. But this is only one side of the story. The psychological theory of illness, which redraws the boundaries and borders of disease and experience, turns any chronic illness into a deception. The re-making of sickness as some kind of lifestyle choice – and the wrong, irresponsible, lazy choice – reflects a fundamental ideological resistance to the fact that many chronic illnesses are permanent. To the state, you live as an ill person – a choice rather than a forced reality – that is unacceptable under neoliberal capitalism.

The 'sick role' was conceived as a kind of moral corruption, rather than the effects of an unequal society, of people forced to eke out a life from the dregs. Disability benefits is not even enough to live on.

We lived off my mother's disability benefit, and council tax and housing benefit, reliant on charity assistance and care work, reliant on a state that did not care about us, that had decided my mother was a burden that cost too much and deserved a precarious life for not being able to contribute to the job market. To say we 'lived off the state' is to say we – a family of one disabled adult and two children – lived off around five thousand pounds a year.

In 2011, a group of nineteen researchers, led by Peter White, including Michael Sharpe and Trudy Chalder, published their findings during the largest ever trial into the treatment of ME/CFS. They purported to show that cognitive behaviour therapy and graded exercise therapy were effective treatments for chronic fatigue syndrome, despite reports by ME/CFS patients' organizations that these exact treatments were ineffective and even harmful. Funded by the Department of Health for England, and the Scottish Chief Scientist Office, part of the Department for Work and Pensions, UK Medical Research Council, the five-year-long 'PACE' trial appeared to prove adaptive pacing, a treatment modality rooted in the premise that ME/CFS was a potentially irreversible and biological condition, was not as effective as therapies that assumed ME/CFS was reversible and behavioural, the consequence of avoidance of activity, rather than its cause. The work of Chalder and Sharpe, alongside Wessely, on 'functional somatic syndromes' and psychological symptoms in CFS had been cited in the 'Malingering and Illness Deception' monograph references. White and Sharpe had also attended the conference, with White actually thanked in the acknowledgements for contributing to the re-thinking of illness as deception, 'directly and indirectly, knowingly and unknowingly' in the opening pages.

Cognitive behaviour therapy had become a treatment recommended by NICE in its 2007 guidelines for CFS/ME (as it was called), based almost solely on Wessely's randomized controlled trials, despite them relying on subjective outcomes in unblinded studies. CBT – as a treatment rather than a management tool – is based on the 'fear avoidance theory' of chronic fatigue syndrome, which states that cognitive responses, such as fear of engaging in activity, and behavioural responses, or the avoidance of activity, are linked and interact with physiological processes to perpetuate fatigue. 'The aim of CBT was to change the behavioural and cognitive factors assumed to be responsible for perpetuation of the participant's symptoms and disability,' wrote the authors of the PACE trial. Crucially, the CBT provided was not aimed at helping people

165

with chronic illness, but guided participants to 'address unhelpful cognitions, including fears about symptoms or activity by testing them in behavioural experiments'. Graded exercise therapy (GET) was done on the basis of 'deconditioning and exercise intolerance' theories of chronic fatigue syndrome. Both theories – that people with ME/CFS are deconditioned or have unhelpful illness beliefs – assume that the syndrome is perpetuated by 'reversible physiological changes of deconditioning and avoidance of activity', or an increased perception of effort, leading to further inactivity, and causing chronic fatigue, which could be reversed if patients changed their 'unhelpful' behaviours. The aim of graded exercise therapy was to help the participant 'gradually return to appropriate physical activities, reverse the deconditioning, and thereby reduce fatigue and disability'. 'Adaptive pacing therapy', on the other hand, regarded CFS as an organic disease process resulting in a reduced and finite amount (or 'envelope') of available energy. APT Participants had to plan and pace activity, reduce or avoid exacerbations, schedule regular rest and relaxation, and prioritize activities in order to adapt to their illness. Participants were advised not to undertake activities that demanded more than seventy per cent of their perceived energy envelopes. The concept for APT reads as purposefully vague. There wasn't even a manual for this therapy, distinguished from 'pacing' as a way that patients have learnt to manage their illness independently, so the PACE trial investigators wrote their own.

Participants were asked to rate their symptoms using the Chalder Fatigue Scale, developed at King's College London in 1993, which was grounded in the same unproven theory that patients were plagued by unhelpful beliefs, and could recover by increasing activity to counteract their supposed 'deconditioning'. Originally the scale comprised fourteen questions but following a principal component analysis (PCA), three items were excluded. The scale has its own biases, based on the theories of those who developed it.

Do you have problems with tiredness?
Do you need to rest more?
Do you feel sleepy or drowsy?

166

Do you have problems starting things?
Do you lack energy?
Do you have less strength in your muscles?
Do you feel weak?
Do you have difficulties concentrating?
Do you make slips of the tongue when speaking?
Do you find it more difficult to find the right word?
How is your memory?

The deleted items from the 14-item scale are:

Do you start things without difficulty but get weak as you go on?
Do you think as clearly as usual?
Are you still interested in the things you used to do?

The questions are so subjective, describing illness as a set of difficulties and problems – as pure, personal experience. The Chalder fatigue scale has been shown to have 'good internal consistency', and therefore works as a scale to compare cases to one another, but as a series of propositions, it is confusing to the person answering. Are you supposed to rate your difficulties and problems based on how you felt before you were sick, compared to 'healthy' people, or since the last time you took the test? What is *usual* anyway?

There is no evidence that 'slips of the tongue' and other cognitive difficulties, which relate to half of the questions in the Chalder Fatigue questionnaire, correlate to severity of overall fatigue. The same goes for the number of symptoms a patient reports. 'These assumptions are untested and their basis is unclear,' reads a critique of the CFQ, written by members of the online forum Science for ME. Besides, the scale makes it impossible to report a worsening of fatigue if participants have already recorded the maximum score, a phenomenon that is called 'the ceiling effect'. This is not necessarily a problem when screening for fatigue syndromes, but it is when the scale is used in randomized trials, such as the PACE trial, as only improvement will be visible on the questionnaire. There is also the issue of its bimodal scoring system – one way of scoring the test counts the number of symptoms, while the other weighs the intensity of those symptoms, which can produce two different outcomes. In the PACE trial, both scoring schemes of the Chalder fatigue scale were recorded. The data showed that twenty-two participants showed improvement at the primary trial endpoint based on one scoring method, while the other scoring method showed a decline. Besides, feeling *tired* or *sleepy* or *drowsy* is not adequate language for fatigue, which is experienced not as a 'lack of energy', but something more active, akin to feeling *full of exhaustion*. PACE used the Oxford Criteria to determine inclusion in the trial, which is an intentionally broad definition based on self-reported fatigue for six months.

As the largest trial of ME/CFS treatments, the publication of the PACE trial was highly anticipated, but the results ran counter to many patients' experiences of both CBT and graded exercise therapy. Many find energy management or 'pacing' to be a far more effective, not to mention less dangerous, way of managing their condition. For anyone with post-exertional fatigue, exercise makes all of their symptoms much worse. Pacing is the activity of scheduling rest and low-activity periods, to either reduce the likelihood of a period of high pain or fatigue from occurring, or to enable you to do other higher-energy tasks as much as possible. It involves stopping any activity well before you have exhausted your resources – your perceived 'energy envelope'. Pacing is not spending everything you've got while you have it, not burning through your resources without thinking about tomorrow, or next week. You have to keep pacing and resting even when you have windows of improvement. Sometimes pacing is forced by pain or fatigue, and sometimes it is way of coping with fluctuating capacity. It can be read as both rejection of chronic pain and fatigue and embrace of disabled life.

Patients and researchers needed access to the raw data, without which they could not prove the PACE trial was flawed. Keith Geraghty was amongst those who asked to see it but was refused access. 'Doctors like me working in this world knew those treatments were ineffective,' he said. 'You know, a condition that is defined by excising tolerance is hardly going to be treated by exercise. It's an oxymoron.' Alem Matthees requested a Freedom of Information

168

Act in 2014, and after several attempts by Queen Mary University of London to reject the request, the raw data was eventually made available, but not before a tribunal ruling. It had taken a year and a half, and QMUL still appealed. Open-source re-analysis of the raw data revealed much fewer positive results than the investigators purported to show. Geraghty discovered that they had changed the goalposts of recovery, so much so that thirteen per cent of people recruited would have been deemed 'recovered' at the start, meaning they would never have been eligible for the trial in the first place.

David Tuller initially reported on the PACE trial for the *New York Times*, when only the authors had access to the data, noting the problem with using the Oxford Criteria for CFS. The Oxford Criteria requires fatigue to be the main symptom, accompanied by 'significant disability', in the absence of an exclusionary medical or psychiatric diagnosis'. Besides blurring the 'syndrome' with general 'chronic fatigue', the criteria elides the cognitive, neurological and physiological symptoms associated with ME/CFS diagnosis, and post-exertional malaise, and is more inclusive than other definitions, making it unclear what illness they were actually investigating. Effectively, they were not actually studying ME/CFS.

Tuller used to be a reporter for the *San Francisco Chronicle* and is now a senior fellow in public health and journalism at UC Berkeley's Center for Global Public Health. In 2015, he started investigating misleading research into treatments for ME/CFS, which he has published under the series title 'Trial By Error' on Virology Blog, a site hosted by a microbiology professor at Columbia University. Tuller is known for ripping up printed copies of the 2011 PACE trial report during his talks, an action he refers to as 'academic performance art'.

Sharpe accused Tuller of conflicts of interest because he funds his investigations into bogus ME/CFS trials via Berkeley's crowdfunding platform. (In April 2019, Tuller raised $183,283. It was his second crowdfund. From his two crowdfunding campaigns he's raised 12 per cent of the total income raised on the platform. As far as he knows, he is the only person in the US with a crowdfunded academic position.)

'I was trashing the PACE trial long before I asked anybody for any money at all,' explained Tuller, at a talk hosted by an ME group in Oxford; 'I was happy to do it for free until my funding ran out, and this is what I was invited to do by the Dean of Public Health at Berkeley.' Besides, he added, 'Professor Sharpe has undisclosed conflicts of interest of his own.' Sharpe has done voluntary and paid consultancy work for legal and insurance companies and for the UK's Department for Work and Pensions, conflicts of interest disclosed in the publication of the PACE trial but not to participants in the trial, or, in Tuller's words, 'the people you are experimenting on'. None of the main PACE investigators chose not to include their long-standing links to disability insurance companies and government agencies. To Tuller, this is a direct breach of the Declaration of Helsinki, the World Medical Association's statement of ethical principles for medical research involving human subjects, including research on identifiable human material and data, which *The Lancet* had promised to follow. According to the declaration, the PACE investigators should have disclosed any *possible* conflicts of interest to participants, not just the journal. Tuller insists that he has made this point 'many times', but it hasn't made *The Lancet* retract the trial.

Tuller actually received a $10,000 jump in donations after Sharpe tweeted a link to his initial crowdfund page. 'He doesn't realise you shouldn't tweet a link to someone's crowdfund (page) if you're protesting it,' joked Tuller. 'I have to thank him.'

In 2013, Tuller published a 15,000-word investigation of the PACE trial, having consulted with colleagues at Berkeley, Columbia and elsewhere. He gathered more than one hundred experts' signatures for his most recent open letter to *The Lancet* in August 2018, citing the trial's 'unacceptable methodological lapses' in the request of a fully independent investigation. A key issue with the subjective nature of the PACE trial outcomes, and the open, unblinded nature of the trial itself, is that both GET and CBT, at least as described in PACE, actively encouraged patients to believe the treatments will work, making it reasonable that the treatments themselves may have informed the reporting of their success. 'The validity of the treatment approach achieved hegemony largely through the status and prestige of those who promoted it,' wrote Tuller, 'not through the power and integrity of the research.'

The *Journal of Health Psychology* published a special issue on the PACE trial in 2016, which aimed to present both sides of the debate, except no papers supporting the trial were considered worthy of publication. The dispute led to resignations from *The Lancet* editorial staff, and some name-calling between them, with one scientist referring to another as a 'disgusting old fart neoliberal hypocrite'.

White, Chalder and Sharpe et al stood by their PACE trial findings, insisting CBT and GET were safe and effective treatments for chronic fatigue syndrome, insisting their findings were 'good news for patients who, in our experience, just want to get better'. 'Of course, we need further trials, not only of CBT and GET but also other treatments,' they added. 'To this end, we hope that editorials such as that by Dr Geraghty do not discourage others from doing such research.' The response – a rebuttal rather than re-assessment, or re-presentation of their results – was a clear attempt to silence their critics and position themselves as allied to those patients who 'just want to get better', and with medical research itself, and associating their critics with 'activism', 'trolling' and conflicts of interest.

Wessely had announced he would no longer work in the field of ME/CFS in 2011, having been accused by respected doctors and academics of 'blocking proper research into ME for years' (Dr Ian Gibson), blaming threats of violence by 'activists' and patients who contested his research. 'Wessely's employers at King's College London have taken advice on the potential risk and have instituted X-ray scans of his mail, he says,' reads a Reuters article from the time. 'Everything I say and do in public, and sometimes even in private, is pored over and scrutinised,' he said. Freedom of information requests to King's College for evidence of these threats were all denied, and the death threats have never materialized. Wessely still insists he is the subject of what he describes as 'relentless internet stalking'. Michael Sharpe also no longer conducts research into CFS/ME treatments, having decided to focus instead on helping severely ill cancer patients. 'It's just too toxic,' he explained.

Although not an author of the PACE trial, and claiming to no longer work in the field of ME/CFS at the time, Wessely backed the results, labelling the concerns of the trial's critics as 'not unimportant, but not likely to affect the fundamental integrity of a trial, nor the confidence with which we can view the results'. Wesseley compared a large trial like PACE to an ocean liner, leaving Southampton to sail to New York. 'Very occasionally there is a shipwreck, but this is very rare,' he wrote. 'Few trials suffer the fate of the Titanic, but sometimes the ship gets to the USA, but not to New York, but some other place; destination changed en route, which is considered bad form.' The trial's findings were not so drastically off to disregard. 'HMS PACE,' he argued, 'did make it successfully across the Atlantic. Small corrections to the route taken were made on the way, but these were of little significance.'

When I read Wesseley's blog post, fourteen-year-old Greta had just sailed the Atlantic on an eco-catamaran. His romanticized image of a cross-Atlantic steam ship with its hardy crew doing a valiant job of sailing its passengers to the New World seemed out of touch with our current reality. 'Storms continue to buffet the ship even as it remains in harbour,' he continued, 'but none of these have damaged the ship to impair its seaworthiness.' Since when does a trial need arguing if it sailed safely to its destination? And isn't the point that a ship has a specified destination, but a trial doesn't? No one would care if the ship took a slightly different course but ended up in the different destination to the one planned; surely the destination should be determined by the journey, not vice versa. And who gives a shit about how well the trial stands up, or weathers criticism, apart from the authors and their conflicts of interest, when the published findings inform the way people are treated, and whether they receive benefits and insurance. The Titanic didn't just sink – we've all seen the movie – there was a whole underclass of people who drowned locked inside its bowels; there were not enough lifeboats to go round.

The psychiatrists conducting £5 million trials with public money are the same psychiatrists who advised the government on theories of illness as an experience rather than a health problem, and they are the same psychiatrists who were paid consultants for insurance companies, which found themselves increasingly burdened by the financial cost of symptom syndromes. (Despite public perception of an increase in benefit claims, they have actually fallen.) The PACE trial authors declared several conflicts of interest with respect to the research, authorship and/or publication of the report: their group contained a member of the Independent Medical Experts Group, which advises the Ministry of Defence regarding the Armed Forces Compensation Scheme, an unpaid consultant for the Department for Work and Pensions, a paid consultant for a re-insurance company, and royalties from several publishers of academic books. Another was a director of the company Vitality360, a private 'rehabilitation provider' for people with persistent tiredness and fatigue, namely ME/CFS and fibromyalgia, which now offers courses for rehabilitation from post-viral fatigue following Covid-19 infection. A cynic would assume that the idea that ME/CFS – and that in fact any long-term condition – is an *experience* of illness without a real cause was adopted by the government in order to limit the amount of benefit claimants, encouraged by insurance companies that benefit from the lack of a welfare 'safety net'.

A Cochrane review of CBT for CFS published on 7 July 2020 claimed that people attending CBT were 'more likely to have reduced fatigue symptoms at the end of treatment than people who received usual care or were on a waiting list for therapy' (forty per cent of people in the CBT group showed clinical improvement, in contrast with twenty-six per cent in usual care). After treatment ended, people who had completed their course of CBT continued to have lower fatigue levels, but when including people who had dropped out of treatment, there was no difference between CBT and usual care. Nevertheless, the average national recovery rate of all referrals to IAPT (achieving a reliable and substantial reduction in their anxiety/depression) is actually closer to sixteen per cent rather than the supposed sixty-seven per cent. This is why Paul Atkinson, counsellor and Jungian psychotherapist who helps run the Free Psychotherapy Network, has called CBT 'an archetypal neoliberal scam'.

'My goal is to completely discredit the PACE trial,' Tuller told Reuters. 'And if they have moved out of the research field, then that's great. They shouldn't be in the field. They shouldn't be doing research at all.'

Who gets to speak in public – on matters that affect policy, benefits, and treatments offered to the general public – without being scrutinized? Who is available for public scrutiny and who is not? In what world should that scrutiny be suppressed? These were medical professionals working in public with public funds, alongside their roles advising government departments and insurance companies, and running their own private clinics and therapy providers. Wessely protested. 'It would be nice to think that perhaps we can now all move on,' he wrote, on his blog. 'The PACE trial will not be the last word. But it is the best we have for now.'

Tuller and Geherty see the retreat of some of the PACE researchers from public health and ME/CFS research as a positive in itself. Their funding deserves to go elsewhere. But maybe the whole thing was a scam – the idea that medical trials could determine how people were treated, and those trials could be determined by arguments and debates, one person's word over another's; Wessely's whole idea, of PACE 'not being the last word', did not make it a valid contribution to medical research. What's more, it didn't seem like the patients mattered at all, just who was more right than someone else, what was more or less useful in reducing the number of disability claimants. I could hear that voice: *You cannot be disabled by it.* Just because something is the best we have doesn't make it good enough. It doesn't validate a way of thinking about illness as a social defect, or treating sick people as toxic, as a problem that needs to be cured.

174

In the UK, it looks like the funding is finally moving towards biomedical research. In July 2020, four months into the Covid pandemic, it was announced that £3.2 million funding from the Medical Research Council and National Institute for Health Research had been awarded to DecodeME, a DNA study looking at samples from 20,000 people with ME/CFS. The study had been designed to find out if there were tiny differences in DNA that may affect the risk of developing the illness, and therefore aid the development of diagnostic tests and targeted treatments. The project was to be facilitated by the ME/CFS (CureME) biobank at the London School of Hygiene & Tropical Medicine.

The work Eliana Lacerda and her colleagues are doing at CureME is at odds with what I had been made to believe twenty years ago – that our illness was related to my social and familial situation, that my environment and psychology were causing our hysterical symptoms, which had no biological root cause. The ME Biobank project was established with the aim of enhancing biomedical research into ME/CFS.

'When we started this,' Eliana told me, in February 2020, 'the research that had been done and consequently, the therapeutic approaches to patients with ME/CFS in the UK were based on a specific way of thinking, which was that it had psychosocial causes, and not only causes but the actual reference in terms of the pathophysiology. What I mean is that the disease was seen as within the remit of mental health issues.' Like the many researchers working in this area, Eliana's interest in ME/CFS stems from personal experience: one of her best childhood friends in Brazil, where she is from, got ill, and then two medical doctors she was friends with.

Eliana does not see how any disease can be easily divided into the remit of either mental or physical health: 'As a medical doctor myself, I don't understand this division of body and mind, or body and psychology. We are entities in terms of mind and body, and to be alive, you have both, so there is no distinction there.'

Any chronic illness has consequences in mental health, and any mental health disease will have some consequences in the physical body, but Eliana does not consider ME/CFS a mental health disease because there are some physical dysfunctions that cannot be explained by mental health issues alone. Besides, Eliana doesn't see depression in people with ME/CFS any more than you would expect with chronic illness. Even before they asked participants to fill out mental and physical health questionnaires, they knew just from spending time with them that they were not depressed. Now they are able to analyze self-report questionnaires, the physical components are always worse than the mental components. 'Some of them have mild depression,' says Eliana, 'which is very common in any chronic disease, but the majority of them don't.' This is the case for the most severely affected patients, as well as the mild or moderately affected.

'When you have a patient that is depressed, and you ask them: "If I gave you a pot of energy tomorrow, what would you do with it?" What do you think a depressed person would say?' she asks me.

'They would say that it wouldn't make a difference,' I respond. 'Whereas it would for an ME/CFS patient.'

'They would give you a list of what they want to do.'

I spend the following days and weeks regularly asking myself: what would I do with a pot of energy, if Eliana gave me one? The answer changes, depending on my mood.

I would stay up all night.
I would walk really far.
I would swim in the sea.
I would cycle across London.
I would lie down because I wanted to, not because I needed to.
I would give it back.
I would finish this book.

CureME started recruiting patients in 2012 for their biobank project, for which they collect medical data and blood samples from three populations: people with ME, people with MS, a disease that has a similar symptom language and can be validated by imaging tests, and people who are considered healthy. These biospecimens are

176

processed, frozen and stored at the Royal Free Hospital biobank. Samples from a participant have to reach the biobank within six hours, where they are processed into forty-four aliquots, taken from different parts of blood: serum, plasma and PP cells, and blood in a 'specific tube that is very expensive' for extraction of ribonucleic acid (RNA), which carries instructions from DNA for controlling the synthesis of proteins.

Inclusion in the biobank depends on strict diagnostic criteria that can be used across populations: the CDC 94, CCC and the IOM criteria, as well as the International Criteria (called the ICC, a new version of the CCC). There are so many definitions, with similar sounding acronyms, that even Eliana mixes them up, going through the list twice before getting it right. If every research group working on the biology of ME/CFS is using a different diagnostic criterium, it is impossible to validate research. 'You cannot say "my findings are the same, or my findings are completely different," because we are looking at different things,' says Eliana.

Eliana has sent blood samples all over the world. There is a map on the wall of her office with red strings spanning out from London: Spain, USA, Brazil, Austria, Scotland. They are in collaboration with Australia, where a mirror-biobank will be set up soon. The red strand for Israel has fallen out so she pins it back in. It looks like something you would find on the wall of a child's bedroom: handmade, naïve and a bit broken, except it is the colour of blood – *unidentifiably diseased* blood.

'Where is the research going?' I ask her, gesturing to the map – the blood spilling out of London. I think of the spider-diagram my mother drew in therapy, with the outline of a person at the centre to signify herself, connected to all the people in her life – children, girlfriend, friends (givers and takers), mother, ex-husband, carer – by lines projecting outwards.

Each line on Eliana's map ends at a location in the world, but also represents a different avenue of research, a separate subtle finding in a bodily system, a research group with speciality looking at a specific pathway of disease.

'We know there is something that is at the core of it, but we don't know yet what it is,' she explains. 'It's like a jigsaw, where everyone is finding a small piece. I think we are heading towards a better understanding with research complementing each other. Based on what I've seen lately, I think there are some promising findings, interesting findings, but we are not there yet.'

I've never really pictured medical research like this, of findings as a jigsaw puzzle, or a fractured image, that need to be seen together for the picture to emerge. I always had the sense that it was more about the pursuit of a finding, a 'major breakthrough', an abnormality or reaction staged in a lab, which could be replicated on bigger samples. I don't know why I believed this – why scientific research would be different from any other kind? I feel closer to them than anyone else – that my work is like theirs. Perhaps Eliana and her colleagues at CureME see medical research in this way because of their relation to the biobank as a means of facilitating research.

It might be that advances in technology will make it possible to diagnose and treat ME/CFS through a biomarker, as was the case with MS and the development of neuroimaging. Alternatively, researchers might find evidence of a genetic disposition – tiny differences in DNA that may affect the risk of developing the illness – rather than a biological marker of disease.

'It could be that you got glandular fever as a teenager, or you were in a road traffic accident in your forties. There is not much in common with those events, but a genetic predisposition could mean you have similar symptoms,' explains Eliana's colleague Caroline. If you were looking for a biomarker, you wouldn't necessarily find it.'

A genetic predisposition sounds so similar to a feeling: we have been *triggered*.

When an illness appears to influence all these different systems, it doesn't submit to the usual logic of cause and effect, it is left behind. Research ends up siloed, with some groups looking at natural killer cells or B cells, and others looking at inflammation in the brain.

The first paper the biobank published themselves was on 'natural killer cells', a type of white blood cell that is activated to contain viral infection in the body, while the adaptive immune response generates antigen-specific cytotoxic T cells to clear it away. Some small studies had found that these 'natural killer cells' were higher in people with ME/CFS, and others found they were lower. Using their large sample, the researchers at CureME didn't find either was the case. They did, however, find a specific subset of cells that were 'different'. 'I wouldn't say abnormal,' says Eliana, 'but *different*.'

Eliana and Caroline want specialists to talk to each other more, because that will influence what they *make* of the results of their tests and trials. It takes a multidisciplinary approach to medicine to understand a disease like diabetes – it should be the same for all diagnoses. As Caroline says: 'You have genetics, you have the environment, you have physical bodies, and this interaction, for every disease.' The problem with ME/CFS, it seems, is that it was siloed into one system – mental health – that could account for many but not all symptoms or physical abnormalities.

'What we definitely know is that it's a very complex disease that affects different systems in the body,' says Eliana. 'Research is able to show there are some abnormalities in people with ME/CFS that you don't find in people that are healthy, or people with other diseases with similar symptoms.' This is why the networking, as well as the collection and dissemination of samples, is important. Part of their work as a biobank is about raising awareness of the need to comply with a specific combination of criteria to minimise bias in medical research. It is essential to standardise procedures for diagnosing people in order to make the research results more reliable in terms of comparisons.

Biobanking projects like this one are archives of samples that, if stored correctly, and shared with enough research teams, have the potential to produce new knowledge of the biology of an illness that has predominantly been investigated by psychiatrists. The physical ME/CFS biobank is the site at which the desires of many individual participants and researchers meet – the desire to find a cause, and even a cure, possible through extraction, and anonymization, or the stripping of identity. Unlike a paper archive, which will deteriorate, or a film archive, which can self-destruct, this one is literally frozen in time, storing matter to be interpreted and tested, used by generations beyond our own.

The term 'biobank' first appeared in scientific literature in 1996. By 2009, *Time Magazine* had claimed biobanking was a 'world changing' idea. Biobanking entailed the need for biorights – the ongoing right of research participants to control their research samples, to benefit directly from the research, and/or to be financially compensated for their contribution. Consent is an important issue in what is a relatively new research process.

CureME consider themselves guardians of the samples, and they have to be sure they will be used by bona fide researchers with the right experience. Each research application is reviewed by a steering committee made up of patients and charity representatives as well as researchers. Then there is always an ethics review, and a final agreement between the legal teams at the School that represents the biobank, where the samples are stored, and the same for the destination. The whole process takes four to eight weeks, which is a time- and cost-effective way of doing research.

There is, however, no consensus as to their legal and ethical appropriateness, and biobanking consent issues are hyped by the press, mainly because there is money to be made – 'Human Biobanking Ownership–Market to Witness a value of $37.1 Billion by 2020'. Industry is inevitably involved in projects that produce technologies and drugs for healthcare contexts, creating the potential to erode public trust. Then there is the issue of data breaches, and the concern over the protection of illegal accessing of personal health information. And the case of Henrietta Lacks, a Black woman who was the source of the HeLa cell line after her uterine cells were taken without her consent.

There is an ethics to collecting samples, and institutions to enforce them. According to the Declaration of Helsinki, the individual should be respected above everything else, meaning physicians and researchers must seek informed consent for blood collection, storage and/or reuse of their samples. Research may be done only after consideration and approval of a research ethics committee. At the ME biobank, the samples that go to the pathology lab for routine testing are eponymized, and the samples that go in the biobank are anonymized. A unique ID is assigned to each set of samples, which is unrelated to the patient's paperwork. (All patient data taken during the patient's appointment, including health questionnaires, clinical assessment and the blood tests they take to exclude other conditions, are anonymized.) An archive of anamnesis – patient history – is stored in one place, and the blood from their body in another, anonymized to reduce bias and ensure privacy. The individual is lost in the process, labelled with a code from the biobank which bears no relation to the participant's history, leaving only the consent forms.

As early as April 2020, it was announced that data on the health of 500,000 UK Biobank participants – funded primarily by the UK's Medical Research Council and the Wellcome science and health charity – was being made available to scientists tackling the Covid-19 emergency. This included test results (both positive and negative) and inpatient, death and critical care data, in addition to the wide range of other data about health and lifestyle, including genetics, that had already been made available to its 14,000 registered researchers.

In 2019, the ME Biobank received £99,766 of funding from the Ramsay Research Fund via the ME Association 'to continue their development of a blood test for ME, based on how a person's immune cells respond to stress'. The funding would also ensure a steady supply of blood samples to ME researchers around the world. Initially funded by three ME charities and an anonymous donor, their application for funding from the NIH in the UK was rejected, so they are funded by the US.

'We have to have funding to do the research,' says Eliana.

This research could be done by researchers working in other countries or with commercial companies who are looking for new treatments or lab tests, but the biobank does not sell samples or data. Each sample is a gift, for which the donor doesn't receive any payment. Each donation is a token of trust in scientific invention, a contribution to a gift economy in the hope that one day that invention could lead to a greater understanding of ME/CFS.

'The community of geneticists worldwide do this all the time in different diseases,' said Chris Ponting, leader of the new genome-wide association study into the genetics of ME/CFS, during a

Decode ME webinar attended by two thousand people during the first nation-wide lockdown. 'They form international consortia and they have studies in their own countries and then they come together to compare their findings and that's what we will do.' He says he hopes that the money from the Medical Research Council and National Institute for Health Research in the UK would act as a catalyst for change in other countries, so that more research could be compared. Genome-wide association studies have established the identity of numerous genes involved in Type II diabetes, revealed that microglia – the immune cells of the brain – play a key role in Alzheimer's disease and improved treatments for ankylosing spondylitis (an inflammatory type of arthritis that primarily effects the spine) by identifying the immune-regulating molecule called IL-23, which plays a significant role in several autoimmune conditions. Like many complex diseases, the research team expects the risk of having ME/CFS is altered by many different DNA letters scattered around the human genome.

The day I went to the biobank in February 2020, there were already three patients being treated at the Royal Free Hospital for Covid-19. Outside the entrance to the UCL Biobank, the CureME research nurse Dio showed me the blood taken from just one person that morning, briefly fanning them out in his hands as if performing a magic trick. Fourteen vials, one hundred millilitres each, taken with care – gifts from a sick person that could contribute to forty-four potential biomedical studies into their disease.

I had always suspected that the reason why biomedical research into ME/CFS was undervalued and underfunded had something to do with the siloed nature of medicine, with purposeful splitting up and isolating. Silos are for grain, but they are also for weapons, or information. A 'silo mentality' is when employees don't share information across divisions within a company, which usually involves a waste of energy for everyone involved. But the real reason for the neglect and corruption of illness is the consolidation of centralised power, the consecration of neoliberal politics and endemic resistance to socialised care. The ME/CFS biobank offers a model to think about gathering, storing and disseminating, rather than the quarantining of knowledge. I confess, I do not know enough about this. This is not my 'specialism'. But I know it in my body.

This is what my mother and I say to each other sometimes, when our knowledge of our own experiences and sensations are dismissed, when we don't know if we have made something up or it really happened, because we are supposed to question that lived reality, to believe it to be fiction, unevidenced and illegitimate.

I know it in my body.

Our bodies are our archives, the storehouses of our shared knowledge. I know it in her body, and in mine.

When I first told my mother I was writing about our shared experience of 'medically unexplained' illness, she didn't challenge me, or ask me not to, but she did remember that she still hadn't given me some books by Sarah Myhill that she had told me about ages ago. One was called *Sustainable Medicine* (2015), in which Myhill argues that the use of 'symptom-suppressing medications' have resulted in an escalation, rather than eradication, of disease. Myhill, who trained at Middlesex Hospital in London, and worked in general practice for twenty years until starting an independent practice in Wales in the early 2000s, aims to 'empower people to heal themselves' by addressing the 'root causes' of their symptoms, asking *why* they feel ill, not just *how*. She believes we are 'addicted' to carbohydrates and develop metabolic syndromes as a result – to the extent that 'it is more dangerous to follow your doctor's advice on diet and take symptom-suppressing medication than to smoke twenty cigarettes a day'. Myhill describes how suppressing symptoms with medication only make our problems worse, and when those drugs are ineffective, the patient is often blamed, or labelled as having 'false illness beliefs', while the actual root cause(s) of their symptoms is ignored. This is not what I was expecting to read in a book by a GP. Maybe it should have been – Myhill had of course left general practice for a reason.

'Myhill actually gets it,' my mother said, in response to my pointing out that she had been struck off the medical register twice. In 2010, she was suspended by the General Medical Council, and banned from prescribing drugs for eighteen months, having recommended vitamin and magnesium injections to patients with 'suspected chronic fatigue syndrome'. At the subsequent hearing, Myhill told of how one patient with a diagnosis of chronic fatigue syndrome took his own life because he mistakenly believed she would no longer able to treat him.

As suggested by Myhill's book, my mother started a ketogenic or 'stone age' (paleo) diet, which she had nicknamed 'the pork chop diet'. My mother was no longer eating potatoes or pasta or bread – the staples of her meals, and mine. No starchy vegetables, no caffeine, and certainly no sugar, lots of expensive bottles of special oils she couldn't afford. In fact, the whole thing was costing her a fortune.

'If she found a treatment that worked,' said my mother, 'the NHS would have to pay for it.'

It wasn't just people with ME/CFS who were trying the keto diet, all kinds of people were desperate to 'reach ketosis', and 'stay in keto', testing their urine with strips bought online. Later, my mother told me the diet made her miserable, and that the benefits did not outweigh the depression it also caused. 'You don't get hungry on it,' she said. 'I wanted to kill myself, but I didn't get hungry.'

Virginia Woolf's second serious breakdown started in May 1904 after her father's death. Initially taken care of by three nurses at 22 Hyde Park Gate, the family house, she was taken to Burnham Wood, Welwyn to stay with Violet Dickinson, where she tried to jump out of a first-floor window, and also came down with scarlet fever. From there she stayed with the Stephen Family at Teversal, Nottinghamshire. She was then prescribed the rest cure by Dr George Henry Savage, an old friend of the family and Virginia's physician since childhood.

'Oh how thankful I shall be to be my own mistress and throw their silly medicines down the slop pail!' she wrote to Violet in October. 'I never shall believe, or have believed, in anything any doctor says.' They all behaved as if they knew what was best, knew exactly how to make her miserable, and were still powerless to make her well: 'I don't expect any doctor to listen to reason,' she wrote; 'If only that pigheaded man Savage will see that this is the sober truth and no excuse!' To Virginia, aged 22, a doctor was 'even worse than a husband'. She had learnt their 'utter helplessness' during her father's protracted illness. 'They can guess at what's the matter, but they can't put it right.'

November, complaining to Violet again of everyone else's fool-ishness: 'That silly old Nessa has been absorbing Savages theories as usual. I cant (sic) conceive how anybody can be fool enough to believe in a doctor. I know he will soon climb down and tell me what is the fact. That I am quicker and better in London than

185

anywhere else – just as he had to give in about walking alone, and being isolated. My life is a constant fight against Doctors' follies, it seems to me.' Virginia was discharged from Savage in January 1905, labelled 'cured'. She published a review within a month, out of brilliant spite. 'Rather amuses me to write,' she wrote in her diary, 'since I have been ordered not to write for my brains health.'

Savage sent her to Burley House, a nursing home for women with nervous disorders at 15 Cambridge Park, Twickenham, in 1910. She had spent time in Lelant, Cornwall in March but returned ill. At 29 Fitzroy Square, where she had been living since 1907, Virginia had the whole of the second floor to herself and could spread out as she chose; her drawing room mourned, 'like the sea, with flowing purple', her sitting room filled with 'great pyramids of books, with trailing mists between them; partly dust, and partly cigarette-smoke'. As master of her own domain, she could furnish the rooms as she liked, with bright green carpets, red brocade and later purple curtains, and a pianola. By June, Vanessa found herself unable to look after Virginia, and appealed to Savage for help.

Kept in a darkened room, Virginia was prescribed a diet of milk and meat, fresh air, limited excitement, no communication with family and little access to letters, and was dosed with sedatives. The effects of her treatment were more powerful than her symptoms, and further fuelled her resistance to the rest cure. As Hermione Lee argued in her biography: 'her intellectual resistance to tyranny and conventionality, derived to a great extent from her experiences as a woman patient'.

The walls of Miss Jean Thomas's nursing home were mottled green and red. Thomas was 'always culminating in silent prayer'. A person who Vanessa thought might be a homicidal maniac turned out to be a nurse. Virginia would return to Burley House, which Vanessa's son Quentin called 'a polite madhouse for female lunatics', three more times over the next decade.

'I really don't think I can stand much more of this,' Virginia Stephen (not yet Woolf) wrote in a letter to Vanessa at the end of July. 'Sick of all the eating and drinking and being shut up in the dark. What I mean is I shall soon have to jump out of a window.' She jokes with her sister: 'you can't conceive how I want intelligent conversation – even yours.' 'I shall tell you wonderful stories of the lunatics,' Virginia wrote to Leonard from Burley in 1910. 'By the bye, they've elected me King. There can be no doubt about it.'

Once they were married, Leonard Woolf went to see Dr Savage in early 1912. He was impressed, but 'more as a man of the world than as a doctor'. It was Dr Savage who first recommended to Leonard that Virginia *go to bed*. Leonard's impression of Savage led him to consult with several other 'brilliant doctors', including neurologist Henry Head, T.B. Hyslop (an expert in eugenics and hypnotism who had previously worked at Bethlem Hospital), and Sir Maurice Craig, all of whom, according to Leonard, 'had not the slightest idea of the nature of the cause of Virginia's mental state, which resulted in her suddenly or gradually losing touch with the real world, so that she lived in a world of delusions and became a danger to herself and other people.' Not knowing how or why this had happened to her, 'naturally they had no real or scientific knowledge of how to cure her'. The doctors told Leonard she was suffering from neurasthenia and that, if she could be made to eat and rest, and if she could be prevented from committing suicide, she would recover. Leonard came to believe Virginia was not neurasthenic at all, but manic-depressive. He watched and studied her, making obsessively detailed notes on her behaviour in a way no doctor thought, or had the time, to do.

Leonard thought Henry Head, recommended by Roger Fry, was more of an intellectual, and would therefore 'understand a person like Virginia better than a man like Savage'. Virginia saw him in July 1913 as she was finishing *The Voyage Out*. According to Leonard, Head told her she was mistaken about her condition, that she was, in fact, ill, 'like a person who had a cold or typhoid fever', but her symptoms would disappear if she took his advice and did what he prescribed, which Virginia must have thought predictable, even by this time: she had to go back to the nursing home and stay in bed for a few weeks, resting and eating. According to Leonard, Miss Thomas was 'somewhat emotional' and adored Virginia, 'a combination which had its disadvantages', but 'Virginia liked her up to a point' and was 'willing to go to her for a week or two'.

Leonard consulted with Savage again in 1913 and Virginia

187

was returned to Burley for a short period in the summer during which she sent six letters, all to Leonard, each a few lines long. She didn't want to be there, but knew it was 'for the best'. She told him she loved him, in spite of her 'vile imaginations'. That she was trying to read a tall American's magazines. Maybe a husband isn't quite as bad as a doctor, if love was a way she could secure escape. Virginia believed her illness was a kind of punishment. And who wouldn't, after several rounds of treatment by doctors who consistently prescribed forced rest and 'stuffing' at a nursing home.

28 July: 'I'm very well, slept well, and they made me eat all day.'

2 August: 'I want to see you, but this is best.'

3 August: 'Here it's all so unreal.'

On 5 August, Savage went to see her at the nursing home, and told her she could go home the following Thursday. 'Nothing has happened,' she wrote. She sounds blank, empty.

Back at Vanessa's house on Brunswick Square, Virginia swallowed a large dose of veronal tablets, powerful synthetic barbiturates Leonard gave her when she could not sleep, usually kept in a locked box. Friend Katherine (Ka) Laird Cox discovered her unconscious. Virginia had to have her stomach pumped. Her action had risked being certified, sent to some 'dreadful, large gloomy' building 'enclosed by high walls, dismal trees, and despair' – these are Leonard's words, written after he visited some nursing homes – but she survived. Two years on, in November 1915, and having had another collapse, and another visit to the nursing home, no letters for six months, she was 'very well and enjoy sitting in this mound of flesh', as she wrote to Ka from Hogarth House in Richmond, now 33. 'I spend my spare time in bed, but I'm allowed out in the afternoons, and thank God the last nurse is gone.'

Sick of all the eating. To refuse to eat as Virginia did is to refuse the men who force you to eat, who repress you, whether you are a female hysteric or a soldier with shellshock, feminized and ignored – it is to refuse doctor and husband both, to channel the anger you felt twenty years previously, when you spent the most wretched eight months in your life never expecting them to see reason.

188

My mother has bookmarked several pages in her copy of *Diagnosis and Treatment of Chronic Fatigue Syndrome and Myalgic Encephalitis: It's Mitochondria, Not Hypochondria*, Myhill's second book on ME/CFS. My mother has written out the pertinent section titles – 'Holes in the Energy Bucket' – on slips of paper in her own distinctive script. According to Myhill, there are two holes where energy drains out rather than being used for the body's necessary functions, one is emotional and the other immunological, and both need to be plugged. As a consequence of ME/CFS, your energy drains due to stress, worry and anxiety about your situation. To need to plug a hole means there is a leak. There is a fault with the system, causing unnecessary waste. The hole is a problem that can be solved – although the bucket itself will never not be broken, just fixed. It's a difficult metaphor, because if there was a hole in your bucket you would probably just throw it away and get a new bucket, or use it for storing something that won't leak away.

Once again, the body is a bank account. 'Imagine that a normal healthy person has £1000 worth of energy to spend in a day,' writes Myhill. 'The CFS/ME sufferer only has £100. What is more, this has to be spread out throughout the day in such a way that there is £20 "change" at the end. This allows energy for healing and repair.' If someone with ME/CFS was to spend their energy on walking or swimming or cycling, but also 'mental activities' such as reading and writing, studying or watching TV, they could easily empty the reserves they need to digest their food, and keep infections at bay, or their heart pumping regularly. 'Remember,' she writes, 'two thirds of all energy production goes into housekeeping duties.' By 'housekeeping duties', she means the basic functions of the immune system, liver, brain, gut and heart.

As a role that encompasses cleaning, cooking and shopping, but also managing the household accounts, housekeeping, to my mind, is very Victorian, in that there are books about it for the emerging middle classes, who had to learn how to do it themselves. According to Isabella Beeton, 'there is no more fruitful source of family discontent than a housewife's badly-cooked dinners and untidy ways'. Most of *Mrs Beeton's Book of Household Management*, first published in 1861, is taken up with recipes, for which she was later accused of plagiarising, but there is also advice on managing servants, frugality and household economy.

Where Beeton lists recipes, Myhill lists basic supplement plans and additional 'bolt-ons' as needed. (She has also written a cookbook of paleo recipes.) Myhill advises the use of valerian and rescue remedy over SSRIs – 'addictive drugs', which carry the risk of suicide ideation. Diazepam – also addictive, but in an epidemic way – is a 'get out of jail free card'. There is a chapter on understanding the need to care and be cared for. This book was practically written for my mother, I think. (Not to mention that diazepam is my 'get out of jail free' drug of choice, with which to self-medicate, designed not to constantly suppress but *relieve*, at the worst times, so as to continue living.)

In *Mrs Beeton's Book of Household Management*, Beeton likens the mistress of the house – the good housewife – to the commander of an army, or the leader of any enterprise. A mistress starts the day early with a cold or tepid bath. She must be economic and frugal, 'whether in the possession of an income no more than sufficient for a family's requirements, or of a large fortune, which puts financial adversity out of the question'. A housekeeping account book should invariably be kept, 'and kept punctually and precisely'. The housekeeper is the housewife's second in command. She is watchful, and disciplined, overlooking all that goes on in the house, constantly on the watch for any wrong-doing on the part of the domestics. She should thoroughly understand accounts, and spend her evenings 'duly writing a statement of moneys received and paid, and also for making memoranda of any articles she may require for her storeroom or other departments'. Like 'Caesar's wife', she should be 'above suspicion', and her honesty and sobriety unquestionable, 'for there are many temptations to which she is exposed'. A housekeeper should be clean, healthy and strong. Although her hands show a degree of roughness, due to the work she has undertaken, they should have a nice, inviting appearance.

190

Unlike Alice James, who said she was expected to be her own doctor, nurse and straight jacket, Beeton instructs how to act during 'the interval that must necessarily elapse from the moment that a medical man is sent for until he arrives'. For liver complaint and spasm, she advises braising and boiling four ounces of dried dandelion root, one ounce of the best ginger and a quarter ounce of columba root together in three pints of water till it is reduced to a quart: strain, and take a wine-glassful every four hours. When an attack of palpitation of the heart arises from nervous irritability, Beeton advises the excitement must be allayed by change of air and a tonic diet. 'Should the palpitation originate from organic derangement,' she writes, 'it must be, of course, beyond domestic management. Luxurious living, indolence, and tight-lacing often produce this affection: such cases are to be conquered with a little resolution.' Mrs Beeton's housekeeping guide also contains chapters of medical advice, suggesting the role of housewife involves a responsibility over the health of those housed inside.

Towards the end of her guide, Beeton provides an antidote to opium poisoning, (and its preparations, laudanum, etc.): 'Tickle the top of the throat with a feather, or put two fingers down it to bring on vomiting, which rarely takes place of itself. Dash cold water on the head, chest, and spine, and flap these parts well with the ends of wet towels. Give strong coffee or tea. Walk the patient up and down in the open air for two or three hours; the great thing being to keep him from sleeping.' Mustard Poultice – equal parts of dry mustard and linseed-meal in warm vinegar – must be applied in the days that follow. (Did Elizabeth ever overdose? Did anyone ever need to tickle her throat with a feather, and smear mustard on her skin?) Beeton also includes a substantial entry for how to treat hysteric fits, which take place, 'for the most part, in young, nervous, unmarried women. They happen much less often in married women; and even (in some rare cases indeed) in men.' These fits are the result of 'false illness beliefs': 'Young women, who are subject to these fits, are apt to think that they are suffering from "all the ills that flesh is heir to;" and the false symptoms of disease which they show are so like the true ones, that it is often exceedingly difficult to detect the difference. . . . In every case, amusing the mind, and avoiding all causes of over-excitement, are of great service in bringing about a permanent cure.'

Housekeeping in a middle-class Victorian home was not necessarily done by a substantial group of people, so the reader could be entertained by imagining taking charge of a substantial household of servants. To imagine themselves not only as the head of the household, but in command of others: the housekeeper, the maid, a doctor. Realistically, 'housewife' would have embodied nearly all who had to learn how to manage a household, turning a paid role into unpaid domestic labour.

Housekeeping is what sticks to us as sick women, as mothers and daughters – it is the work we are expected to do, without pay. It is conversely the work disabled women do not have the capacity or physical capability to do, making them less than women. The social ideal of not only living independently but having the ability to look after others at all cost. Housekeeping is mirrored in the immune system, whose cells have historically been assigned class and gender. T-cells or 'killer cells' sit at the top of the hierarchy, as they have masculine warrior-like qualities, with B-cells associated with upper-class women. Macrophages on the other hand are associated with a feminized labour: enveloping, housekeeping and other kinds of low-paid domestic and care work.

The leftover energy from pacing all day and surrounding oneself with energy givers is used for recovery – banking energy for repair or 'housekeeping'. Sufferers can face 'multiple mild organ failure' as a result of not having enough energy for basic bodily tasks. With less energy for brain function, you become foggy-headed, and find it difficult to concentrate in the short term, which could, in the long term, lead to dementia; with less energy for your immune system, you are more susceptible to infection and, later, cancer; with less energy for your heart to function, you become fatigued, you feel better lying down, and you get chest pain from angina or lactic acid burn, and long term, your heart can fail; with less energy for your gut and liver function, you are at increased risk of poor digestion and fermenting gut, leading to bowel cancer, and are more susceptible to toxic stress from the outside world. A messy household, a chaotically run home, in which the day-to-day housekeeping duties are not carried out, is an unhealthy home. We too must be economic and frugal, duly writing a statement of energy received and energy paid. Housekeeping is also keeping time. It is living within your means. According to Myhill, housekeeping is the starting point to prevent all disease. Essentially, she says, she is slowing down the ageing process of mitochondria, which can live 'theoretically, up to 120 years'. Myhill attributes this number to the lifespan of Jeanne Calment.

Having lived for 122 years and 164 days, until her death in 1997, Calment is still the oldest person ever known to have lived. She claimed to have met Van Gogh and was known for charging around Arles in her old age. But was she authentic? A mathematician called Nikolay Zak developed the theory that the person known as Jeanne Calment was actually her daughter, Yvonne, and the family had presented Jeanne's corpse to the authorities as Yvonne in order to avoid inheritance taxes in 1934. 'In the course of more than six decades,' reads a 2020 *New Yorker* article on the story, 'he posited, a family secret had metastasized into a national conspiracy.' A biobank in France supposedly holds 'secrets' to her real age but could not be legally accessed in the absence of informed consent in accordance with the Declaration of Helsinki. It seems absurd to aim to live for this long, as if anything less is a failure on our own part.

To plug the Emotional Hole, an important part of recovery, we have to reduce the demands on the system, to rest and pace. 'Energy borrowed has to be paid back at 300 per cent interest,' Myhill writes, to 'avoid the loan shark.' According to Myhill, resisting the tendency to push yourself to your limits, is vital in ME/CFS to start the process of recovery. In the 'boom and bust' pattern, the body 'borrows' energy it doesn't have – hasn't *earned*? – to keep going when it really should be resting. She advises keeping to a strict routine, by the clock, and doing activities in short bursts. Varying tasks is less tiring. Some of her advice reads like she is channelling Marion Hilliard. We have to reduce the load and stop spending unnecessary energy. She suggests making a list of tasks in order of importance, and then just stop doing the bottom fifty per cent. Plus, their names happen to be similar. Except Myhill has left out all the stuff about women, and duties of care. 'To recover you must be emotionally ruthless and selfish,' Myhill says; 'surround yourself with "energy givers" rather than "energy vampires".'

A vampire's bite harbours contagion, which is why Silas Weir Mitchell wrote: 'A hysterical girl is, as Wendell Holmes has said in his decisive phrase, a vampire who sucks the blood of the healthy people about her; and I may add that pretty surely where there is one hysterical girl there will be soon or late two sick women.'

Mitchell would have called my mother and me vampires. He would have called my mother 'over-loving', and our apparent influence on each other – that we were making each other feel ill – 'a form of evil'. In his 1877 book *Fat and Blood and How to Make Them*, Mitchell dedicates whole paragraphs to the parts on a woman's body where a woman gains flesh when 'subjected' (his word) to the rest cure: the back, flank, belly, and lastly the legs. The case studies at the end of the book are numerous, each around two lines long: women of twenty-six, or thirty-two, their height and weight listed, who went to bed for two months and were back to work as a clerk, or a teacher, when they arose, if their profession and activities are listed at all, anonymous bar their marital status: Miss R., Miss E., Mrs. L., all fed a pungent diet of mutton chops for midday dinner, four pints of milk in place of water, butter largely, raw beef and hydrochloric acid in water twice a day – the smell of meat and milk and fat lingering in the air, emitted by the food itself, but also, I imagine, by their skin and hair.

Following the death of her parents, my mother was one of those cases for which, in Mitchell's words, 'illness is the cause', but was also enduring my grandfather's bizarre everyday existence and imminent death. She implemented care that he had already surpassed the need of, and then went along with the fiction that he lived at home when he didn't. He thought he was living in his own house, surrounded by demented old ladies and cared for by nurses who took him for blood transfusions once a week.

194

'I see every week — almost every day — women who when asked what is the matter reply, "Oh, I have nervous exhaustion,"' declared Mitchell, in *Fat and Blood*. These exhausted women, often suffering with spinal irritation, wasting, anaemia and emotional manifestations, were, he believed, unnecessarily called 'hysterical'. These were women for whom exertion causes nausea and 'quickens the pulse curiously', 'the tire shows in the face, or sometimes diarrhoea or nausea follows exertion'. Mitchell also observed a smaller number of cases, people – still women, especially – 'subject to a host of aches and pains, without notable organic disease', 'feeble and forever tired'. Prevented from reading, they were left to study themselves, and obsess over their 'accumulating aches and distresses'. They might have undertaken the 'hard task of nursing a relative', 'swayed by hopes and fears', or physical strain, 'such as teaching'. There were also cases for which 'illness is the cause'. No matter how it came about, 'every effort is paid for dearly, and [the patient] describes herself as aching and sore, as sleeping ill'. 'Emotional' women became more so, but even the firmest fell apart, 'lose self-control at last under incessant feebleness'. The healthy life became entirely absorbed by the sick, the normal obscured by the pathological. If nothing was done, their fate was 'the bed', and with it, moral degradation:

> I have heard a good deal of the disciplinary usefulness of sickness, and this may apply to brief and grave, and what I might call wholesome, maladies . . . I have seen a few people who were ennobled by long sickness, but far more often the result is to cultivate self-love and self-ishness and to take away by slow degrees the healthy mastery which every human being should retain over her own emotions and wants.

Mitchell believed all these women needed was a liberal gain in fat and blood through the ingestion of copious amounts of milk and fatty meat, or 'excessive feeding', made possible by 'passive exercise' (lying down most of the day), combined with 'the steady use of massage' (what he termed 'manipulation') and electricity, and insisted on the fact that it is the use of these means together that is wanted. They lacked what could be put back in, or built back up.

195

The first listing in the index for Mitchell's *Fat and Blood and How to Make Them* reads: 'Advantages of seclusion in emotional cases', but the chapter it refers to – 'Chapter III Seclusion' – is less about the advantages of treating hysterical patients away from home than comparing sick girls to fictional monsters and the difficulties of fattening persons at rest during the summer months. The need for seclusion was nevertheless necessary, as Mitchell found it was impossible to treat his neurasthenic patients in their own homes. For his treatment to be successful, the patient had to be free from the influence of their habitual surroundings, disentangled from contact with 'the willing slaves of their caprices', and the moral and physical surroundings that have become 'a part of her life of sickness'. In breaking ties between family members, carers, friends or companions, Mitchell meant to destroy the 'drama of the sick-room', the 'habit' of sickness, and the sympathy and indulgence that seemed to feed it. According to Mitchell, the exacerbation of feebleness could be ascribed to: 'The self-sacrificing love and over-careful sympathy of a mother, a sister, or some other devoted relative.' This particular symptom was trickier to treat, especially if that relative's temperament was also nervous and they were 'impatient or irritable'. 'Two such people produce endless mischief for one another.' Some mothers and daughters will always be considered naughty children, whatever their age.

Perhaps by seclusion what he really meant to achieve was *separation*.

In 1936, Virginia wrote in her diary that not since 1913 had she felt so above the precipice. Precariously balanced, about to slip and sink down and down, going under. A few months later, Virginia and Leonard made friends with Octavia Wilberforce, a doctor with a practice in Brighton – the other side of the South Downs. Octavia was living with Elizabeth Robins, an actress, whose book the Hogarth Press had agreed to publish. Virginia was very interested in Octavia's adolescence, and her family, who, Virginia wrote in her diary, had forced her to stay at home: 'Only through a great struggle did she break off and become a doctor.' Leonard had been privately consulting with Octavia, and urged Virginia to be taken on as a patient.

On 17 March 1941, the day before she died by suicide, Virginia was persuaded by Leonard to consult with Octavia, who advised complete rest. Virginia admired Octavia for leaving the family house and working. Sadly, Octavia prescribed to the views of the male physicians Virginia had encountered. She had even brought cream and cheese from her dairy to Monk's House.

For Myhill, human bodies are 'battlefields', and our immune systems are made up of cells that require advanced training and strategic defence tactics. She sees a lot of ME/CFS in people who had chronic sore throats, toddler diarrhoea, tonsillitis, then glandular fever – an acute infection from which they never recovered, and 'the immune system stayed switched on'. Her advice, given during an online workshop I attended: 'Strike soon, strike hard, because time is of the essence.' Myhill has a habit of using really specific historical events as metaphors for infection. 'It's a bit like Henry V at Harfleur, when he was assailing the French,' she says, an elaborate extension of the image of the immune system as an ancient fortress. 'They were holed up in a castle, and they were well defended, and he didn't just get them out of the castle by lobbing a few spears over the top, he was throwing big rocks at them, he was poisoning the water, he was starving them, he was scaling the battlements, he was hitting them all the ways he could. And it's the same with these microbes.' One of her more haunting – and more concise – metaphors goes: 'Life is an arms race.'

It is as if Sontag had never written how illness is explicitly *not* a metaphor, 'and that the most truthful way of regarding illness – and the healthiest way of being ill – is one most purified of, most resistant to, metaphoric thinking' – in 1978.

Our bodies are not even systems that maintain self and other. The immune system is always in a state of dynamic internal responding, never passive or at rest. 'The immune system is everywhere and nowhere,' writes Donna Harraway. 'The genetics of the immune system cells, with their high rates of somatic mutation and gene product splicings and rearrangings to make finished surface receptors and antibodies, makes a mockery of the notion of a constant genome even within "one" body.' There cannot be an 'invader' that the system has not already 'seen' and mirrored, a series of endless interactions across immunoglobulin molecules.

I have never thought of the battle in my own body. I have never thought of it as a battle at all. I imagine it flowing out to meet its alien guest.

198

During the same workshop, Myhill mentioned another potential root cause of ME/CFS: parasites, specifically Giardia – the parasite I contracted aged two, which went undiagnosed for many months, passed off by our GP as 'toddler diarrhoea'. In the early 1990s, Leo Galland published a series of papers which noted the presence of active Giardia infection in a high percentage of cases of ME/CFS. 'Most of the patients with Giardiasis had only minor gastrointestinal symptoms but were really ill with muscle pain, muscle weakness, flu-like feelings, sweats and enlarged lymph nodes,' Gallard wrote, in 2011, on the *Huffington Post* blog. According to Gallard, sixty-one per cent of fatigued patients with Giardiasis had been diagnosed elsewhere as suffering from chronic fatigue immune dysfunction syndrome (CFIDS, *another* name for ME/CFS), compared to only nineteen per cent of fatigued patients without Giardiasis.

My immune system can't still be fighting *G instertinalis*, can it? That Giardia infection was treated thirty years ago – my very own root cause.

'I'm not surprised,' my mother says later. 'It was then that your symptoms started. Your legs would suddenly give way underneath you. You had such bad fatigue. It went undiagnosed for over six months because the GP kept fobbing me off calling it toddler diarrhoea. I'm so sorry darling. I fought and fought to have it taken seriously and when they finally tested it and found Giardia they were horrified.'

Parasites are fundamentally horrifying. That you are hosting something you cannot see, that it is inside you, gobbling up your resources.

My mother is sorry for my childhood experiences of physical illness, always holds herself accountable. She *fought and fought*, and failed to make them believe her, before they eventually found my body under siege by – or reaching out to meet – a parasite. It is not only an immune system that is trained to fight, a mother must be ready for battle too, although without the chance of winning power or valour. It is a lose-lose situation.

G. intestinalis was first noted by Antony van Leeuwenhoek, having examined his own faeces:

199

All the particles aforesaid lay in a clear transparent medium, wherein I have sometimes also seen animalcules a-moving very prettily; some of 'em a bit bigger, others a bit less, than a blood globule, but all of one and the same make. Their bodies were somewhat longer than broad, and their belly was flatlike, furnished with sundry little paws, where with they made such a stir in the clear medium and among the globules that you might e'en fancy you saw a pissabed [a type of bug] running up against a wall; and albeit they made a quick motion with their paws, yet for all that they made but slow progress.

My parasite has a confusing character. It is quick and yet slow, and *pretty*. It has little paws.

My waiting immune system reached out to meet this *exterior antigenic structure*, it recognised and responded, and in responding, it would never be the same as it was before. I will never not contain the antibodies it produced. They have maintained and transformed me. My body was not born; it was made. In this metaphor, my own hand touches a mirror – image and reality never quite meeting. Little paw touching little paw.

Some 500,000 cases of Giardiasis are diagnosed each year, with people typically picking up the disease by drinking infected water or contaminated food. Symptoms include severe diarrhoea, stomach pains, bloating, flatulence and fatigue and can last weeks or months without treatment. In medical drawings, Giardia looks like a face with googly stick-on eyes, like a kite flying, or two parrots kissing. Sometimes it is pictured walking, its four pairs of flagella as its limbs, the two nuclei for eyeballs, the central karyosomes for pupils, its median bodies forced into a smile. In the earliest rendering of the parasite, it looks like a seed pod, or nut. Through an electron microscope it looks far sinister: like a skull, or a brain with weedy tentacles, or the *Scream* mask.

Giardia excels at evading the defences of the infected organism. It alters the variant-specific proteins on its surface, confounding the infected body's immune system, rendering it unable to recognize and respond to the parasite, an RNA interference mechanism called antigenic variation. New discoveries about the parasite happen all

200

the time. In 2018, Dr Kevin Tyler from UEA's Norwich medical school found that Giardia parasites mimic human cell functions to break apart cells in the gut and feed inside, which allows bacteria already present in the body to join in and feast from the same nutrients. The supposed hard boundary between self and other dissolves, as the body feeds on itself in their unknowing interaction.

In the 2011 article, Galland refers to an epidemic in Placerville, California, which was followed by 'an epidemic of Chronic Fatigue Syndrome, which swept through the town's residents' in 1989. He thought that the cases of CFS were due to 'failure of some people to eradicate the parasite'. I don't know if this is true. Galland includes four references at the end of the blog post, but all of them are to his own work, published between 1989 and 2005 in journals about 'nutritional medicine' and textbooks on ME/CFS. A closed loop, rather than an opening to a web of knowledge. The article ends with a disclaimer, saying that the information provided is for 'general educational purposes only' and is not intended to constitute medical advice and links to more information on leaky gut syndrome and how to reduce the risk of infection next time you travel abroad, as well as an invitation to 'learn how to assess your digestive function and the presence of intestinal toxicity in my book *Power Healing: Use the New Integrated Medicine to Cure Yourself.*'

More questionable is that Galland has a profile on Goop.com, Gwyneth Paltrow's modern lifestyle website, the 'wellness' section of which was immediately flooded with articles on Covid-19 that included links to buy their products alongside information from the WHO. A Q&A with Galland published on the site, titled 'The Allergy Epidemic – And What To Do About It', is labelled 'speculative but promising', meaning: 'There's momentum behind this concept, though it needs more research to elucidate exactly what's at work.'

There is some evidence linking Giardia and ME/CFS. Norwegian studies showed that at least five per cent of patients with confirmed Giardia enteritis reported failure to recover after a large waterborne outbreak in Bergen in 2004. Their unexplained fatigue and accompanying symptoms corresponded with ME/CFS, meaning it was at least eight times higher than in the general population. A comparative study in 2017 did not find increased immune responses including T-cell activation or cytokine responses, but did find higher levels of a key immune marker called sCD40L implicated in inflammation and in severe symptom flares in ME/CFS patients after exercise. In each paper, further study is recommended.

My Giardia infection, which occurred exactly when Galland began publishing on the correlation between Giardiasis and CFS – in 1989 – becomes another blind alley, a possible cause with momentum behind it, that remains, as Goop would say, *speculative but promising.*

According to Myhill, immune response is not only analogous to war. During the workshop, she compared her approach to building a house: 'the groundhog acute regime is the foundations, the absolute fundamentals'. If it is like building a house, that house would be a self-build: 'For many people all they need is groundhog acute regime,' she says – you have a good chance of curing yourself. Do it really well and give it a chance to work. Take a daily dose of vitamin C, follow the paleo-ketogenic diet (high fat, high fibre, very low carb, probiotic foods like kefir and sauerkraut, no dairy or grains. Two meals a day; no snacking), take nutritional supplements, sleep eight–nine hours, take lots of herbs and heat, avoid risky actions like kissing and unprotected sex. Avoid vaccinations (alarming advice). Travel with care. You may consider a fast – this is essential for any acute gut infection. Take two drops of Lugol's iodine 12% in a small glass of water every hour until symptoms resolve. Rest – listen to your symptoms and abide by them. Sleep is even more important with illness.

Myhill's approach to ME/CFS – that you can treat it without paying for dozens of consultant appointments and expensive herbal treatments – is accessible, and homespun. (For most people, she says, her 'groundhog acute regime' is enough: changes to diet, taking vitamins and supplements, sleep and rest, herbs and Lugol's iodine.) It does not promise a cure for hundreds or even thousands of pounds. She doesn't want you to spend loads of money. A copy of her book and some big bags of vitamin powders are, in theory, all you need. Myhill is putting control back in the hands of the patient – something that is both empowering and concerning.

Prescribing off-label has got her into trouble with the General Medical Council. She's currently waiting for a hearing, having been reported as practising 'dangerous medicine' to the General Medical Council by a GP for prescribing valacyclovir to someone with EBV, despite evidence provided by Martin Lerner – who claimed to have cured himself with valacyclovir and published four studies before he died. Valacyclovir is licensed to treat some but not all of the herpes viruses, including EBV.

'The fact that the patient is better is of no consequence whatsoever.'

It strikes me that prescribing ketogenic diet and natural supplements – products that cannot be licensed as medicine and therefore cannot be regulated as such – is a less problematic way for her to practise medicine, despite her beliefs that these drugs can improve peoples' conditions. She lists herbal treatments for EBV, such as Chinese skullcap or Japanese knotweed, which she terms affordable, accessible and safe. (Skullcap has been linked to liver damage, though it is suspected that the source of damage was actually from Germander being substituted for skullcap. It should however be used with some caution since in overdose it causes giddiness, stupor, confusion and twitching. I am growing it in the garden.)

Should I change my diet? Can you even be keto, grain-free, dairy-free and vegetarian? Even Florence Nightingale doubted the reputation of meat as a panacea, stating that it was a common error to believe that it was the most nutritious foodstuff that a patient could be given.

My mother and I went to a presentation about a new approach to recovering from ME/CFS at the local Quaker Meeting House in the early 2000s. I was a teenager and my mother would have been about forty. Unfortunately, it had nothing to do with Quakerism. The meeting was held by people who had been cured, who were well enough to stand up and talk for a long time and had enough energy to persuade people that this treatment could work for them too, that they were still sick but did not have to be. It was the nature of the presentation that stuck with me. They looked so healthy they were practically glowing. As far as my mother and I could tell, this new 'cure' was CBT with graded exercise thrown in, but it was all under wraps, and secretive. There was so much unexplained it sounded like brainwashing, like an introduction to join a kind of cult. They promised we could be cured in a matter of weeks, we just had to *want* to be better and believe that we could be.

There were so many questions from the audience – potential clients: What about my daughter who cannot get out of bed – how would she get to the sessions in person? Would it work? What does the treatment actually involve? And so many others, unspoken: Can we really think ourselves well, and does that mean we thought ourselves sick? Would we get 'as bad' as that woman's daughter, and become bound to our beds, unable to even get to a lecture about how to achieve complete recovery, if we didn't pay up to get our lives back? Were our lives as we were living them not worth anything?

My mother and I were sceptical, like many people in the audience, not necessarily because the treatment wasn't convincing, but because these people were trying to sell a mysterious cure to a room full of desperate people in the first place. At the time, I thought we had only gone so we could call it out as bullshit, but that would have been such a waste of energy. My mother went because she too wanted a cure. As we were leaving, my mother introduced me to someone she knew: a woman a little older than her, who was there with her daughter, a few years older than me. Like my mother and

I, they both had a CFS diagnosis. The four of us stood there for a few minutes, unsure of whether we were living proof our illness was hereditary, contagious, or maybe just endemic. Maybe we should have pushed ourselves to do more exercise, and were we snobs to think that wouldn't work on us. By refusing to pay money – that we didn't have – for an unknown treatment meant we didn't want, to get 'better', we had accepted our illness as part of our bodies and ourselves, as something that could not be cured.

Is the mind really powerful enough to cure physical ailments?

'I had to my surprise a week ago a call from Mrs Lucian Carr who was as dropping of eyelid and pallid of face & manner as ever,' Alice wrote to William in November 1889. '(S)he, in truth, made me rather sick & lessened somewhat that protesting patriotism wh. is so ardent within me.' According to her caller, Alice's symptoms were not due to her 'physical anaemia', but the power of her mind.

Mrs Lucian Carr, whose very proximity made Alice feel more ill, followed 'The Mind Cure': a course of twelve lectures, each two and a half hours long, which Alice dismissed as distasteful imbecility. 'When I asked her what the attitude of mind was that she assumed in her wrestle with fate the poor lady cd. not make an articulate sound notwithstanding her thirty hrs. of instruction, she finally murmured "to lose oneself in the Infinite," wh. process seems to bring one rather successfully to the surface in the finite as the Curer "says her power is the same as Christ's only less perfect".'

At the time, Alice was living in rented rooms at 11 Hamilton Terrace in Leamington Spa with her 'better half', Katharine. Leamington had become a popular spa town in the early 1800s. It was claimed that the water from saline springs could cure a number of disorders, including 'the effects of gout and rheumatism and various paralytic conditions'. Here, Alice spent mornings in bed, in a south-facing room, and afternoons in the north-facing living room, where she would write her diary, taking occasional trips around Lillington, an area of the town she called 'a microcosm of England', in a bath chair – what she called her 'invalid chair', a gift from Kath, wheeled by a man named Bowles. 'It has rubber tyres & bicycle wheels so that there is absolutely no jar & one can lie out in it like a bed if necessary.'

'The Mind Cure' had another name: New Thought, a movement that emphasized the healing power of positive emotions and beliefs. People appeared to be regenerated via their faith, despite having exhausted their energy reserves and will. William James defended the cure: 'life-long invalids have had their health restored'. In the context of a conflicted society in which success and achievement was a question of mind over matter, they thought themselves well. They *believed*, and had, as a result, been saved: 'Science gives to all of us telegraphy, electric lighting, and diagnosis, and succeeds in preventing and curing a certain amount of disease. Religion in the shape of the mind-cure gives to some of us serenity, moral poise, and happiness, and prevents certain forms of disease as well as science does, or even better in a certain class of persons.'

Alice squarely refused to fit into this class. 'Accepting the infinite' seemed, to Alice, to sound a lot like accepting illness without a struggle, which made no sense to her at all.

Most people with ME/CFS will know that the basic principle of the Lightning Process is that our thoughts and beliefs can influence our immune system. It is notorious in the ME community for its secrets, lack of scientific basis and exorbitant costs. It even sounds like the twenty-first century version of The Mind Cure.

I remember watching Martine McCutcheon talking about her recovery to Loraine Kelly on morning TV. Their TED talks are called things like: 'Breathe to Heal' (Phil Parker) and 'Listening to Shame' (Helen Harding). The Lightning Process is not listed in the 'Treatment' sections of ME forums, and is the subject of remarkably few discussion threads. It is not technically a *treatment* at all. Those first-hand experiences of the Lightning Process refuse to go into detail about the process itself, not wanting to 'get into trouble'. People who have reported recovering with help from Parker and his team have been told that they never had ME/CFS in the first place. Responses to a positive account on a forum, which claimed anyone who failed to recover had not committed to it properly, anticipated a troubling level of backlash: 'World War Three may be about to hit.'

In a video on YouTube, a woman crouches on the floor in her bedroom. She has just been doing physio exercises to improve the strength in her legs and is nervous about attending a five-hour course when she feels so unwell. Two days later, she says she has been swimming, and gone out to dinner afterwards. The next day, she walked 'much further than usual', has been swimming again, and travelling around London. It's 11pm and she's 'Still. Got. Energy!'

'It's the most amazing, lifechanging thing I've ever done,' she says. 'It's amazing how powerful the brain can be. I've got my life back. If you're committed to it, and work hard at it, and believe it will work, it works. I'm well, I'm okay. If you're watching this thinking it's unbelievable, it really is. It's crazy but it's true.' By day four, she is almost shouting with enthusiasm, utterly transformed from the fearful, sick person she was before she started the Lightning Process. She has spent the day giving out food, gloves and socks to homeless people – her way of 'giving back' because she was 'given hope' by Phil Parker and his team. That day, she had run to catch a bus for the first time in a year. 'It was amazing,' she says. I look for more videos recorded by people who had attended the sessions in London, but it turns out, for the first five pages of results at least, all the videos have been uploaded by Phil Parker himself.

It is said that the Lightning Process will work if you have tried everything. You have to 'want it to work'.

'The Lighting Process takes three half-days to "unfold",' says Helen, who is introducing a group of potential clients, including me, to the process. 'It's like going back to school', except they teach you 'softer skills', like how to 'manage yourself' and 'how to look after yourself emotionally'. At the end of those three days, clients can use these soft skills – unlike the 'hard' ones you learn as a child in actual school – to 'influence your health through the mind-body connection'. It sounds more like going to university: twelve contact hours in a small group of four to seven people costs £775. That's £65 per hour, per person. These courses can bring in £5425. The same course costs £1997 with Phil 'because he is the designer of The Lightning Process', and £2500 if you want to learn the process one-to-one. Phil Parker – the designer of the Lightning Process, an osteopath with a PhD (in the Psychology of Health from London Metropolitan University) 'so he keeps reminding us all' – is in high demand and has 'other projects' so he only holds sessions once every three months. £1997 strikes me as a weird amount of money.

'He sees himself as a bit of a rock god,' she says, meaning that he plays music, but this seems to reflect his personality too. 'He is relentless. He will not take no for an answer.' The rest of the team who 'work out of Head Office' comprises Jude, who had PTSD before training as a practitioner; Kate, who had ME for seven years; and Helen, who has osteoarthritis and a history of chronic perfectionism, and who reveals she had been working with clients all day before we arrived – an impossible feat for anyone with even mild ME/CFS. Like Jude and Kate, Helen is also is a hypnotherapist and life coach. She managed her pain after a hip replacement with techniques learnt through the process. Many years ago, she explains, Phil Parker had an accident with a caravan which severed a nerve and left him with a 'claw hand', which he healed himself. 'His hand is completely normal-looking now,' she says. 'You would never know.'

They want us to be 'the best versions of ourselves'. Helen says a version of this sentiment – that they can teach us how to be *the best versions of ourselves* – six times over the next forty minutes. She also introduces us to two concepts: PER – the fight or flight response of the sympathetic nervous system – and neuroplasticity, or the ability to re-learn unconscious patters that lead to anxiety, pain and low self-esteem.

Helen says PER means that any perceived threat – a tiger in the room becomes a thirty-five-year mortgage – can switch on the fight or flight response, which, if not switched off compromises our immune systems. The Lightning Process is about teaching you how to 'switch on' your parasympathetic nervous system. 'Symptoms create their own symptoms,' she says. They want to teach us how to 'calm that system down'.

To explain neuroplasticity, how the brain can change in response to experience, she asks us to interlink our fingers and then switch them so the little finger on the 'wrong hand' is at the back. Phil Parker's Lightning Process can teach us how to pull these unconscious patterns into a conscious level, she says; how to 'step in and re-learn to be able to be happy and healthy'. Children and young people do particularly well at the Lightning Process because they are 'used to learning things'. My fingers feel weird for ages after.

What *is* the Lightning Process? I still do not know.

It incorporates different steps, through language, posture, movement, mindfulness and visualization.

It requires discipline, but it's not difficult.

To begin with, you do it fifty times a day. Helen now does it a couple of times a week.

It is also 'not for everyone'; participants have a range of conditions, from anxiety to chronic regional pain syndrome. 'It's all linked,' says Helen, 'anxiety, pain, confidence.' Sixty per cent of people have fatigue.

Crucially: 'It is not a treatment.'

They are not doctors; they are offering skills and tools to be *the best version of ourselves*. 'We can't do it for you,' she says. I would imagine physiotherapy, or CBT, cannot be 'done for you' either, but they are still considered treatments.

When it's time for questions, the woman from the sofa revealed she paid for one-to-one sessions for her daughter because she was bed bound. She wants her younger daughter to hear more about it, so she can try it for self-esteem – to be *the best version of herself*. The man sitting next to me is twenty-two and has had chronic fatigue since he was fifteen. His mum arrived late so I am accidentally sitting between them. She leans out from her chair and asks him if he has any questions over me. He has made notes on his phone, which is switched to night-mode, like mine.

'I am *thirty*-two,' I want to say to him.

I will always be suspicious when asked to pay nearly £800 for someone to teach me how to make myself better. Maybe I am too old, and not plastic enough.

When I ask if Helen knows how many people respond well to

the process, she says that they haven't done any studies *because it's not a medical treatment*, but she estimates eighty per cent of her clients have had a positive experience. I think my question sounds too knowing, suspicious, but I don't know if it's paranoia, if I should have stayed quiet or asked a different question. I want to ask more questions, but I am afraid to speak, or that I will not stop speaking.

As we file out of the small room, where the Lightning Process – whatever that is – has been taught a few hours earlier, I notice a collection of small coloured plastic ducks on top of the filing cabinet by the door. I want to know what role they play in The Process, but I also never want to know what they are for. I never want to be in that room again. To me, in that moment, they too look like a trap.

Why is having an illness something that needs to be unlearnt – like something has gone wrong, or broken, something won't turn off or on properly, the computer-that-is-my-brain is not receiving messages, or my nerves are misfiring. Why is thinking like this another way of 'wanting to be ill' or 'not wanting to get better'?

Lightning is dangerous, electric, natural. It strikes 'out of the blue' for us watching, and sometimes defies our understanding. Lightning can strike ten miles away from the storm cloud in which it was born. When two electrically charged regions of the atmosphere or ground temporarily equalise, because one – lower clouds, for example – is more positive than the other (steeples, trees, the Earth itself). Lightning is a release of energy. Lightning is hotter than the sun. It can and does strike the same place twice. When it strikes a person, they have a nine in ten chance of surviving, albeit with memory loss, dizziness, weakness, numbness and other life-altering ailments.

Lying in bed unable to sleep because my sides and my middle and my legs hurt and fizz, having failed trying to soothe my pain with massage and walking, I think maybe body-work isn't the answer, or maybe the answer is not in my body at all, but in the power of the mind to overcome it. I visualize a shining needle puncturing my skin and muscle and injecting some liquid that would melt what was inside. Botox blocks neuromuscular transmission, selectively paralyzing whatever muscle it is injected into, alleviating spasms

210

and tension. Botulism would quiet the signals that my brain reads as pain, but the mechanism is not exactly melting: botulinum toxin works by binding to the nerve-muscle junction, blocking the nerves that cause muscle contraction. It is not a permanent solution to pain. Nerves wake up again, stimulating the muscle within two months or so. I find myself back in my body. I barely left it. Maybe I should do this fifty times a day.

In September 2017, the *British Medical Journal*'s *Archives of Disease in Childhood* published a paper by Esther Crawley, Professor in Child Health at the University of Bristol, which purported to show that the Lightning Process is effective in treating children with ME/CFS (SMILE). David Tuller found several problems with this trial too. SMILE was an open-label trial with a subjective primary outcome: self-reported physical function, which is highly vulnerable to bias, even if perfectly conducted. (Observer bias means participants are more likely to exaggerate their recovery during an unblinded trial compared with blinded assessors.) Tuller also took issue with the trial results because Crawley had switched the primary outcome from school attendance after six months to self-reported physical function once the feasibility study was conducted. According to Tuller's investigation, if school attendance at six months had remained the primary outcome of the official trial, the results would have been null. Furthermore, over half the participants in the trial – 56 out of 100 – were participants in an earlier 'feasibility study', before the full trial had an officially assigned registration, meaning data was carried over into the official trial. To Tuller, this all meant that Crawley could report more impressive results. Researchers switch outcomes and report subjective outcomes because it is harder for a study reporting negative results to get published. Trials with positive outcomes are twice as likely to be published than trials with negative outcomes, which makes a difference when half of all cohort studies go unpublished, meaning relatively few trials make a meaningful contribution to patient care. In the case of the SMILE trial, as Tuller wrote nearly two years later, in June 2019, having charted his and others' investigation into the trial's discrepancies since December

211

2017, 'It is way past time for *Archives of Disease in Childhood* to consign the paediatric Lightning Process study to the trash bin.'

There is an argument for testing how effective the Lightning Process is. Crawley's patients were already using it, and paying for it, without any scientific evidence it worked – didn't it need to be properly trialled? Michael Sharpe thought so, claiming that rigorous testing was 'especially important' for an illness about which 'much misinformation is spread using social media'. He stressed the need for 'more studies and less polemic', avoiding the issue of the trial's inadequacies. Dorothy Bishop, Professor of Developmental Neuropsychology at the University of Oxford, expressed the opposing concern: 'that this report will in effect act as positive publicity for a programme that is being proposed for a wide range of physical conditions and has to date been promoted largely through celebrity endorsements'. The problem was not that Crawley's trial had been done at all, but that it had been done badly, and on children, and that the positive results it purported to show were reported in the international press without issue. Press releases by the Science Media Centre focused largely on the positive results for the self-reported physical function outcome and not the null results for the original primary outcome. Other positive-outcome trials by Crawley have made headline news, including one treating teenagers with online CBT.

What happens to all the trials with negative outcomes – aren't they just as useful to patients and care providers as the positive ones? Shouldn't we know if something makes no difference?

'Do you know how you got yours?' Crawley asks me when I meet her in Bristol.

This question comes out of the blue – less of an aside, more of a way to integrate my experiences into her argument. I hesitate, not wanting to say, 'a parasite in my gut when I was two years old', out loud, in a public place.

'I don't know,' I say, because I don't actually *know*. 'I was diagnosed when I was ten.'

'Right, so you got it at eight,' she says, with certainty.

Crawley explains her theory that some people have genes that predispose them to chronic fatigue, which seems to me like a good-enough explanation. Children who get ME/CFS would therefore be considered more genetically 'loaded'. Crawley also has a theory that sleep cycles play a role, that children and teenagers can get into detrimental sleep patterns, which affects cortisol levels.

'It's a bit hard to teach someone about this at primary school,' she says, referring to my case history, 'but if you just taught everyone at secondary school about sleep, and they knew to look after their sleep if they get the flu or pneumonia when they start to get better, I think we would stop getting so much chronic fatigue syndrome.'

I forget that her idea of chronic fatigue syndrome could be different from mine.

Crawley mentions some unpublished research she has done by screening children who have TATT, or 'tired all the time' in their medical notes. These are children who do not have an official diagnosis of CFS, despite recurrent GP visits, but who might meet the criteria for treatment at her clinic. GPs often don't recognise the symptoms, or don't want to diagnose a child with a syndrome because of the lack of treatment provision. Crawley tells me that she has done a review of the world literature that found that the chance of recovery from ME/CFS (in children) is around six times higher if a child has access to medical treatment of some kind, irrespective of the treatment modality. Currently only around fifteen to twenty per cent of the country have access to a local ME/CFS service.

'It's really heartbreaking,' she says. 'It's a really big problem. That's why I'm talking to you. It's *awareness*.' Crawley wants to offer these children *some* kind of treatment. I am struck by her potent mix of wanting to do right by her patients, children with no other options, and her intelligence, privilege and personal ambition.

I wonder if I have 'tired all the time' in my notes from when I was a child, having been repeatedly taken to the GP by my mother. It sounds so trivial, a niggling complaint rather than symptom – just something a mother would say about their child that could easily go undocumented, and unexplained.

Two days of work later and I am back in bed thinking: how much does it cost me to do a research trip? I have budgeted £100, but what does it *cost* me?

I am so used to thinking that if I didn't have to do other jobs to earn a living I wouldn't be so ill – in my case that illness is a feeling of illness, of feeling ill – that I rarely think about the effects of working on writing about illness. I type some notes into my phone, thoughts that keep me from resting, 'new connections and things I want to do', but I cannot be anything other than horizontal for more than a few minutes, cannot look at my laptop or think about reading or writing anything. What if I had no ill feelings – what would I be doing? Everything comes back to them – all the reasons I cannot do anything and all the meaning in my life. I open a parcel from my mother that arrived days ago containing the swimming costume I left at her house. The message on the card is about a university lecturer who had to stop teaching because they had become chronically ill. When I speak to her on the phone, she tells me about all the stuff my brother is helping her with, like managing her bank account and picking things up from the supermarket. Is the only reason I can work and write and get opportunities that I don't have to be there? Is my ability to care for myself predicated on not having to care for her?

When I attempt to articulate what I am writing about to someone who asks, I get a sense of recognition from most people; they have heard of ME or chronic fatigue syndrome, by one or other name. This recognition might be vague, or searching, or mildly disinterested, or it might be fearful, or wary, but sometimes, the best times, it makes space for the other person to tell me about their concern for their own mother, or their friend, or their partner, even themselves.

¶ *More harm than good*

Alice's health didn't deteriorate during their three-year stay in Leamington, but that didn't stop Henry regarding Katharine's care-taking as doing 'more harm than good'. He was clearly *bothered* by their relationship, in part because he had no influence over it: 'even if it were a much worse prospect than it is,' he wrote in a letter to Aunt Kate, 'there would be no possibility of averting it, for it is a matter between themselves.' No one could deny that Katharine had a positive influence on Alice's life.

Alice and Katharine were introduced to hypnosis therapy by Dr Charles Lloyd Tuckey via William, to whom Alice described her experience: 'What I do experience is a calming of my nerves & a quiescent passive state, during which I fall asleep, without the sensations of terror which have accompanied that process for so many years, and I sleep five or six hours, uninterruptedly.' Katharine administered hypnosis from late 1890 until Alice's death using Tuckey's machine. The therapeutic contraption looks like a domestic object, like a music box or sewing box, and the electric nodes look like dessert spoons with carved wooden handles. 'The sensations Katharine is able to facilitate are transformative,' she continued. 'K. turned on the hypnotic Tuckey, the mild radiance of whose moon-beam personality has penetrated with a little hope the black mists that enveloped us.'

In her diary Alice recorded a visit with two characters. One was 'a typical British matron', who believed 'the manipulation of such a delicate organ as the brain' to be very dangerous, but the other, 'a typical Mind-cured Jamaica Plain' (a reference not only to the Mind Cure but also surely to the Boston asylum where Alice had stayed) was already a convert, saying: 'You call it here hypnotism; we call it the science.'

Based on the description of Dr Ambroise-Auguste Liébeault's 'Treatment by Suggestion' in Tuckey's book *Psycho-therapeutics*, published in 1889, Katharine would have told Alice to 'think of noth-ing at all', and to fix her eyes and attention on some special object, maybe Katharine's face or one of her hands, or the pattern of the

215

carpet, or a mark on the wall in their living room. (This would not have been a mark like the one on Woolf's wall, which made her mind swarm, 'lifting it a little way, as ants carry a blade of straw so feverishly, and then leave it . . .' – Alice needed to make her mind as blank as possible.) Katharine would have then encouraged Alice into a natural sleep–

Your sight is growing dim and indistinct.

Your eyelids are becoming heavy.

A numbness is creeping over your limbs.

My voice seems muffled to you.

You are getting sleepy.

You cannot keep your eyes open.

At this point, Alice's eyes would have closed, or else Katharine would have closed them herself, before continuing with the treatment proper: directing Alice's attention to the affected area, her legs for example, or the part of her head that was causing her pain, and suggested an amelioration or disappearance of the morbid condition and symptoms. Katharine would have gently rubbed the affected part, attracting Alice's attention to it, telling her the pain will soon disappear, that she will wake up without it. A few minutes later, Katharine would tell Alice to open her eyes and awake, to some relief.

K's hands, the same that transcribed her dictated diary entries, even stopped Alice fearing death in her last days: 'physical pain however great ends in itself and falls away like dry husks from the mind, whilst moral discords and nervous horrors sear the soul. These last, Katharine has completely under the control of her rhythmic hand, so I go no longer in dread.' There was no suggestion that hypnosis could cure Alice, but it did help her manage her pain.

By the time they commenced Tuckey's hypnosis, Alice and Katharine had moved to 41 Argyll Road on Campden Hill, off Kensington High Street. Katharine had been living in America, but had returned when Alice's health declined. After all, she 'had to get a little worse in order to lose all conscience about absorbing K. as a right'. Alice needed to be sick to surpass the love of men, but she also needed to be *ill enough* to draw Katharine back to her.

216

'Through complete physical bankruptcy, I have attained my *"ideel"* as nurse calls it,' she wrote.

Alice and Katharine moved in on 12 March, when London was only beginning to warm, once Katharine had 'levelled all the rough places and let the sunlight into the dark corners of suggestion'. When I walked to 'the decidedly silly little house' from Kensington High Street tube station, past the 4x4s and other white stucco, four-storey buildings, I felt far away from home – the wrong side of the West End, the City, the river. I had been staring at the house on Google Street View for a while, but the image had been taken a year and a half before, in the bright August sunshine. From the outside, the house didn't look like much had changed since 1890, except they were now worth £10 million, probably more. Several had scaffolding cladding their exterior. Their owners were probably digging into the basements. These houses were no longer rented by invalid sisters of famously intelligent American men.

It was a house of women: Alice and Katharine, a teetotal cook who refused to put wine in the sauces and came included in the lease of the house, 'the excellent Louisa', busy transforming herself into a London parlour maid, who Katharine had 'transported from Leamington', and Alice's nurse, whose 'sorest trial' was the 'low intellectual level at the dinner table'. Alice wrote how happy she was in the house, except she didn't, having dictated her diary entries to Katharine since the end of the previous year. Katharine became Alice's pen, as well as her healer, bed, her legs, her heart, but to Alice, Katharine was always a 'simple embodiment of Health'. 'Katharine can't help it,' Alice's last diary entry (4 March 1892) reads, 'she's made that way.'

Katharine was Alice's protector and carer, embodying both masculinity and femininity, or what Alice saw as the best of both. 'I wish you could know Katharine Loring,' wrote Alice in a letter to Sara Darwin years earlier from the Adirondack mountains in the Keene Valley, New York, where she had gone to try William's 'panacea for all earthly ills': 'she is the most wonderful being. She has all the mere brute superiority which distinguishes man from women combined with all the distinctively feminine virtues.' Katharine was

Alice's ideal person, for there was nothing she could not do, 'from hewing wood & drawing water to driving run-away horses & educating all the women in North America'. And, like Alice, Katharine did not need to seek 'refuge in matrimony', like so many of her female acquaintances, including Sara herself. Alice's illness, her constant need for treatment, and her financial independence, kept her out of marriage to a man. Alice admonished men and women alike for their decision to marry over any other arrangement, and loved Katherine for her mastery of both masculine and feminine virtues. Alice refused her brothers' wish for her to be marriageable, to be visibly charming and visibly well.

It is so clear to me that Katharine and Alice's relationship was a partnership, but in almost everything I've read, there is a refusal to name it as such. When I told my mother about this, she reminded me that there was no such thing as a *lesbian* at the time. No one believed women could be sexually attracted to one another: sex without men was utterly inconceivable. This admission does not negate the fact that when we write now of Boston marriages and female companionship, of ladies opting out of marriage for a life with another woman, we deny the fact of that life as whole and complex. Of all the people who have written about Alice, none have really questioned her 'companionship' with Katharine, positioning their relationship as compliant with the social standards of the time. If I am wrong, and Alice and Katharine were not in a loving *lesbian* – in the modern sense – relationship, then I risk historical inaccuracy, which is a small price to pay in the face of queer erasure. This is my refusal, on behalf of Alice, and all the other sick queer women who lived through their refusals before me.

Can the category of lesbian not be expanded to include 'companions'? Can Queer? Is the re-writing of history not driven by the same resistive force as queerness – and a way to resist being written out again?

For decades, Woolf's biographers insisted that Virginia's love for Vita was rooted in the loss of her mother when she was thirteen, and seems to have been compounded by Quentin Bell's characterisation of his aunt Virginia as a 'sexless Sappho'. Their relationship deepened through Virginia's illness in the 1920s – it seems to have become more familiar, more intimate. Hermione Lee thought so at least, quoting Woolf's diary: 'the best of these illnesses is that they loosen the earth about the roots. They make changes. People express their affections.'

Mitchell Leaska: 'What Virginia meant by "intimacy" was really the maternal coddling she wanted from Vita.'

And James King: 'Vita wanted to become a male lover who could compete for and win her mother's embraces, whereas Virginia's desire was to be hugged and cared for by a maternal woman.'

I can't find any desire for maternal coddling in Virginia's letters to Vita, but there is certainly desire.

28 February 1927. Virginia is ill and lovesick. Each condition has its own bodily expressions and medicinal relief: 'Dearest Honey . . . It gets worse steadily – your being away. All the sleeping draughts and the irritants have worn off, and I'm settling down to wanting you, doggedly, dismally, faithfully – I hope that pleases you. It's damned unpleasant for me, I can assure you.'

Vita is concerned and protective, encouraging and empathetic. Neither truly motherly or husbandly, she occasionally takes on these roles, encouraging her to go out, she also puts her to bed: 'at ¼ to 10'. Vita tells Virginia she wishes she could know how she feels, and could make her feel better. 16 August 1929: 'I wish I knew REALLY how you were – at least I have my head left free, whereas yours aches – or ached.' Going out – rather than staying in bed – might be a temporary remedy for Virginia's ill feelings when a more permanent cure is impossible – 4 February: '. . . I wish for nothing in the world so much as that I might look after you – short of being able to work a miracle to make you instantly better. Instead of that, we have to go to The British Colony Ball!' There is so much wishing around illness – wishing for relief, for access, and understanding. From my health archive, her therapy diagram and our conversations, I have come to understand that my mother wished everyone would believe me when I said I felt ill, and that did not stop her wishing I was not ill at all.

That Vita played the role of mother or husband necessitated by the death of Virginia's mother, but also her father and brother, limits female companionship through illness to the role of ideal caring parent – giving your own desires up for the sake of another's bodily and emotional needs. It belies the complexities of love beyond gender and health – that women can only love other women one way: as a mother. Vita, like Katharine for Alice, transgressed gender roles, embodying both male and female, confined to neither.

Virginia only remembers her mother Julia Stephen, nurse and author of 'Notes from Sick Rooms', in company; 'of her surrounded; of her generalized; dispersed'. Her mother was 'the centre', or 'the whole thing', in the sense that Virginia lived 'so completely in her atmosphere that one never got far enough away from her to see her as a person'. Julia was at once presence, life force and building – 'Talland House was full of her; Hyde Park Gate was full of her' – and therefore not a person at all: an absence. Virginia's loss is also dispersed, shared with the world: 'her death was the greatest disaster that could happen', she wrote in 'Reminiscences'.

Most of the people in this book lived a queer life – queer also meaning contested, much like our illnesses. Florence's biographer disputes that she was a lesbian. Still, she lived a queer crip life at home, working from her sofa, living with women, refusing marriage. (In a letter to Vanessa, Virginia writes of finding 'the master of biography' Strachey's Nightingale life narrative 'very amusing'– him having read it aloud to them in the spring of 1916.)

Sontag thought of her sexuality – another thing she never spoke about publicly – in relation to her desire to write, rather than the absence of motherly love: 'I need the identity as a weapon, to match the weapon that society has against me . . . I am just becoming aware of how guilty I feel being queer.' (Sontag's enemy was also her ex-husband; I remember the therapy diagram and my father's refusal to acknowledge my mother's breakup with her girlfriend L.) 'Being queer makes me feel more vulnerable. It increases my wish to hide, to be invisible – which I've always felt anyway.' As if queerness is a kind of illness – living an unacceptable life.

Woolf transformed her feelings into bodily metaphors because that was the way I assume she – and I, my mother and so many others with 'invisible illness' – experienced those feelings: through her body. This does not mean her love for Vita – like Alice's love for Katharine – was a metaphor for an infantile longing for maternal nurturance. Besides, as is well known, Virginia attached Vita not to her lost mother, but the character of *Orlando*, 'the kind of shimmer of reality . . . the lustre on an oyster shell'.

Psychoanalytical readings of female relationships aside, any loving relationship between women can easily be read as a bad influence, and blamed for illness, whether that love is between family or friends, companions or partners. A visit to see Vita in Berlin in 1929 put Virginia to bed for two weeks. 'But of course, the Dr and Leonard say it's all the Berlin racketing . . .' wrote Virginia. He – doctor or husband – may as well have said Vita did more harm than good. 'I can't believe it's the "racketing" of Berlin; really, you might have spent every night for a week til 5 in the morning indulging in orgies . . .' replied Vita. 'Do you know what I believe it was, apart from "flu"? It was SUPPRESSED RANDINESS.'

Illness can conceal as much as it encourages affection – 'illness often takes on the disguise of love', wrote Woolf in 'On Being Ill'. What of maternal ambivalence? – A mother's nurturing affection doesn't come without pain, as Sontag reminds us in her diary. The joy and curse of the daughter is that you will forever be a part of your mother, whether they are alive or not. A daughter never has a mother; she is had by her.

My mother has been invited to talk about trans histories at an event at Monk's House. She mentions her friend, who told her once that he is trans in the sense that he is 'both genders, not one or the other'. This was the weekend I introduced her to the term 'queer feminist crip' because I have been reading Alison Kafer's book about how the disabled/abled binary fits into all the other binaries: body/mind, natural/unnatural, them/us. Kafer 'crips' queer theory, which historically responded to 'the future' through refusal. Rather than imagining the future only through overcoming disability, she imagines futures that 'cultivate disability', a practice she describes as 'imagining disabled

221

futures differently'. 'I am yearning for an else-where – and, perhaps, an "elsewhen",' she writes '– in which disability is understood otherwise: as political, as valuable, as integral.'

'You're a queer feminist crip!' I tell my mother, as if it is an identity you can claim for someone else, if at all. I meant it as a gift.

'The change of sex, though it altered their future, did nothing whatever to alter their identity,' wrote Woolf in *Orlando*.

That evening, we watch the Angela Carter documentary. 'Being a showgirl is being a metaphor for women,' someone says; 'for what you have to do to negotiate the world as a woman.'

This sentence doesn't register with my mother, who, unlike Angela Carter, was, at one time, a showgirl. (She will never go back to Worthing or Great Yarmouth because of the seasons she had to endure at the end of the pier.) I look to her for flickers of identification and find none. Then again: how would she identify with being a *metaphor for a woman*. Why would anyone?

During my last visit, we watched the documentary Paula Rego's son made about her. Maybe this is who documentaries are made about now – the *grand dames* of art and literature.

'Everyone should put money aside during their lifetimes for their children's therapy after they die,' my mother says, out of nowhere.

In May 1891, Alice consulted with Sir Andrew Clark, who diagnosed her with cardiac complications, a spinal neurosis affecting the legs, a 'delicate embroidery of the most distressing case of nervous hyperesthesia', and rheumatic gout in her stomach. These diagnoses satisfied what Alice called her 'pathologic vanity'. She found 'enormous relief' in his 'uncompromising verdict', saying: 'one becomes suddenly picturesque to oneself'. Clark also found a lump in her breast he thought to be malignant, but another physician, William Wilberforce Baldwin, confirmed breast cancer, assumed to be spread from her liver. No surgery was optioned, but Alice was prescribed morphine for the pain, which Henry encouraged her to take. After decades of treatment, Alice finally had the pathological disease she longed for out of desperation and 'pathologic vanity', the disease that would take her life. In that moment, she became truly untreatable.

'To him who waits, all things come!' Alice wrote. 'Ever since I have been ill I have longed and longed for some palpable disease, no matter how conventionally dreadful a label it might have, but I was always driven back to stagger alone under the monstrous mass of subjective sensations, which that sympathetic being "the medical man" has had no higher inspiration than to assure me I was personally responsible for.'

In the face of her own death, Alice felt sorry for Katharine and Henry, who would actually *see* her die – she would only *feel* it. Witnessing discomfort is worse than experiencing it. ('Poor dear William with his exaggerated sympathy for suffering isn't to know anything about it until it is all over.') You can forget your own headaches, but living with your mother's pain seems unbearable. Just as there is some pleasure – as well as distress – in knowing your body is mystifying, there is relief in pathology, of knowing a disease has taken root in a specific organ.

Alice wrote of vanishing, always likening herself to domestic objects. Katharine's care was healing to Alice, like the homes they made together. When Alice felt like a collection of 'fantastic *un*productive emotions enclosed within tissue paper', just the sight of Katharine made her spirits rise, in the hope that 'the unremitting and various nature of her muscular contractions may shed a glamour over her humiliated appendage'. Elsewhere in her diary, she called herself 'an appendage to five cushions and three shawls', and regarded her own body as a 'little rubbish heap'. I think of Katharine as her bed, her home.

Like Henry's fictional Bostonians Olive and Verena, Alice and Katharine were engaged with culture and social betterment – female virtues that formed the basis of the life they shared. Immersed in the emerging feminist movement, Olive and Verena are in what was referred to as a Boston Marriage, an ambiguous same-sex relationship, or a 'union of soul'. Olive even proposes: '"Will you be my friend, my friend of friends, beyond everyone, everything, forever and forever." Her face was full of eagerness and tenderness.' (The pair live together in their 'peculiar friendship', financially independent from any man, until Olive's cousin Basil – the outsider

223

– elopes with Verena.) Unlike Henry's fictional Bostonians, Alice and Katharine were partners, thoroughly attached to one another in sickness – the type that has no beginning or end, no clear origin and therefore no cure.

'Of what matter can it be whether pain or pleasure has shaped and stamped the pulp within,' Alice dictated to Katharine, in the last days of her life, 'as one is absorbed in the supreme interest of watching the outline and the tracery as the lines broaden for eternity.'

I often feel *dragged* – to use Alice's word – by so much of the literature around illness. I am so aware of the energy I spend on seeking out papers and collections, and reading through them, that I feel that energy running out, my bank account draining. When I read Alice's diary, I felt strengthened. She energizes me. Alice's diary is a record of her desires and the affects they had on her body. It was the site of their shared love – Alice's mind, Katharine's hand. It was Alice's way of leaving her body entirely, knowing it was nothing of lasting significance. When I work now, I am *Alice in Bed*: propped up, and protected, by three cushions and two blankets. Alice's diary speaks to the power of care, rather than the mind; to what someone can live through if their desire is met by another's.

'You know that illness you're writing about?' she says jokingly. 'I think I have it.'

My mother has come to stay with me for one night, with the dog who doesn't get travel sick. She wants to see her friend E-J Scott speak at the third annual Queer History Lecture at Goldsmiths College, which is very close to where I live in South East London.

In his lecture, titled 'Expose Yourself in Public', E-J talks about the energy it takes to do work of activism, and his project the 'Museum of Transology', for which he invited people to send him any object they wanted to include in the collection. E-J describes the emotionally draining work of making the personal public, of curating oneself as well as the experiences of others. Not knowing what was going to arrive through the letter box was like playing 'trigger warning roulette', he says. One object was Lynx Africa, a purchase that marked the time when the owner wasn't afraid to 'smell like a boy' anymore. E-J says he had to be prepared to share his experience if he was asking others to do the same, so he displayed his breasts in a jar. 'Besides,' he says, 'my girlfriend wanted them out of the house.'

'Curating means care,' he says, and we have to be careful not to perpetuate the same ways of telling history that wrote us out in the first place, that erased our identities as queer people.

'The more you uncover,' he says, 'the more you realize you don't know.'

My mother and I are excited to hear E-J speak, but his lecture is also a reminder for my mother that she has not been able to work for some time now. She has to some extent, 'recovered' from a recent severe relapse, during which time she could barely walk or stand, and had excruciating pain in her spine. Her rollator had helped her get around, and she could sit on it for choir. I was amazed we had walked the fifteen minutes to Goldsmiths and back. Both of us are stronger than we have been recently, and I feel stronger now I am with her. But she is not giving lectures about queer histories at institutions, or sharing her research into the lives of queer designers and performers and everyday people, and making quiet jokes about her own life while doing so. She's been reading something on the Optimum Health clinic website about the different stages of ME/CFS, and how they respond to treatments differently. The test results came back, and she doesn't have campylobacter, so the GP put her symptoms down to 'anxiety'. She's nearing the end of her series of free occupational therapy sessions. She's listening to podcasts about the nervous system on her noise-cancelling headphones, except the man in John Lewis said she can't wear them in the street because someone might want to get her attention. 'That's the whole point,' she had replied, 'I don't want anyone to get my attention.' Being outside, in the street, with so much going on, is overwhelmingly exhausting.

I have these scraps of paper with notes of what she says on the phone to me, but I can't really understand any of it and I don't really know if she is okay.

can't stand, can't walk.

£150 on a credit card for a hoover you don't have to push

no seats at Disability Pride, and the music was too loud

Some of the notes I find seem to bear no relation to any memory of what we talked about, but she must have said them.

I am feeling apart from her. I am not there. I do not go to her. I am writing this book, and I don't have the energy

Blue light affects women really badly

I googled it and I don't think it's even true.

I feel like I've been robbed of myself

If someone were to find these notes, they would not know which ones were my thoughts and which ones were hers. I cannot be sure either.

The night she comes to stay with me in London, she tells me she understands 'what it takes' for me to go to see her. That it's a big journey, and not being in your own bed is exhausting. She had been in a place where she was quite scared. She couldn't walk, but she was out of it now. She had got herself out of severe relapse by scaling back, and saying 'no' to everything and everyone. Saying No to the choir festival with the LGBT group you sing with. Saying *No* when a friend wants to visit. Saying *No* when your new friend has an open studio and wants you to come.

'It makes a difference, even just doing it for a week. There's no option. You have to say No to everything. Because the years just roll by.'

My mother used to teach BA students about the history of design. When I was a child, she taught aerobics and studied for her GCSEs. Before that she was a dancer and a singer. She is still all these things, my mother, but not 'on paper'. This does not make her less of a person.

'I'm sorry I gave you this ghastly thing,' she says, knowing there is a connection between my ill feelings and hers, even if the *how* is unclear. I know that I am demanding on her when I go to see her, in a way that sometimes she has been demanding on me. I know it works the other way, and we don't feel as bad about ourselves when we have each other to relate to.

The more I talk to my mother and research our diagnoses -- the more I uncover – the more I realize I don't know.

When we hug goodbye in the entrance to my flat, our loops joining to become an infinity figure of 8, what I don't know is: I will not see my mother again for a very long time.

As it spreads throughout Europe, overwhelming healthcare systems in Italy and Spain, the UK government initially doesn't seem to care about its citizens, only its economy, as though the deaths of thousands of disabled, chronically ill and elderly people would be no bad thing.

The drained are already called a drain.

The healthy – the undrained, or not-yet-drained – seem not to care, as though it does not affect them, only those who have already been given a second chance at life, with transplants and chemotherapy and medications that supress their immune systems.

Advice columns on how to stave off boredom when stuck at home appear, except no one asked disabled and chronically ill people how they have dealt with 'missing out' for years. Will the sick become sages, dispensing advice based on years of experience, or will we be ignored over the ableds who have spent a mere two weeks inside? The more pressing concern seems to be: will Covid-19 bring more people into our sick community, expanding and enriching it, transforming a society intimately tied to the market into one bound to networks of care, or would our government let the virus eradicate us entirely?

There is hope and there is pain.

The fear associated with the spread of disease, around what will happen if my mother contracts it – another bad case of pneumonia for sure, her lungs weakened by decades of repeated infection, caught from being anywhere near anyone with a virus – and the post-viral fatigue that would inevitably follow, forces her to rest. Doing less becomes a valid option for well and sick alike. Rest seems to be what everyone is doing – there are advice columns about that too.

'Head ringing for two days,' reads a note from 18 March. 'Waves of heat and tingling, prickling sensation. Have to lie down. Don't feel better, just have to.'

When the first UK lockdown is announced, the impending doom is coupled with relief. The state I despise has sanctioned my isolation. What keeps my mother inside during a pandemic is what has kept her out of work, limited her social life and affected her relationships with other people, for several years. What keeps her inside during a pandemic are all the usual factors that are passed off as *anxiety* – an illogical physical response to what is really going on.

The isolation and loneliness that comes with chronic illness, and an endless, daily grief for what you could be doing, is now a shared experience, as everyone now knows what it feels like to not be doing what they want to be doing, and frankly, the crips don't want to hear about it. It feels like more and more effort to accept a life spent mainly inside now no one else can do the things they want to do either; when they long to meet up with their friends, go on trips and holidays, go out whenever they want and get whatever they want from the shop, as usual. This was always the 'normal' for a lot of people with ME/CFS, who suddenly seem seen and invisible at the same time: just like everyone else. It makes us touchy, and easily upset. It is not about *you*, I want to scream, do not make this about *you*. Your isolation is not coupled with nausea, pain and unreasonable exhaustion.

During the first lockdown, people keep asking my mother how she is doing. They text her when she was resting, and then call up when she doesn't answer. Everything is normal for her, she says, and 'you weren't bloody checking up on me before!' I am angry for her. We are pissed off and laughing at it all on FaceTime. But I also know this is my truth too.

'It's a relief not to hear the traffic,' she says. 'I find it so exhausting.'

I too am relieved it is so quiet. Walking outside, along a usually busy road – inevitable for anyone living in a town or city – is not too much anymore.

'Like the world has slowed down to join us,' she writes. Except there are no food deliveries available, which we usually rely on. My mother and I are suddenly anxious about this most of the time. It uses all of our energy and banishes our crip joy.

Anxiously made plans to attend conferences and trips to archives and libraries are cancelled. Initially this is disheartening, but those feelings quickly turn to relief. I do not have to find the energy to go anywhere at all. All the things I have put off for months because of fatigue suddenly can't happen. Everything now needs to be done

229

from bed – including all the research I have left to do. No visiting libraries, no ordering archive material. I must rely solely on digitized documents, online articles, remote interviews – as I am used to, with so little energy to spare. The world has *slowed down to meet us* – and it has also migrated. My way of researching and writing – as much from bed, from home, as possible – is *the new normal*.

Everyone becomes housebound – the reality for so many people living with chronic illnesses, including thirty per cent of people with ME/CFS. There is a sense we are good at this, that this is as much as we can do anyway, that time has slowed down, that we are limited to an indoor life. One walk with my dog a day is enough to put me back on the sofa, where I do my work. More than what the state now mandates – stay at home, one walk a day – will put me in a two-day crash, unable to do anything at all. I need to be lying down a lot of the day. I am not *taking to bed*. If I lie down often I am able to do more.

These were things we were told we could not do. I used to have to go to work like everyone else, even though going in even two or three days put me in bed – not lying down, actually crashed-out, in bed – for the rest of the week. Accommodations that would have enabled people with chronic illness, mental health issues and disabilities to continue their social life, education and meaningful employment, in certain sectors that already relied on internet technology anyway, swing into action for able people in a matter of days. In-person meetings are replaced seamlessly with Zoom calls; we email each other as we did before, when we worked in the same building. Online, disabled ex-students mourn the college degrees they dropped out of because it was insisted that their teaching could not be accessible online.

To be bound to one's house or bed or sofa is not necessarily shit in itself. It is shit because you don't have access to medical care, and the job that could give you financial security, and the relationships you want to have. It is not shit because you are disabled, but because the world is ableist. It usually excludes you on the basis of your limitations. For so many who have been housebound for years, even decades, hearing everyone desperately wanting things to 'go back to normal' is just a reminder of how long their grief has gone on for. *Going back to normal* means being left behind. They have heard it all before – 'Twice as many people on graded exercise therapy and cognitive behaviour therapy got back to normal,' said investigator Trudie Chalder, at the PACE press conference.

As lockdowns continue, data shows people are taking more car trips, travelling further, going out more and staying at home less, a phenomenon referred to as 'quarantine fatigue'. 'It just seems that people are getting a little tired collectively of staying at home after we passed that one-month mark,' says Dr Zhang, as quoted in the *New York Times* on 27 April. But fatigue is not *getting a little tired*. It is not something you fight off, or combat. Fatigue is not waning discipline in adhering to restrictions.

What is fatigue anyway? – I have often thought back to the question my mother asked that day, all those years ago. I still can't tell you what it *is*.

'What is fatigue?' asks the Guy's and St Thomas' post-polio syndrome pamphlet. Answer: 'This is not the same as tiredness.' In order to define what fatigue actually is, social scientist Karon Cook is invoked: '"an overwhelming, debilitating, and sustained sense of exhaustion that decreases one's ability to carry out daily activities, including the ability to work effectively and to function at one's usual level in family or social roles".' – this is, as far as I can tell, a definition Cook and others developed as part of the NIH's Patient Reported Outcome Measurement Information System (PROMIS) for measuring self-reported fatigue. Another endless loop: self-reporting necessitating a definition for self-reporting; clicking through links looking for a source only to find more and more research papers. 'Physical activity is an essential part of a healthy lifestyle,' reads the pamphlet. 'Inactivity leads to the "de-conditioning" of your body. This, in turn, leads to weakness and fatigue.' Unlike ME/CFS, post-polio patients are advised to rest during activity before you become exhausted and need days to recover. How many other symptoms of illness are measured according to the sufferer's ability to work effectively?

'Fatigue' during periods of lockdown is used to mean being *fed up*, justification firstly for defying the rules so you can do what you want, so you can go about your 'normal' day, and to excuse the actions of government officials flouting the rules. 'Fatigue' does not refer to crippling exhaustion, or actually feeling ill – it means 'sick' of *not doing whatever you want to do*. 'The term "fatigue" conjures up middle-class sacrifices,' reads a *Guardian* article, 'such as feeling cooped up at home and being unable to visit friends or shops.' I think of the ME patients Eliana spoke of, who give her lists of things they want to do.

The striking thing about the use of the word 'fatigue' is not what it says about the government – that any excuse would do to keep things as 'normal' as possible and prevent full economic collapse – but that fatigue can be assumed as an excuse for breaking the law because it doesn't really exist.

I still don't know what fatigue is. I cannot explain it. But I know what fatigue feels like. I know its effects.

Fatigue is being worn out, but it is not a fair consequence of exertion. Fatigue is not a lack of energy, it is its total absence. Fatigue is not exhaustion because exhaustion belongs to the healthy, to the productive; it is the result of doing. Fatigue is the total negation of productivity. It is a force on your body. It is dragging downwards. Fatigue is not doing what you want to be doing, and then it is not remembering what that was to begin with. It is the opposite of enjoyment, of joy, meaning fatigue is a category of *feeling*, except it is a feeling you have in your *cells*. Fatigue stops you working, and it is work. It is laborious and laboured. Fatigue is punishing and a kind of punishment. Fatigue is not worth googling. Fatigue is an effect; it is exhaustion, sometimes without cause, and without solution. Fatigue is *exhausting*. Fatigue fucks your 'cause and effect'. It is made worse by further exertion, and, sometimes, it is relieved by the same means. It might be relieved by long periods of inactivity or compounded. Fatigue is being awake for three days. It is mystifying, and, in some cases, deadly. Fatigue is not restful; it is the body in resist.

If pain sounds like screaming and wailing, fatigue sounds like silence, like nothing, *zero*. It can't be stabbing or burning or thready or loose. It is not something you can measure, or change, or fight.

I used to think there was no language for illness when the body fails. I believed that it was near-impossible to speak about pain, and therefore fatigue, but that's not true, and not because there is already a literature of illness. Crips know how to verbalize their pain and fatigue, but no one cares to listen. It has been co-opted to mean 'bearable' or 'minor' or 'waning discipline'. It has been stolen and trivialized, another erasure. If there is no language for pain and fatigue it is because of this suppression. It is ableism, not pain and fatigue, that structures the disabled experience.

It was obvious to anyone with ME/CFS that post-viral fatigue would rise as people recovered from the Covid infections. As early as May, ME Action warned of the impending spike of ME/CFS in the months and years ahead. US action groups appealed to Congress, warning that cases of ME/CFS could double globally. Would all those people be offered antidepressants, graded exercise and cognitive behavioural therapy too?

Covid-19 presented a rare opportunity to research how our bodies recover – or don't – from serious infections. It had happened with SARS in 2003. And it had happened with polio. Many people who had recovered from polio infections in the 1950s as children reported weakness and pain decades later, despite their immune systems having rid their bodies of disease decades previously.

My father contracted polio in 1954 as a child in Sydney. His grandmother, who had a house in Parsley Bay, took him to see the Queen during her Coronation visit. Much like in the particular moment of the pandemic we're currently in, people were advised not to gather and to avoid excessive handshaking. Although he spent two weeks in the hospital and was severely ill, my father was not one of the children who depended on an iron lung to breathe or subsequently used a mobility aid. He remembers his left leg was an inch shorter until his teens and admits he is 'still a bit weak in the legs'. It too was a stigmatized condition, and for many people had long-term effects. It is only then that I realize I have witnessed that weakness in all the time I have known him, that he is often, I think, in pain, and despite that weakness and pain has always moved around, trained as a dancer, still sails and surfs and hikes where he now lives, back in Australia, in order to be in nature, away from crowds and technology, but also to fend off early death.

In early June 2020, *The Washington Post* reported that some were

233

testing positive and then negative and then positive again. 'Many scientists believe the tests are likely picking up dead virus — in studies, it has only been active nine to eleven days. But a few autopsies have shown the virus lurking in puzzling places like the spleen, creating continuing uncertainty.' Melanie Montano, a thirty-two-year-old woman from New Jersey, had been ill for ninety-two days, and was documenting her journey on video. People's symptoms were cycling but also changing, shifting from fatigue one week to sore throats or weakness or fever the next. No one knew whether people with extended symptoms were facing a long recovery from a disease that affected multiple systems in the body, due to damage to different organs that have not repaired themselves, or whether their illness would come to resemble something like ME/CFS. Except ME/CFS also seems to affect multiple systems in the body. It was impossible to know if the long-tail phenomenon was more pronounced with Covid-19 than any other virus. The radio shows and articles in major magazines might only evidence the heightened awareness of societal effects and the global nature of the disease, rather than the significance of extended recovery from the virus.

On a BBC 5 Live Breakfast 'Your Call' discussion in July, callers revealed they had already been ill for up to four months, having contracted Covid in March. Despite reports of slow recoveries, there didn't seem to be much support or treatment offered to those who hadn't recovered from their illness. Dr Charles Shepherd, a Medical Adviser for the ME Association, proposed the idea of a 'post-Covid syndrome': 'Most people thought this was just another infection which you got over. Then we found out there were people going into hospital who were seriously ill. But there's this huge group in the middle who've been self-managed, who are fit, young adults who've never had any problems with their health before, and they're just not getting over it.' He thought there were two groups of people who seemed to fall into what he described as 'post-Covid syndromes': 'We've got the group who have got symptoms relating to Covid and the complications that it's caused with breathing and the respiratory system. We've just heard from someone who sounds as though they probably had neurological involvement with this as well. Then there's the other group who are fitting much more into the picture that we're used to dealing with, [who are] getting a post-viral syndrome, which is very much like ME, with unrefreshing sleep, brain fog, fatigue, dizziness.' Based on his experience, Shepherd advised complete rest initially to aid recovery.

Three days later, during an International AIDS Society Covid-19 press conference held on 9 July, ME and HIV activist Terri Wilder took the opportunity to ask Dr Anthony Fauci, Director of the National Institute of Allergy and Infectious Diseases and member of the White House Coronavirus Task Force, what the NIH is doing to address Covid-19 'long-haulers'' risk of developing ME/CFS. 'You can see people who've recovered who really do not get back to normal that they have things that are highly suggestive of myalgic encephalomyelitis and chronic fatigue syndrome,' he replied. 'Brain fog, fatigue and difficulty in concentrating, so this is something we really need to seriously look at because it very well might be a post-viral syndrome associated with Covid-19.'

The parallels with ME/CFS were undeniable. The first instances of ME occurred concurrently around epidemics of polio and affected a large number of healthcare workers. Viruses have caused other outbreaks: in one 2006 Australian study, eleven per cent of people infected with Ross River virus, Epstein-Barr virus, or the bacterium behind Q fever, were diagnosed with ME/CFS after six months. In a study of 233 Hong Kong residents who survived the SARS epidemic of 2003, about forty per cent had chronic fatigue problems after three years or so, and twenty-seven per cent met the CDC's criteria for ME/CFS. Psychiatric morbidities and chronic fatigue persisted and continued to be clinically significant after four more years. In 2011, eight years after the SARS outbreak in Toronto, sleep disorders specialist Harvey Moldofsky noted that chronic post-SARS patients looked very much like ME/CFS and FM patients, characterized by persistent fatigue, diffuse myalgia, weakness, depression and nonrestorative sleep. A group of fifty healthcare workers were still unable to work, experiencing 'musculoskeletal pain, profound weakness, easy fatigability, (and) shortness of breath that accompanied psychological distress'. After a sleep study comparing them with ME/CFS, fibromyalgia and healthy controls, he proposed that the virus had produced a chronic neuroinflammatory state affecting sleep, pain sensitivity and energy levels.

Post-Covid patients were reporting similar bodily symptoms and signs to ME/CFS, with an emphasis on post-exertional fatigue and disordered cognition. What was more, some people with lingering and at times incredibly debilitating post-Covid symptoms were also experiencing what most people with ME/CFS or FM have gone through at some point in their illness: friends and family could not believe they were still ill when the tests came back normal. David Tuller even discovered that the Oxford Health NHS Foundation Trust had issued a pamphlet promoting graded exercise and cognitive behaviour therapy as treatments for post-Covid. 'This dung heap read is if it were written by Simon Wessely, Trudie Chalder, and Michael Sharpe way back in the early 1990s,' he wrote on Virology Blog. 'It was credited to something called the "psychosocial response group" – a mysterious-sounding phrase that did not yield any results when I searched for the term on Oxford Health's website. But the acronym–PRG–is kinda cool-looking.'

A professor of Tropical Medicine who had contracted Covid in early March was still ill. Paul Garner used his prominent platform to call for the provision of more support to people experiencing a more protracted illness, and who needed help to 'understand and cope with the constantly shifting, bizarre symptoms, and their unpredictable course.' The symptoms he was experiencing post-Covid are familiar to many people with an ME/CFS, or indeed fibromyalgia, diagnosis: 'A muggy head; acutely painful calf; upset stomach; tinnitus; pins and needles; aching all over; breathlessness; dizziness; arthritis in my hands; weird sensation in the skin with synthetic materials. Gentle exercise or walking made me worse – I would feel absolutely dreadful the next day.' It sounded like post-exertional fatigue/malaise – a defining characteristic of ME/CFS. On the radio, he spoke about being tearful in the mornings, an emotional component of the syndrome, which cleared by the afternoon. 'Sometimes I felt better and became optimistic; after all, the paralytic state had not recurred; but then the next day I felt as though someone had hit me around the head with a cricket bat.' He started talking to others and joined the Facebook group 'Covid-19 Support Group (have it/ had it)', where he met a marathon runner who collapsed with rigors and slept for twenty-four hours after trying to run 8k, and spoke to others experiencing 'weird symptoms, which were often discounted by those around them as anxiety, making them doubt themselves'. Their two weeks for the illness – determining the length of time off work – was up: 'people report that their families do not believe their ever-changing symptoms, that it is psychological, it is the stress'.

It's not that chronic Covid-19 is post-viral fatigue, or ME/CFS, even if the symptoms are similar. These are names, tools of categorization, with their own histories. Regardless, it must be acknowledged that if the biological actions at play in the causes of ME/CFS had been researched more thoroughly to date, rather than the psychosocial aspects, which hadn't seemed to have gone anywhere and were plagued with vested interests, people with post-Covid might have a better understanding of their condition. We might even have a language for fatigue, beyond cricket bats, crabs clawing, being hit by moving vehicles.

Ultimately, the accounts of chronic Covid-19 included in Garner's posts reflect an endemic attitude to chronically ill people. It is our fault for not getting better, which is what *should* happen with illness. They showed an unwillingness on the behalf of society to accept anything other than a total return to health and productivity – to get back to work, to running marathons, to getting back to normal.

What also becomes clear is that when it comes to physical symptoms that map onto anxiety, or are exacerbated by rational fear, and are too changeable to be believable indicators of disease and its effects, and you're female, you will be told it's all in your head. Vonny LeClerc reported relief that a man had written about post-Covid to *The Atlantic*: 'I've had messages saying this is all in your head, or it's anxiety,' she said. It didn't seem long before a mother would be told that she and her daughter have *a shared hysterical language.*

¶ Combing through

A full-scale revision of the NICE guidelines for ME/CFS (NICE used CFS/ME) was launched in 2018, and its publication has been delayed for a third time, due to the Covid-19 pandemic, to April 2021. At the biobank, Caroline had explained the guidelines review process to me: 'They bring a group of people together and go through all the research with a fine-tooth comb. If there is no evidence for something, they can't recommend it. If there is evidence that something is harmful, they can caution against it. It's a really, really meticulous process.'

ME advocacy groups wanted the graded exercise taken out of the guidelines, and CBT for 'erroneous illness beliefs', which is not the same as CBT that helps you cope with a potentially chronic, fluctuating and disabling – not to mention stigmatized – illness. The previous guidelines – published in 2007 – stated that GET and CBT for erroneous illness beliefs should be offered to people with 'mild or moderate CFS/ME'. Both treatments involve challenging thoughts and expectations that may affect symptom improvement and outcomes, developing awareness of thoughts, expectations or beliefs and defining fatigue-related cognitions and behaviour, and addressing complex adjustment to diagnosis and acceptance of current functional limitations, identifying perpetuating factors that may maintain or exacerbate symptoms to increase the person's sense of control over symptoms, and addressing any over-vigilance to symptoms and related checking or reassurance-seeking behaviours, and addressing any unhelpful beliefs about sleep. With GET, post-exertional malaise – the exacerbation of symptoms after exertion – is even written into the guidelines, with encouragement to advise the patient that increasing their level of exercise 'may mildly increase symptoms for a few days'.

'Unfortunately, there are a few papers that might have something, but they haven't been repeated, or been conducted on the wrong populations,' Caroline continued. 'But of course, we don't have a biomarker, and there aren't many treatments, and very few of them are evidence-based, so . . .' she trailed off.

'So, what *are* they combing through?'

According to Tuller, the panel that created the 2007 guidelines was dominated by GET and CBT proponents, which is why those interventions ended up as core treatment recommendations. On Virology Blog, he compared the group that consulted on the 2007 guidelines to destructive invaders on indigenous land: 'They have sought to colonize what one might call the "fatigue space" in some of its many manifestations – cancer-related, MS-related, HIV-related, and so on.' He warned of more colonization to come: 'Post-Covid fatigue could represent fertile new ground to plough with their failed biopsychosocial template.'

With the emergence of post-Covid syndrome or long-Covid as a major public health concern, which often presented as extreme fatigue, post-exertional malaise and cognitive problems, there was concern that GPs, patients and policy makers would turn to the outdated 2007 CFS/ME guidelines. 'If some or many post-Covid syndrome patients respond to over-exertion the way ME/CFS patients do,' wrote Tuller in July, 'then pushing them to exercise could easily make them worse.' NICE put out a statement warning against using the outdated ME/CFS recommendations on graded exercise therapy as they may change. It had been three years since the CDC quietly removed all mention of CBT and GET as treatment or management strategies from its public access pages.

NICE published an initial version of the revised guidelines (for ME/CFS now, not CFS/ME) in November 2020 as part of its consultation stage. GET and CBT (as a treatment option) were out, and 'energy management', or pacing, was now to be advised. The committee had considered the qualitative evidence and their own experiences of GET and CBT for erroneous illness beliefs and found it wanting, recommending not to offer graded exercise therapy, structured activity or exercise programmes that are based on deconditioning as the cause of ME/CFS. The message on illness beliefs was also clear. CBT was now only to be offered to people with ME/CFS who could use it to support them in managing their symptoms and reduce the psychological distress associated with having a chronic illness: 'Do not offer CBT as a treatment or cure for

ME/CFS.' It was a positive outcome, but a lot of damage had already been done – decades of misguidance and neglect, funding treatments that regarded the diagnosis as symptomatic of a 'culture of illness', justified by the notion that people with ME/CFS were deconditioned, that their illness experience was a metaphor for unproductiveness under neoliberalism, rather than backing patient-forward biological research.

'I learnt that in convalescence after a severe assault, the body goes into protect mode, so if it isn't getting space to recover, it shuts you down by bringing an embodied memory of the illness,' read a follow-up post by the Professor of Tropical Medicine with long-Covid. Total convalescence, not graded exercise, was being advised to anyone with long recovery times. If any good was going to come out of the neglect of ME/CFS patients, it was that long-Covid patients were not going to suffer the same fate. Nevertheless, total rest, and therefore recovery, is not accessible for everyone who contracts a virus like Covid: 'What about people less privileged than us articulate middle classes mobilizing ourselves, writing to MPs, and talking to journalists?' Garner asked. 'Pushing themselves because they have no choice will lead to further illness, suffering, and distress. They are being left behind.' He also highlighted the inequalities at work in recovery: 'What about the minority groups, the single parent households, people on zero hours contracts, where long convalescence is not an option?' These people – the ones without job security, who are raising children on their own, who are already disabled, or belong to ethnic and racial minority groups – have always been the most maligned. They have always been more *at risk* because of the choices made by leaders, and now they were more at risk of both contracting Covid and of a longer recovery. *It's chronic.*

On 25 January 2021, nine months after contracting Covid-19, Garner published another post on the BMJ blog: he had recovered from long-Covid, and also CFS/ME – as he had also been given that diagnosis and referred to a specialist – through the power of his mind. Garner had been introduced to someone who had 'completely recovered from post-viral fatigue syndrome (CFS/ME)' and learnt how to retrain his bodily reactions – 'dysfunctional autonomic responses being stimulated by our subconscious' – with his conscious thoughts, feelings and behaviour. 'I suddenly believed I would recover completely,' he wrote. 'I stopped my constant monitoring of symptoms. I avoided reading stories about illness and discussing symptoms, research or treatments by dropping off the Facebook groups with other patients. I spent time seeking joy, happiness, humour, laughter, and overcame my fear of exercise.' It sounded like the Lightning Process. When Garner's recovery was 'tested', having developed dengue fever while on holiday (during a pandemic), he thought: 'let's do it: I will either die or recover'. He got out of bed and went to a military fitness session, resisting death. Military fitness is an appropriate activity for those who believe in choosing between complete recovery or death; it is training for actual war, where the options are winning or losing, literally between life or death. 'I feel that I have looked down the barrel of the ME/CFS gun,' he said, 'and disarmed it.' Even as the possibility of delayed recovery is increasingly recognized amongst the medical community, the belief that our minds can cure our ill feelings persists.

The same psychologists who conducted the PACE trial, and informed the government on illness as an experience, continue their research into chronic fatigue as a biopsychosocial phenomenon, and their ideas easily transfer to long-Covid. It is uncertain how resilient their ideas about illness, which have been so useful to the political elite, will be in our post-viral world.

There are some scenes we are not let behind.

241

Lockdowns have afforded those in the kingdom of the well insight into the kingdom of the sick. Even before the news of long-Covid recoveries, it felt like everyone was hovering on the edge of crip time, characterized by uncertainty, disbelief and loss. Most people would pull themselves back into normative time. Some would stay forever.

Maybe I am projecting.

Everything in between is warped, officially sick.

The 'afternoon' is the forty-five minutes I spend outside with my dog before the cemetery at the end of the road shuts at 6 pm. Some days, I try and go to the allotment where I have three raised beds and then the whole day is fucked: before and after. During is bliss. Now all time is sick time, everyone is going to get good at knowing the only two times you need to know: what time your clock radio alarm turns off and what time the cemetery closes.

Ocean waves, tides ebbing and flowing in constant, turbulent change.

I am back where I began.

If grief is time without its flow – only things happening – then sickness is flow without time. When the chronically ill grieve, they grieve for event-based time, for the sense of one thing after another, for planning for the future, for a day that is not like any other day.

And this is what everyone feels in quarantine, inside, inhabiting the fear and loss before the grief can begin. Except some of us have already been grieving for a long time.

In April 2021, NICE revised guidelines for treating chronic pain. GPs were advised to stop prescribing painkillers because there was not enough evidence they work, and to prescribe antidepressants, exercise and acupuncture instead. I don't know where the evidence is that antidepressants, exercise and acupuncture work for chronic pain, but you cannot get addicted to them in the same way as opioids.

My medication is working for my pain, but I don't think NICE would say there was enough evidence for that either. I can hear the psychologist at the specialist outpatient clinic: *Don't you think you are in less pain because you're less depressed?* I still don't. Like almost everyone, my mental health suffers during periods of lockdown, but I do not necessarily feel more ill – or less. Again, the diagram blurs and warps.

There is no medical evidence for pacing either, the kind crips do on their own, rather than the 'adaptive pacing' tested by the PACE trial investigators, which was 'trialled' and found wanting.

Just before the first UK lockdown, the *Scandinavian Journal of Disability Research* published a special collection on 'cripping time', which included a paper by Emma Sheppard. During her study, she found that pacing can be read as both a 'rehabilitative normalizing practice' and 'a practice of crip self-care', a 'trickster strategy' – a way of passing as non-disabled while simultaneously embracing a disabled life – and a site of conflict and internalized ableism simultaneously. 'As a way of moving in/through time, pacing is both normative and non-normative, read in opposing ways at once.'

Pacing makes sense because it is based on living in between normative and non-normative experiences of time. That there might be no such thing as a future in which you are well.

Sheppard's participants revealed tensions between the pressures of performing as 'normal' – as able body-minded individuals without pain or fatigue – and the desire to be as close to 'normal' as possible, 'to be in/move through time in normative ways'. As one participant explained: 'I can choose to work from home giving myself that much more energy that by . . . Friday evening, I could have a night at the club.' Why should she push herself to go to work every day without doing something she enjoys? Why are we not deserving of that?

There is pleasure in control, and relinquishing that control up to the unreliability of rest as a panacea. Pacing is one of the strategies some of Sheppard's participants engaged in, in order to re-orientate themselves normatively, to pass as 'normal', as abled, unidentifiably – *invisibly* – ill, and pain free. It is also a way of living with your disabled body-mind – 'those who fail to perform heteronormative, flexible, independent, proper bodiliness, at the right time and in the right amount of time'. Some of us with disabled body-minds – 'too slow, too fast, too uncontrolled, too reliant, too different, too much and also not enough' – can pass as normatively orientated in time if we have to, or if nobody looks too closely. Pacing is like hacking time, rather than your immune system.

Pacing could be seen as a way to be more productive within a fast-moving neoliberal workplace, a way to appear as 'normal' as possible during working hours, rather than succumbing to the 'boom and bust' cycle of modern capitalism. ('It is perhaps ironic that pacing programmes present a critique of capitalism as a way to become a better capitalist worker.') Pacing is a trickster strategy, where it is difficult if not impossible to tell where normativity ends and crip begins, what is normal and what is abnormal: 'There could be joy and pleasure in pacing, and in deliberately engaging with their bodyminds.' But pacing is never enough. It is never going to get you *back to normal* (when normal is defined by a forty-hour working week). It is never going to get you back to 100 per cent, whatever that is. Inevitably, pacing fails, in that you might-probably-won't fully recover.

Crip time is not productive. Those of us who live by it have to deal with the limitations of rehabilitative practices such as pacing, but they do not give you resources to resist internalized ableism – the shame of not being enough or doing enough.

Pacing as a strategy for managing the illness experience has never been advised to me, as such – it is a practice developed by patients rather than doctors. It is also almost impossible unless you work from home, which was not 'normal' until the coronavirus pandemic.

Pacing enables crip joy: gladness of missing things sometimes, or most of the time; pleasure in the rejection of the norms and pressures of social engagement; delight in not being curable, even pushing beyond what you feel the boundaries of pain and fatigue are, because every activity hurts in some way. I embrace this re-orientation to crip time – that extended, warped kind of movement through time. I embrace a disabled future, rather than a cure, 'a distinctly crip outlook', in the joy of occasionally doing something on that list of things I want to do, even if it looks, from the outside – in heteronormative time – like I am saying *No* to almost *everything*.

Pacing is a form of politicized self-care, an act of resistance against ableist social structures. We find joy through listening and learning from our bodies, of knowing their limits. Occasionally, there is joy when there is also pain.

During the women's movement and the civil rights movement, self-care became a political act. In the late 1960s, the Black Panther group set up nationwide 'survival programmes' to provide basic preventive care and test for illness and diseases that were chronically underdiagnosed within the Black community, including lead poisoning and sickle-cell disease, due to medical racism. This racial and ethnic inequality in health persists. Black, Asian and minority ethnic people have been disproportionately affected by Covid-19, which socioeconomic factors alone do not account for.

Audre Lorde wrote about the act of self-care as a radical act of liberation within a racist and capitalist world that targets Black women. In the series of diary entries that comprise the 1988 essay 'A Burst of Light', Lorde figures her struggle with cancer as another facet of her continuing battle for self-determination and survival as a Black woman: 'Caring for myself is not self-indulgence, it is self-preservation, and that is an act of political warfare.'

As she processes the impossible – a death that could only be delayed, her cancer not curable – Lorde comes to feel that diagnosis through her whole body, and beyond it. The *burst of light* she feels is 'that inescapable knowledge, in the bone, of my own physical limitation'. No matter how sick she feels, and in the face of death, she is still 'afire with a need to do something for my living'. In this sense, as Sara Ahmed explores in the text 'Selfcare as Warfare', Lorde's self-care is not about her own happiness; 'It is about finding ways to exist in a world that is diminishing.' Self-care is not a way to improve your own well-being, as is often touted by the wellness industry; it is crucial for people who are marginalized. It is an act of survival.

'I want to live the rest of my life, however long or short, with as much sweetness as I can decently manage, loving all the people I love, and doing as much as I can of the work I still have to do,' writes

Lorde. 'I am going to write fire until it comes out my ears, my eyes, my noseholes — everywhere. Until it's every breath I breathe. I'm going to go out like a fucking meteor!'

Crip pacing is not just management, it is the time needed to engage with the body-mind in meaningful ways. I am not trying to *be recovered*, I am claiming my self-worth.

Ahmed writes: 'Sometimes, "coping with" or "getting by" or "making do" might appear as a way of not attending to structural inequalities, as benefiting from a system by adapting to it, even if you are not privileged by that system, even if you are damaged by that system. Perhaps we need to ask: who has enough resources not to have to become resourceful? When you have less resources, you might have to become more resourceful.'

In *The Cultural Politics of Emotion*, Ahmed describes growing up with a mother with ill feelings, diagnosed first with MS and then re-diagnosed with transverse myelitis, a non-fatal condition that is no less painful. For Ahmed, living with her mother meant 'living with her pain', which she perceived as 'unliveable'. Ahmed imagines her mother's pain as her own: 'I love you,' she writes, 'and imagine not only that I can feel how you feel, but that I can feel your pain for you.'

To live with someone else's pain – your mother's pain – is to imagine you can feel it for them. To say 'No' is to consider yourself worthy of care.

There is something so decidedly *un*romantic about pacing. Quite frankly, it is *boring*. And it is counterintuitive. When I do manage to pace myself, I feel I deserve a reward, which for me would be *not* having to *pace myself*. Rest and relaxing after activity throughout the day is a hard thing to do in the abled world, but it is the only thing that helps. I don't have to eat it, or actively avoid it, swapping it for animal products or raw food and expensive oils. I don't have to buy it in the online shop when it's back in stock. I don't have to pay for classes or stand shivering in a swimming costume. I don't even have to collect it once a month from the pharmacy and remember to take it twice a day, and only because I have been trusted to *not take them* *all at once.* I can't say I won't do any of these things again, or in the next week, or that I haven't done them today, but at the moment, it is the best option I have.

I am not much better or worse, more normal or abnormal. I still have pain, am still fatigued. The difference is: I can cope with that. It's absolutely *fine.* Most days aren't great, but the days after I don't pace are *the worst.* I can of course, choose *not* to pace if I want to – a privilege knowing many people are entirely housebound and bedbound.

How many 'usable hours' you have depends on what you're using them for. I can garden, with enough breaks, for hours sometimes, and feel fine the next day. I can't rest at the allotment, so I'm there for less than an hour each time I go, and I have to walk there and back, and talk to people while I'm there – meaning I will hurt afterwards and have less usable hours the following day. I might have to work more hours one day because I have to teach a seminar, or run a workshop, or call in to meetings, or am close to a deadline, in which case I will lose the next two days to fatigue. So how many hours are we talking, over a week? Who knows.

Crip joy is not the same as having a happy disabled identity – to be cheerful in being disabled. Not every part of being disabled needs to be celebrated, including improvement in ability. The pressure to be happy, to say that your fatigue and pain are not awful, to *not* say 'I feel like shit', is ableist in nature – the kind of ableism that is reflected in the willingness to make pain 'indescribable' rather than undesirable or hard to hear, and the idea that to medicate oneself is to attempt normalization, to succumb to the pressure to pass as abled, rather than control your own pain. It is this kind of attitude that upholds the invisibility in invisible illness – and the idea that you are not really ill at all.

¶ Unrecovery

Sickness narratives do not always start with symptoms and end in recovery. Treatment does not always follow test. A new diagnosis might arrive at any time, or never. Sick time is not linear time. It is circular. It lapses and relapses, it drags, loops and buffers.

I desired a singular narrative but the form, with its need to end in a place it did not begin, refused to accept my version of events. I originally proposed an order that followed the medical narrative that started with 'Symptoms' and ended in 'Recovery', hoping to 'recover' illness from 'Cure'. My version resisted order, or could be ordered in any number of ways. There was my own story of illness, which started in childhood, seemed to stop and start throughout my young adulthood, and was also unfolding in the present, and there was my mother's story, which was inextricably entwined with mine. My diagnoses had their own timelines, their own futures and histories, which allied us with previous centuries of nervous illness, but also belonged to the present, all the new theories tested by research studies and treatment trials, all the contested evidence of controversial treatments and greatly anticipated treatment guidelines.

Chronic illnesses are bound to time; the time of being sick, most probably without end. You might not feel acutely ill every day. You might feel well-enough for a few months or years, and later relapse back into being severely unwell – as if you had never got any better. It will make you think that sometimes you have never been well, even if, at times, you believed you were *well-enough*. Sometimes it will make you think you are too well to be sick, and too sick to be well.

I live in sick time, inside my loop of pain. And in that time, I gather.

Science fiction writer Ursula Le Guin thought of books as carrier bags or containers; humanity's first tools being the bag, the sack, the net, something to hold it all together, rather than weapons of domination with spear-like narratives. Carrier-bag books are 'full of beginnings without ends', holding initiations and losses, transformations and translations, containing 'far more tricks than conflicts,

248

far fewer triumphs than snares and delusions'. If we are to recover illness from capital and from patriarchy, perhaps we need more books-as-containers, books as medicine bags, biobanks and sick rooms.

The more you uncover, the more you realize you don't know. Uncovering is tiring – the sensation that the amount you do know and don't know are increasing at the same rate.

What I know is: you will be told at some point in your life – if you haven't already, which is likely, especially if you present as female – that the ill feelings in your body cannot be entirely explained. They will look for all the things they know the shape of and find nothing. You might be told: you are stressed, or you are anxious, or you need to go to a support group even though they know there aren't any, or aqua aerobics on Wednesdays. You might have different questions to me, or my mother, or the other women in this book. You might come across scraps of fiction that present themselves as fact, and new research and studies that sound made up, because they might in fact be bended truths. Following advice – the small changes and life overhauls – will probably not make you 'well', but it won't mean people will stop giving it to you.

A sickness narrative is a useful structure, but one that could be undermined at any stage. One that insists: you *can* recover from this.

For many of us, there will in all likelihood be no recovery. Some of us still do not know what we need to recover *from*.

As Alice James knew: 'And then these doctors tell you that you will die, or *recover!* But you *don't* recover. I have been at these alterations since I was nineteen, and I am neither dead nor recovered -- as I am now forty-two there has surely been time for either process.'

But there is an ending, and that is: accepting that there might be no end to illness, that your life still has meaning, that you are worthy of care, and that you still have an ability to make something, just because it takes you two or four or ten times longer than 'everyone else'.

This is not a desirable ending – acceptance is not dominant enough. It is not acceptable to accept suffering. Accepting sounds like indulging, like refusing to get better, like a resignation, or a sickness in itself. Except it is not.

Accepting chronic illness is not the same as accepting bad care or bad science or bad politics.

The narrative of recovery – from symptom language to test to diagnosis to treatment and cure, has been co-opted, turning work into a health outcome and incapacitated persons into a scourge, not worthy of equal care. The narrative of cure and recovery is not ours to take back.

I return, relapse and repeat myself. I fall from grace.

I find *un*-recovery more useful, because it holds the potential for crip pain and crip joy.

This un-recovery is each our own. Maybe it looks like rest without the meat, water and milk, or like knowing that you did not *choose to be ill*, and that it is your socioeconomic circumstances that have been chosen for you and naturalized by metaphorical language. Maybe it looks like trying to remember what you knew about the natural world that has been destroyed and colonized by my white ancestors, like *wild lettuce for pain relief* and *yarrow for healing wounds*. Maybe your un-recovery is based in feelings not facts; theories like: there are not different systems in the body, or: flying and fighting are not the only instincts, and: some people need opiates to survive their pain, and some doctors are criminals, and some people think they are just doing the right thing – and in none of these circumstances should the patient be shamed. Maybe it looks like scanning your body as an act of reclamation. Saying *No* but keep asking me in case I say *Yes*, even if I never say *Yes*. Maybe it is addressing the root cause, the reasons for your body's failures, which are probably not 'just anxiety', and maybe it is just not listening to an unsolicited suggestion that starts with *Have you tried* . . .

Sources

3   'illness is the great confessional'; 'things said, truths blurted out, which the cautious respectability of health conceals'; 'let a sufferer describe a pain in his head to a doctor and language at once runs dry': Virginia Woolf, 'On Being Ill', *Selected Essays* ed. David Bradshaw (Oxford: Oxford University Press, 2008), 104, 102.

3   'Did anyone ever suffer as I did?': Virginia Woolf, letter to Vanessa Bell, 18 June 1919, *The Letters of Virginia Woolf, 1912-1922* ed. Nigel Nicolson (Harcourt Trade Publishers, 1975), 369.

3   'the pain not be wasted': Audre Lorde, *The Cancer Journals* (London: Penguin, 2020), 9.

7–8 'a case of genuine hysteria for which no cause as yet can be discovered': Mary James quoted in Ruth Bernard Yeazell, *The Death and Letters of Alice James: Selected Correspondence* (Berkeley: University of California Press, 1981), 12.

8   'my nerves are his nerves and my stomach his stomach': Alice James (25 March 1890), *The Diary of Alice James* ed. Leon Edel (Boston: Northeastern University Press, 1999), 104.

8   'taking up of household duties that her mother laid down': Catherine Walsh [Aunt Kate] quoted in Jean Strouse, *Alice James: A Biography* (New York City: New York Review Books, 2011), 202.

9   '. . . experience the pain, without distraction': Alice James (18 July 1890), *The Diary of Alice James*, ed. Leon Edel (New York City: Dodd, Mead & Company, 1964), 129. Also: 'How well one has to be, to be ill!'

11   'tender and affectionate to Virginia Woolf in her illness . . .': Hermione Lee, 'Introduction to On Being Ill', 'On Being Ill' (Ashfield: Paris Press, 2002), xv.

11   In 2009, six years after the SARS virus infected around 8,000 people . . .: Marco Ho-Bun Lam et al., 'Mental Morbidities and Chronic Fatigue in Severe Acute Respiratory Syndrome Survivors: Long-term Follow-up.' Archives of Internal Medicine, (December 2009) 169(22): 2142– 2147.

11   Funding had been syphoned off to other diseases in the US, and patients felt abandoned: 'The current developments are part of a chain of events that began in 1998, when William Reeves, director of the CDC's viral

251

exanthems and herpesvirus branch, reported that funding earmarked by Congress for studies on CFS had been diverted to unrelated CDC projects. A subsequent congressional inquiry revealed that a total of $12.9 million—as much as half of the funds appropriated for the CFS—had been redirected or improperly accounted for. Reeves has also filed a complaint with the US Office of Special Counsel alleging that his supervisor, Brian Mahy, reprimanded him, reduced his staff and downgraded his performance appraisals after Reeves reported the irregularities.' Alan Dove, 'GAO reports on CFS funding controversy', *Nature Medicine* (August 2000) 6: 846.

12   *One study in Japan suggested people with a diagnosis of ME/CFS had smaller hearts . . .*: [The papers I came across at this time were written by Kunihisa Miwa and include this one] 'Cardiac dysfunction and orthostatic intolerance in patients with myalgic encephalomyelitis and a small left ventricle', *Heart Vessels* (July 2015) 30(4): 484–489. [Miwa is one of the authors of the 2011 International Consensus Criteria for myalgic encephalomyelitis.]

16   *'The subject of pain is the business I am in . . .'*: Louise Bourgeois quoted in Rainer Crone, *The Secret of the Cells* (Munich: Prestel, 1998), 81.

18   *During a symposium at the Royal Society of Medicine in 1978 . . .*: M.J. Dillon, '"Epidemic neuromyasthenia" at the Hospital for Sick Children, Great Ormond Street, London' in '"Epidemic neuromyasthenia" 1934–1977: current approaches', A symposium held by the courtesy of the Council of the Royal Society of Medicine at 1 Wimpole Street, London, W.1, on 7 April 1978', ed W. H. Lyle And R. N. Chamberlain, *Postgraduate Medical Journal* (November 1978), 54.

23   *'never to rest, interminably, from searching for the archive right where it slips away . . .'*: Jacques Derrida, *Archive Fever: A Freudian Impression* (Chicago: University of Chicago Press, 1998), 91.

24   *The first outbreak of what was then called 'epidemic neuromyasthenia' . . .*: J. Gordon Parish, 'Early outbreaks of "epidemic neuromyasthenia"', *Postgraduate Medical Journal* (November 1978) 54: 711-717. [Details of early outbreaks of 'epidemic neuromyasthenia', including the 1934 LA epidemic.]

25   *In October 1957, Medical Staff of the Royal Free Hospital, then located on Gray's Inn Road in London, reported an outbreak of an 'obscure*

illness', which had occurred two years earlier . . .: 'An Outbreak of Encephalomyelitis in the Royal Free Hospital Group, London, in 1955', *British Medical Journal* (October 19, 1957) 2(5050): 895.

26   *The issue is important because other young women have been, and will continue to be, diagnosed as hysterical . . .*': R.E. Kendell, 'The Psychiatric Sequelae of Benign Myalgic Encephalomyelitis', *British Journal of Psychiatry* (1967) 113, 833. quoted in Dr Melvin Ramsay, '"Epidemic neuromyasthenia" 1955–1978', *Postgraduate Medical Journal* (November 1978) 54: 718–721.

26   *He saw fifty-three patients admitted to the hospital from the community between April 1955 and September 1957* . . .: Dr Melvin Ramsay, '"Epidemic neuromyasthenia" 1955–1978'.

28   *This may itself be related to the uncertainty of diagnosis . . .*': Mair Thomas, 'Epidemiological approaches to "epidemic neuromyasthenia": syndromes of unknown aetiology (epidemic myalgic encephalopathies)', *Postgraduate Medical Journal* (November 1978) 54: 768–770.

29   *McEvedy and Beard insisted the disease 'proved relatively benign and though a few of the affected suffered some disability for up to a year, no-one died of it*': Colin P. McEvedy and A. W. Beard, 'Royal Free Epidemic of 1955: A Reconsideration', *British Medical Journal* (January 1970) 1(5687): 7–11.

30   *'One characteristic feature of the disease is exhaustion, any effort producing generalised fatigue . . . '*: 'Epidemic myalgic encephalomyelitis' *British Medical Journal* (June 1978) 1(6125): 1436–1437.

30   *'We still know nothing about the nature and cause of epidemic myalgic encephalomyelitis . . .*': 'Epidemic myalgic encephalomyelitis' *BMJ*, 1978.

30   *In one survey, more than seventy per cent of ME/CFS patients . . .*: 'ME/CFS Road to Diagnosis Survey: Conducted January 2014, 263 respondents', CFIDS Association of America, 2014.

30   *'. . .the victims of ME should no longer have to dread the verdict of, "All your tests are normal. Therefore there is nothing wrong with you"*': Melvin Ramsay, *Myalgic Encephalomyelitis and Postviral Fatigue States: the Saga of the Royal Free Disease*, (London: Gower Medical Publishing and the ME Association, 1988), 59.

31   *Before she wrote about archives . . .*: Carolyn Steedman, *Landscape for a Good Woman: A Story of Two Lives* (London: Virago, 1986), 17.

32 '*My mother's longing shaped my own childhood . . .*': Steedman, *Landscape*, 6.

33 '*the equivalent loop now projected into the external world*': Elaine Scarry, *The Body in Pain: The Making and Unmaking of the World* (Oxford: Oxford University Press, 1987), 170.

37 '*But I supposed all the trouble of body, soul and spirit had been too much for me . . .*': Rose la Touche in *John Ruskin and Rose La Touche: Her Unpublished Diaries of 1861 and 1867* ed. Van Akin Burd (Oxford: Oxford University Press, 1979), 169.

37 '*I used to sit up nights and pray, more for the sadness . . .*': Rose la Touche, *Unpublished Diaries*, 160.

37 '*I was angry sometimes but not then, only so tired I could only rest . . .*': Rose la Touche (diary entry), *Unpublished Diaries*, 168.

37 '*She was a marvellous little thing when she was younger . . .*': John Ruskin, letter to Charles Eliot Norton, 10 March 1863, *The Correspondence of John Ruskin and Charles Eliot Norton*, ed. John Lewis Bradley and Ian Ousby (Cambridge: Cambridge University Press, 1987), 77.

38 '*best in Ireland*': Tim Hilton, *John Ruskin* (New Haven: Yale University Press, 2002), 418.

38 '*tendency to cerebral disease*': Maria la Touche, letter to Georgina Cowper, quoted in Tim Hilton, *John Ruskin*, 430.
    Ruskin dreamed of a beautiful, innocent snake . . .: John Ruskin, *The Diaries Of John Ruskin 1848–1873*, ed. Joan Evans and John Howard Whitehouse (Oxford: Oxford University Press, 1958), 644.
    'March 8th, Monday . . . Dreamed of walk with Joan and Connie . . . Then of showing Joanna a beautiful snake, which I told her was an innocent one; it had a slender neck and a green ring round it, and I made her feel its scales. Then she made me feel it, and it became a fat thing, like a leech, and adhered to my hand, so that I could hardly pull it off — and so I woke. Vermilion dawn, to-day.'

38 '*I can remember distinctly feeling naughty when I was about two or three years old . . .*': Rose la Touche (1 January 1867), *Unpublished Diaries*, 154.

38–39 *She loved Religion . . .*: '*So I got ill and things used to make my head ache constantly . . .*': Rose la Touche, *Unpublished Diaries*, 158–159.
    '*They made me eat, but I could not, for it hurt me so*'; '*I did what they told me but suffered dreadfully and seemed to get worse*'; '*I knew I ought to lie*

quiet and not think and I did it' . . .'They said I could not know.': Rose la
Touche, Unpublished Diaries, 169–170.

39   '– only laughed at me.': Rose la Touche, Unpublished Diaries, 164.

43   'collecting her own archives . . .': Carolyn Steedman, The Tidy House: Little
Girls Writing (London: Virago, 1983), 76.

43   '(L)ittle girls have used written language in order to become the women
they were expected to be': Steedman, The Tidy House, 76.

43   'curious, especially where the elastic spirits and fancies work upon the fixity
of character and situation': Elizabeth Barrett Browning, The Barretts at
Hope End: The Early Diary of Elizabeth Barrett Browning, ed. Elizabeth
Berridge (London: John Murray, 1974), 26.

43   'more than a journal about feelings': Elizabeth Berridge, Introduction to
The Barretts at Hope End, 26.

43   'Unwell, very unwell all the evening!'; 'A strange nervous depressed feeling,
as if I were both soulless & boneless!': Elizabeth Barrett Browning (diary,
12 August 1831) in The Barretts at Hope End, 156.

43–44   'Never mind. I enjoyed my ride.': Elizabeth Barrett Browning, (diary, 20
August 1831) in The Barretts at Hope End, 145.

44   '(M)y constitution and my appetite is as bad as ever . . .': Elizabeth Barrett
Browning, letter to her mother, quoted in Forster, Elizabeth Barrett
Browning, 22.

45   spine crib – 'a kind of hammock'; 'as for a diseased spine'; 'nothing obviously wrong with the spine': Forster, Elizabeth Barrett Browning, 24.

45   '"Ungracious-looking" device':, Mary de Young, Encyclopaedia of Asylum
Therapeutics, 1750–1950s (Jefferson: McFarland & Company, 2015).

46   found EBB to have 'no DISEASE', 'only an excitability and irritability of
the chest which requires precaution': Forster, Elizabeth Barrett Browning,
90–92.

46   'I am better a great deal than I was last week, and have been allowed by
Dr Chambers to come downstairs again, and occupy my old place on the
sofa', EBB to H.S. Boyd (June 1838) in The Letters of Elizabeth Barrett
Browning, ed. Frederic G. Kenyon, Vol. 1, (New York City: Macmillan
& Co., 1897), 71.

The week before: 'The truth is that I have been very unwell . . . The
pain grew worse and worse, and Dr Chambers has been here for two
successive days shaking his head as awfully as if it bore all Jupiter's

255

ambrosial curls; and is to be here again today, but with, I trust, a less grave countenance, inasmuch as the leeches last night did their duty, and I feel much better – God be thanked for the relief. But I am not yet as well as before this attack, and am still confined to my bed . . .': (June 1838), 69.

47 *'You have not thought me ill or—worse still—unkind, for not writing? . . .'*: Elizabeth Barrett Browning, letter to Mary Russell Mitford (October or November 1840) in *Women of letters: selected letters of Elizabeth Barrett Browning & Mary Russell Mitford* ed. Meredith B Raymond and Mary Rose Sullivan (Woodbridge: Twayne Publishers, 1987), 45.

47 *'not answer for the consequences'*: (Autumn of 1838) Forster, *Elizabeth Barrett Browning*, 92.

48 *'It would lessen both the actual fatigue, & the evils consequent upon sedentary habits'*; *'I think I deserve a diploma.'*: Elizabeth Barrett Browning, letter to Mary Russell Mitford (15 August 1837), ed. Betty Miller, *The Unpublished Letters of Elizabeth Barrett to Mary Russell Mitford* (New Haven: Yale University Press, 1954), 18.

50 *'a castle gateway, and two walks, and several peasants, and groves of trees which rise in excellent harmony with the fall of my green damask curtains'*: Elizabeth Barrett Browning, letter to Mrs Martin (5 October 1844) in Percy Lubbock, *Elizabeth Barrett Browning In Her Letters* (London: Smith, Elder & Co., 1909), 45.

50 *'EBB chose the second way, although unconsciously . . .'*: Berridge, *The Barretts at Hope End*, 18.

51 *'My diary is not meant to be read by any person except myself'*; *'but she deserves to be let behind the scenes . . .'*: Elizabeth Barrett Browning (diary, 1831) in *The Barretts at Hope End*, 235.

54 *'As I lay prostrate after the storm with my mind luminous and active and susceptible of the clearest, strongest impressions . . .'*; *'Owing to some physical weakness, excess of nervous susceptibility . . .'*: Alice James (26 October 1890) in *The Diary of Alice James*, ed. Leon Edel (Boston: Northeastern University Press, 1999), 148–150.

55 *'An hysteric woman abandons part of her consciousness because she is too weak nervously to hold it all together . . .'*: William James, 'The Hidden Self', *Scribner's Magazine*, March 1890.

55 *'Get at the secondary personage by hypnotisation, or in whatever way,'* Janet

wrote, '*and make her give up the eye, the skin, the arm, or whatever the affected part may be*': Pierre Janet quoted in Judith Ryan, *The Vanishing Subject: Early Psychology and Literary Modernism* (Chicago: University of Chicago Press, 1991), 66.

55   '*. . . violent revolt in my head overtook me so that I had to 'abandon' my brain, as it were*'; '*When all one's moral and natural stock in trade . . .*'; '*It may be the word commonly used by his kind*'; '*So, with the rest, you abandon the pit of your stomach . . .*': Alice James (26 October 1890) in *The Diary of Alice James*, 149–150.

56   '*an unspeakable disgust for the dead drifting of my own life for some time past*': William James's diary, 1868, quoted in Jean Strouse, *Alice James: A Biography* (New York City: NYRB Classics, 2012), 127. [In the margin I have noted: '*his* diary is so boring'.]

56   '*Let Alice cultivate a manner clinging yet self-sustained, reserved yet confidential . . .*': William James quoted in Strouse, *Alice James*, 124.

56   '*gouty diathesis complicated by an abnormally sensitive nervous organisation*'; '*luminous waves that sweep out of my consciousness . . .*'; '*The headache had gone off in the night and I had clean forgotten it*': Alice James (12 July 1890) in *The Diary of Alice James*, 48.

57   '*I think the difficulty is my inability to assume the receptive attitude . . .*': Alice James, letter to William James in *The Death and Letters of Alice James* ed. Ruth Bernard Yeazell, 112.

58   '*whether straight time means a firm delineation between past/present/future . . .*': Alison Kafer, *Feminist Queer Crip* (Bloomington: Indiana University Press, 2013), 34.

58   '*The present takes on more urgency as the future shrinks,*' Kafter writes; '*the past becomes a mix of potential causes of one's present illness or a succession of wasted time; the future is marked in increments of treatment and survival even as "the future" becomes more tenuous.*': Kafer, *Feminist Queer Crip*, 37.

59   '*always sending its signals, the rough black "No", the golden "Come", in rapid running arrows of sensation . . .*': Virginia Woolf, *The Waves* (Oxford: Oxford University Press, 2015), 103.

59   '*– partly mystical. Something happens in my mind.*': Virginia Woolf, *A Writer's Diary: Being Extracts from the Diary of Virginia Woolf*, ed. Leonard Woolf (London: Hogarth Press, 1953), 153.

'I believe these illnesses are in my case–how shall I express it? – partly mystical. Something happens in my mind. It refuses to go on registering impressions. It shuts itself up. It becomes a chrysalis. I lie quite torpid, often with acute physical pain. Then suddenly something springs. Two nights ago Vita was here . . . ideas rush in me; often though this is before I can control my mind or pen.'

60   *'the drawings of the night / They all emerge from the water . . .; 'why are we here? / How do we manage to appear? . . .'*: Louise Bourgeois, inscription on reverse of drawing *Untitled (Insomnia)*, 1994, quoted in Francis Morris and Philip Larratt-Smith, *Insomnia in the work of Louise Bourgeois: has the day invaded the night or the night invaded the day?* (Edinburgh: Fruit Market Gallery, 2013), 126.

61   *'Love your neighbour as yourself – It is difficult to achieve this ideal when you always feel that / something is wrong with you'*: Louise Bourgeois (October 17 1955) in *Louise Bourgeois: The Return of the Repressed* ed. Phillip Larratt-Smith (London: Violette Editions, 2012), 47.

62   *'I believe insomnia comes from guilt . . .'*: Louise Bourgeois (LB-0445, 28 January 1958), quoted in *Insomnia in the work of Louise Bourgeois*, 117.

62   *'I cannot sleep because I / am angry . . .'*: Louise Bourgeois (LB1345, 1961), quoted in *Insomnia in the work of Louise Bourgeois*, 123.

62   *'I shall never tire of representing her'*: Louise Bourgeois, *Ode à ma mère* (1995).

62   *'The spider – Why the spider? . . .'*: Louise Bourgeois, exhibition catalogue (Tate Modern, 2000).

62   *Spider*, Louise Bourgeois, in *He Disappeared into Complete Silence*, 2nd Edition (New York City: MoMA, 2005).

62–63   Louise Bourgeois, *Spider Woman*, print, 2005.

63   *'like a vertigo at the hollow of the stomach'*: Louise Bourgeois, *The Return of the Repressed*, 47.

64   *'and what's the use of talking, if you already know that others don't feel what you feel?'*: Louise Bourgeois, *Destruction of the Father / Reconstruction of the Father: Writings and Interviews, 1923-1997*, eds. Marie-Laure Bernadac and Hans Ulrich Obrist (Cambridge: MIT Press, 1998).

65   *'the night side of life'*: Susan Sontag, *Illness as Metaphor*, (London: Penguin, 2002), 3.

66 One entry from 1961 . . .: Susan Sontag (24 August 1961), *Reborn: Early Diaries 1947–1963* ed. David Rieff (London: Penguin, 2009), 285.

66 Going home to visit for the weekend . . .: Susan Sontag (25 May 1949), *Reborn*, 29.

67 as her son and editor calls it . . .: David Rieff in *Reborn* , 106.

67 'Notes of a Childhood': Susan Sontag, (January 1957), *Reborn*, 106–129.

67 'DO / Shower every other night / Write Mother every other day': Susan Sontag [Undated, most likely late February or early March 1957], *Reborn*, 140.

68 'The journal is a vehicle for my sense of selfhood . . .': Susan Sontag, 'On Keeping a Journal' (31 December 1957), *Reborn*, 166.

68 Susan Sontag, *Alice in Bed: a play in eight scenes* (New York City: Vintage 1994), 83.

74 Virginia Woolf, 'Blue & Green' in *Monday Or Tuesday: Eight Stories* (Mineola: Dover Publications, 2012), 37–38.

75 'Many patients today have acquired the unshakable belief that their symptoms represent a particular disease . . .': Edward Shorter, *From Paralysis to Fatigue: A History of Psychosomatic Illness in the Modern Era* (New York: The Free Press, 1992), 295.

75 'We have observed that nervous diseases . . .': Sayer Walker, *A Treatise on Nervous Diseases: in which are introduced some observations on the structure and functions of the nervous system; and such an investigation of the symptoms and causes of these diseases as may lead to a rational and successful method of cure* (London: J. Phillips, 1796), 148.

75 Elaine Showalter, *Hystories: Hysterical Epidemics and Modern Culture* (London: Picador, 1998).

76 'Shannon Tiday's mother says her daughter has faced accusations that the condition is all in her head . . .': 'Child with M.E. wants to tackle the stigma', ITV News, Thursday 28 September 2017, 12:03pm.

76 'not dead, but not alive properly': Bridget Kathleen (Kay) Gilderdale quoted in Kay Gilderdale: A devoted mother', *The Guardian*, Monday 25 January 2010.

76–77 'We wanted to believe what they said . . .': Kay Gilderdale, 'Appeal for appropriate care' (no longer available online at 25megroup.org).

77 Extracts of Lynn's online diary: 'The ME victim's diary of despair: "My

body is tired and my spirit is broken. I have had enough, I long to die"',
Daily Mail, 26 January 2010.

77   '*In short, mothers of children with disabilities are subjected to more insti-
tutionalised control . . .*': Susan Wendell, *The Rejected Body: Feminist
Philosophical Reflections on Disability* (London: Routledge, 1997).

78   *Eighty-nine per cent of participants . . .*: Celia Wookey, *Myalgic
Encephalomyelitis: Post-viral Fatigue Syndrome and How To Cope With
It* (London: Chapman & Hall, 1988), 17.

79   *Each one a question that was still unanswered after many years of illness . . .*:
J.C. ('Case History 10'), in Wookey, *Myalgic Encephalomyelitis*, 104–120.

86   '*The same abundant curls framing a face, plain in feature, but redeemed by
wonderful dark eyes, large and loving and luminous as stars . . .*': Harriet
Hosmer, in *Harriet Hosmer: Letters and Memories*, ed. Cornelia Carr
(London: The Bodley Head, 1913), 49. See also: Kate Culkin, *Harriet
Hosmer: A Cultural Biography* (Amherst: University of Massachusetts
Press, 2010).

87   '*Ba's best love and as Robert won't wait, dearest Hattie, at Florence now, and
Rome afterwards. E.B.B.*': Elizabeth Barrett Browning to Harriet Hosmer
(19 October 1857), in *Harriet Hosmer: Letters and Memories*, 93.

87   '*little & black like Sappho*'; '*a very little voice*': Elizabeth Barrett Browning,
letter to Benjamin Robert Haydon, 1 January 1843 (Correspondence,
8.128) quoted in Marjorie Stone, 'Browning [née Moulton Barrett],
Elizabeth Barrett', *Oxford Dictionary of National Biography*, 23 September
2004.

87–88   *a 'blind poet' who knew little of 'life and man'; 'her, ponderous, help-
less knowledge of books, for some experience of life and man, for some
. . .*': Elizabeth Barrett Barrett to Robert Browning (50 Wimpole Street:
March 20, 1845.), in *The Letters of Robert Browning and Elizabeth Barrett
Browning, Vol. 1 (of 2) 1845–1846*, 48. Project Gutenberg ebook.

89   *Woolf knew, without knowing what was really wrong with her, that you
can name a problem – influenza, tired heart – any number of ways, and
still not know how to solve it. 'What is a "murmur"?' she asked in 1922. 'I
don't know – but I gather it's not a thing that matters in the least.*': Woolf,
quoted in Hermione Lee, *Virginia Woolf*, 186.

90   '*Zincum met is often considered where there is restlessness of feet or legs.
This remedy type also exhibits a poor memory, mental exhaustion, sleeping*

difficulties, weakness, headache felt in the occiput or temples, poor sleep and a sore throut.' Robert Medhurst, 'Chronic Fatigue Syndrome and the Role of Homeopathy', hpathy.com, 11 March 2011.

90   'Directly I stop working I feel that I am sinking down, down. And as usual, I feel that if I sink further I shall reach the truth': Virginia Woolf (23 June 1929), in A Writer's Diary ed. Leonard Woolf (London: Hogarth Press, 1953), 144.

90   'I Felt a Funeral, in my Brain': Emily Dickinson, The Complete Poems (280) (London: Faber, 2016). 128.

91   'If she went to bed and lay doing nothing in a darkened room . . .': Leonard Woolf, Beginning Again: An Autobiography of the Years 1911 to 1918 (London: Hogarth Press, 1964), 76.

91   'you cannot tell her not to think, work or write'; 'a quiet, vegetative life . . .'; 'She would argue as if she had never been ill . . .' : Leonard Woolf, Beginning Again, 80.

92   In her 1982 book . . .: Toni Jeffreys, The Mile-High Staircase (London: Hodder and Stoughton, 1982), 172–73.

93   'The more I have learned about medicine . . .': Wendell, The Rejected Body, 134.

94   'I live in the world of the healthy (or fairly healthy) . . .': Wendell, The Rejected Body, 3.

94   'Cellular exhaustion suggests an abnormal condition . . .': Wendell, The Rejected Body, 136.

95   'People without disabilities tend to assume . . .': Susan Wendell, 'Toward a Feminist Theory of Disability', Hypatia vol. 4, no. 2 (Summer 1989) 4(2): 104–124.

95   'I need other people to accept my physical limitations . . .'; 'Everyone is supposed to feel exhausted and overworked . . .': Wendell, The Rejected Body, 4.

96   'I lost the power of sleeping quite . . .'; 'It might strike you as strange that I who have had no pain . . .': Elizabeth Barrett Barrett to Robert Browning (5 February 1846), Letters Vol. 1, 451.

96–97   In the sonnet . . .: Elizabeth Barrett Browning, 'Pain in Pleasure', The Poems of Elizabeth Barrett Browning (London: Frederick Warne and Co., 1850), 426.

101–102 'Despite the objective reality, what becomes a disability is determined by

261

the *social meanings individuals attach to particular physical and mental impairments . . .*': Albrecht, G. and Levy J., 'Constructing Disabilities as Social Problems' in *Cross National Rehabilitation Polices: A Sociological Perspective*, ed. G. Albrecht (London : Sage, 1981), 41. Quoted in: Mike Oliver, The Politics of Disablement (Oliver, M. 1990), 78.

102   '*suffering is diagnosed relentlessly as personal*'; '*we lack a vocabulary for thinking about pain as communal and public*': Adrienne Rich, 'Introduction', *The Best American Poetry* (New York City: Scribner, 1996), 23.

'In the America where I'm writing now, suffering is diagnosed relentlessly as personal, individual, maybe familial, and at most to be "shared" with a group specific to the suffering, in the hope of "recovery." We lack a vocabulary for thinking about pain as communal and public, or as deriving from "skewed social relations" (Charles Bernstein). Intimate revelations may be a kind of literary credit card today, but they don't help us out of emotional overdraft; they mostly recycle the same emotions over and over.'

102   '*The problem is . . .*': Adrienne Rich, 'Contradictions—Tracking Poems', *Your Native Land, Your Life* (New York City: W.W. Norton, 1986), 18.

103   '*I feel signified . . .*': Rich, 'Contradictions—Tracking Poems', *Your Native Land, Your Life*, 7.

103   '*an Element of Blank*': Dickinson, *Collected Poems* (650), 323.

106   J.B. Harman, 'Fibrositis and Pain', *Annals of the Rheumatic Diseases* (December 1940) 2: 101–107.

106   The name '*fibromyalgia*' emerged much later . . .:H.A. Smythe and H. Moldofsky 'Two contributions to understanding of the "fibrositis" syndrome' *Bulletin on the Rheumatic Diseases* (January 1977) 28(1): 928–931.

106   *The first American College of Rheumatology criteria . . .*: Frederick Wolfe et al., 'The American College of Rheumatology 1990 criteria for the classification of fibromyalgia: report of the Multicenter Criteria Committee' *Arthritis and Rheumatism* (February 1990) 33: 160–172.

106   '*To make people ill, to give them an illness, was the wrong thing.*': Frederick Wolfe quoted in Alex Berenson, 'Drug Approved. Is Disease Real?', *The New York Times*, 14 January 2008.

106   '*that borderland between the body and the soul*': J.H. Kellgren, 'Deep Pain

262

Sensibility', The Lancet (June 1949) 1(6562): 943–949. [An address delivered to the Manchester Medical Society on 1 December 1948.]

108 *'Self-reporting is important . . .'*: Frederick Wolfe quoted in April Cashin-Garbutt, 'Fibromyalgia: an interview with Dr Frederick Wolfe', news-medical.net, 22 March 2013.

108 *In 2005, Wolfe conducted a study that showed that the ACR . . .*: Robert S. Katz, Frederick Wolfe and Kaleb Michaud, 'Fibromyalgia diagnosis: A comparison of clinical, survey, and American College of Rheumatology criteria', *Arthritis & Rheumatology* (January 2006) 54(1): 169–176. [Among the 206 patients, the clinician diagnosed fibromyalgia in 49.0%, while 29.1% satisfied ACR criteria and 40.3% satisfied survey criteria.]

108 *The new 2010 criteria . . .*: 2010 Fibromyalgia Diagnostic Criteria – Excerpt', rheumatology.org, 2010. [https://www.rheumatology.org/portals/0/files/2010%20fibromyalgia%20diagnostic%20criteria_excerpt.pdf].

111 *'Such a nervous system I have'; 'my amreeta draught, my elixir'; 'keep the pulse from fluttering and fainting . . .'*: Elizabeth Barrett Barrett to Robert Browning (5 February 1846), *Letters* Vol. 1, 451.

111 *'I shrink before the nameless draught'*: Julia Ward Howe, 'One Word More with E.B.B', *Words for the Hour* (Boston: Ticknor & Fields, 1856), 146.

111 *'All things are poison, and nothing is without poison'*: Paracelsus in Hugh D. Crone, *Paracelsus, The Man who Defied Medicine: His Real Contribution to Medicine and Science* (Melbourne: Albarello Press, 2004), 121.

112 *Laudanum could be produced . . .*: Thomas Dormandy, *Opium: Reality's Dark Dream* (New Haven: Yale University Press, 2012), 48.

114 *'antidepressants can be useful . . .'*: 'Chronic fatigue syndrome (CFS/ME)' NHS Health A to Z. https://www.nhs.uk/conditions/chronic-fatigue-syndrome-cfs/.

114 *in 2016, 64.7 million antidepressant items were dispensed in England*: 'Antidepressants were the area with largest increase in prescription items in 2016', NHS Digital, 29 June 2017.

118 *Her heart, this 'damnable organ'*: Virginia Woolf, letter to Violet Dickinson (12 February 1922), in *The Letters of Virginia Woolf Volume 2 1912–1922* ed. Nigel Nicholson and Joanne Trautmann (New York City: Harcourt Brace, 1976), 503.

118   *'furious, speechless, beyond words indignant with this miserable puling existence'; 'They come in and sit down and produce a bunch of violets . . .'*: Virginia Woolf, letter to Vanessa Bell (20 February 1922), *Letters Volume 2*, 504.

118   *'I get the jumping pulse and pain if I do anything . . .' she wrote in the summer of 1927. 'It's so easy with this damned disease, to start a succession of little illnesses, and finally be sent to bed for 6 weeks.'*: Hermione Lee, *Virginia Woolf*, 186.

118   *'This melancholy', she wrote in 1929, 'it comes with headache, of course'*: Woolf quoted in Hermione Lee, *Virginia Woolf*, 185.

119   *'I am so cold I can hardly hold a pen . . .'; 'Such "sensations" spread over my spine and head directly I give them the chance . . .': 'Never was anyone so tossed up and down by the body as I am . . .'; 'hacking rather listlessly'*: Virginia Woolf (11 February 1928), *The diary of Virginia Woolf, Volume Three 1925–1930* ed. Anne Olivier Bell assisted by Andrew McNeillie (New York City: Harcourt, Brace, Jovanovich, 1980), 174–175.

120   *'literature is no one's private ground; literature is common ground'*: Virginia Woolf, 'The Leaning Tower' (1940) in *The Essays of Virginia Woolf Vol.6 1933–1941*, ed. Stuart N. Clarke (The Hogarth Press, 2011).

120   *'Nature is at no pains to conceal that she in the end will conquer . . .'*: Virginia Woolf, 'On Being Ill', *Selected Essays*, 106.

123   *'I have invented for my comfort a theory that this degenerescence of mine is the result of Alice and Willy getting better and locating some of their diseases on me'*: Henry James: *Selected Letters*, ed. Leon Edel (Cambridge: Harvard University Press, 1987), 53.

124   *'Keep remembering that a short rest at the time you need it is like money in the bank, only it will pay more than dividends.'*: Marion Hilliard, *Women and Fatigue: a Woman Doctor's Answer* (London: Macmillan, 1960), 93.

125   *'Our reserves of adaption energy could be compared to an inherited fortune from which we can make withdrawals . . .'*: Hans Selye, *Stress Without Distress* (Philadelphia: Lippincott, 1974), 40.

126   *'You and I must learn what our pattern is . . . look at your mother, father, aunts, uncles, grandparents, because you inherited your pattern from them. Find out what those inheritances are.'*: Hilliard, *Women and Fatigue*, 17.

129   *'let the dykes break and the flood sweep in, acknowledging yourself abjectly impotent before the immutable laws.'*: Alice James, *Diary*, 149.

130 *'Built with money bequeathed by . . .'*: The will of the founder of the Adams Nervine Asylum provided that it should be 'for the benefit of the indigent, debilitated nervous people who are not insane, inhabitants of the Commonwealth of Massachusetts, as may be in need of the benefits of a curative institution: Mary Norton Bradford, Boston Daily Globe, April 18, 1887.

130 *'be plain, substantial and simple and great attention shall be paid to convenience . . .'*: Seth Adams quoted in: Bradford, 1887.

130 *'queer apparatus for driving the lazy blood into new life . . .'*: Bradford, 1887.

130–131 *'Paralyses, epilepsy, and the different types of manias have been quite resistant to electricity . . .'*: Jean-Baptiste Sarlandiere, *Memoires sur l'electropuncture – treatise on electroacupuncture*, 1825.

131 *'So, take care of your nerves . . .'*: Bradford, 1887.

131 *'either in spite or because of his quackish quality'; 'the lowest of organism with absolutely no insides but a stomach . . .'*: Alice James, letter to Frances Rollins Morse [Spring 1884?], *Death and Letters*, 94.

132 *'a part of the price we pay for civilization . . .'*: George M. Beard, *Cases of hysteria, neurasthenia, spinal irritation, and allied affections; with remarks* (Chicago: J.J. Spalding, 1874), 2.

132 *'The sensations were most marked after fatigue . . .'*: Beard, *Cases of hysteria*, 7.

133 *'not "passed away" yet . . .'*: Alice James, letter to Catharine Walsh, William James, etc. (22 November 1884), *Death and Letters*, 97.

133 *'against my conscience and my purse . . .'; 'We read his book two years ago . . .'*: Alice James, letter to Alice Howe Gibbons James, 8 December 1884, *Death and Letters*, 100–103.

134 *'one of the earliest diseases'; 'unlike any other disease, (gout) kills more rich men than poor . . .'*: Alfred Baring Garrod, *A Treatise on Gout and Rheumatic Gout (Rheumatoid Arthritis)* (London: Lonmans, Green & Co., 1876), 1.

134 *'It is quite true that a patient often feels much relieved by a fit of gout . . .'*: Garrod, *A Treatise on Gout*, 297.

134 *'promote the action of the skin by hot air or vapour bath, or by tepid sponging with water or vinegar and water'*: Garrod, *A Treatise on Gout*, 307.

135   'the administration of some simple alkaline saline . . .': Garrod, A Treatise on Gout, 316.

137   'as often as the lightning broke out . . .': Laura Otis, Networking: Communicating with Bodies and Machines in the Nineteenth Century (Ann Arbor: University of Michigan Press, 2001) 16.

137   'so that they may be considered as continuations of that organ . . .': Walker, A Treatise on Nervous Diseases, 5.

138   'just as little as telegraph-wires, do the nerves betray by any external symptom that any or what news is speeding along them . . .': Emil DuBois-Reymond, 'On the Time Required' (1868), quoted in Otis, Networking, 24.

138   'By comparing the electrical activity in muscles . . .': Otis, Networking, 24.

139   DuBois-Reymond also described his own migraine: Emil DuBois-Reymond quoted in J.M.S. Pearce, 'Historical aspects of migraine', Journal of Neurology, Neurosurgery, and Psychiatry (October 1986) 49(10): 1097–1103.

139   'Fear will produce different actions in the heart and arteries . . .'; 'Epilepsies have been induced by sudden terror . . .': Walker, A Treatise on Nervous Diseases, 43.

141   'I should have thought he would therefore have liked to do something for me . . .': Alice James, letter to Catharine Walsh, 31 January 1885, Death and Letters, 106-108.

145   There is no single definition of ME/CFS..: 'Chronic fatigue syndrome: Report of a joint working group of the Royal Colleges of Physicians', Royal College of Physicians, October 1996.

145   'labels are important to patients as well as doctors . . ..': Charles Shepherd, 'Disagreements still exist over the chronic fatigue syndrome' [Letter], British Medical Journal (January 1997) 314:146.

148   'It is a sad irony that Florence Nightingale . . .': D. A. Young, 'Florence Nightingale's fever', British Medical Journal (December 1995) 311:1697.

149   Her convalescence was inevitably long . . .: Mark Bostridge, Florence Nightingale (London: Penguin, 2009), 281.

149   'I see her at times when she seems hardly able to walk . . .' : Bostridge, Florence Nightingale, 297.

150   'but an invalid of a curious character . . .': Lytton Strachey, 'Florence

Nightingale', *Eminent Victorians* ed. John Sutherland (Oxford: Oxford University Press, 2003), 134.

151   '*No one so carefully concealed the part she played.*': Zachary Cope, 'Miss Florence Nightingale and the doctors', President's Address, Proceedings of the Royal Society of Medicine (6 June 1956), 907.

152   *Not until the twentieth century . . .*: Alice C Evans, 'Chronic brucellosis', *JAMA* (September 1934) 103(9): 665–667.

154   *According to her most recent biographer . . .*: Bostridge, *Florence Nightingale*, 186.

155   *at Malvern you would be called at 5 am* . . . W. H. McMenemey, 'The Water Doctors of Malvern, with Special Reference to the Years 1842 to 1872', Proceedings of the Royal Society of Medicine Vol.46, 1 October 1952.

157   '*When one can only take a passive part in life . . .*': Alice James, letter to Sara Sedgwick Darwin, *Death and Letters*, 84–87.

158   '*one of the greatest medical scandals of the 21st century*': Carol Monaghan, 'PACE Trial: People with ME', *Hansard's Parliamentary Debates* (20 February 2018) 636: col 28WH.

      'The trial was unique in medical research. It was funded by the Department for Work and Pensions to the tune of £5 million, a point to which I will return. From the very start the PACE trial was flawed. In contravention of the World Health Organisation classification, it assumed that ME was psychological and sufferers could recover if they chose so to do. Thus the PACE trial was framed in psychological terms.'

      'Calls to publish the raw data — basic protocol in good research — were ignored. Queen Mary University spent an estimated £200,000 on keeping the data hidden. Finally, after a long battle, patients won a court order to force the PACE authors to release the data. It was discovered that the authors had altered the way in which they measured improvement and recovery, to increase the apparent benefit of the therapies. Re-analysis showed that the improvement rate fell from 60% to 21% and the recovery rate fell from 22% to just 7%.'

159   '*culturally sanctioned expressions of distress*': Simon Wessely, 'Old wine in new bottles: Neurasthenia and "ME"', *Psychological Medicine* 20(1): 35–53.

160   *Professor Gordon Waddell was also in attendance . . .:*Gordon Waddell and
       Mansel Aylward, *The Scientific & Conceptual Basis of Incapacity Benefits*
       (London: The Stationery Office, 2005).

161   *And EBB, who always resented the implication that her illness was imagi-*
       nary . . .: 'Elizabeth longed for a precise diagnosis of a precise disease . . .'
       Forster, *Elizabeth Barrett Browning*, 25.

162   *Not working – which was previously supported by incapacity benefits –*
       was now perceived as 'one of the greatest known risks to public health' . . .:
       Waddell and Aylward, *Malingering and Illness Deception*, 17.

163   *'Psychological theories of illness are a powerful means of placing the blame*
       on the ill . . .': Susan Sontag, *Illness as Metaphor*, 58.

171   *'disgusting old fart neoliberal hypocrite':* Paul Gallagher, '"You're a disgust-
       ing old fart neoliberal hypocrite" – scientists in furious row over ME study'
       inews.co.uk, 1 August 2017.

174   *'The PACE trial will not be the last word. But it is the best we have for*
       now.': Simon Wessely, 'The PACE Trial for chronic fatigue syndrome:
       choppy seas but a prosperous voyage', nationalelfservice.net, 4 November
       2015.

180   *'Human Biobanking Ownership – Market to Witness a value of US$37.1*
       Billion by 2020'; Global Market Watch, 24 February 2017.

181   *ME Biobank received £99,766 of funding from the Ramsay Research Fund*
       via the ME Association: 'MEA Press Release: Vital new research could
       lay bare the cause of one of world's cruellest illnesses', ME Association,
       23 October 2019.

185   *'Oh how thankful I shall be to be my own mistress and throw their silly*
       medicines down the slop pail!': Virginia Woolf, letter to Violet Dickinson
       (30 October 1904), *The Letters of Virginia Woolf Volume 1 1888–1912*
       (Virginia Stephen) ed. Nigel Nicholson and Joanne Trautmann (New
       York City: Harcourt Brace, 1977), 148.

185–186 *That silly old Nessa has been absorbing Savages theories as usual*
       *. . .':*Virginia Woolf, Letter to Violet Dickinson (26 November 1904),
       The Letters of Virginia Woolf Volume 1, 159.

186   *'Rather amuses me to write, since I have been ordered not to write for*
       my brains health.': Virginia Woolf (30 January 1905) in *A Passionate*
       Apprentice: The Early Journals 1897–1909 ed. Mitchell Leaska (London:
       Pimlico, 2004), 230.

186   'great pyramids of books, with trailing mists between them; partly dust, and partly cigarette-smoke': Virginia Woolf, letter to Lady Robert Cecil (12 April 1909), The Letters of Virginia Woolf Volume 1, 390.

186   'her intellectual resistance to tyranny and conventionality, derived to a great extent from her experience as a woman patient': Hermione Lee, Virginia Woolf, 179.

186   'a polite madhouse for female lunatics': Quentin Bell, Virginia Woolf: A Biography (London: Hogarth Press, 1972), 164.

186   'I really don't think I can stand much more of this . . .': Virginia Stephen, letter to Vanessa Bell (28 July 1910) The Letters of Virginia Woolf Volume 1, 431.

187   'I shall tell you wonderful stories of the lunatics. By the bye, they've elected me King. There can be no doubt about it.': Virginia Woolf, letter to Leonard Woolf (5 March 1912), in Quentin Bell, Virginia Woolf.

187   'more as a man of the world than as a doctor': Leonard Woolf, Beginning Again, 82.

187   'Virginia liked her up to a point' and was 'willing to go to her for a week or two': Leonard Woolf, Beginning Again, 82.

188   'Nothing has happened', she wrote . . .: Virginia Woolf, letter to Leonard Woolf (5 August 1913), Letters Volume 2, 34.

188   she was 'very well and enjoy sitting in this mound of flesh . . .': Virginia Woolf, letter to Katherine (Ka) Laird Cox (November 1915), Letters Volume 2, 70.

189   'Imagine that a normal healthy person has £1000 work of energy to spend in a day': Sarah Myhill, Diagnosis and Treatment of Chronic Fatigue Syndrome and Myalgic Encephalitis: It's Mitochondria, Not Hypochondria (London: Hammersmith Health Books, 2017) , 199.

189   'Remember,' she writes, 'two thirds of all energy production goes into house-keeping duties.': Myhill, Diagnosis and Treatment, 138.

189–190   'there is no more fruitful source of family discontent than a housewife's badly-cooked dinners and untidy ways': Mrs. Isabella Beeton, The Book of Household Management,(London: S. O. Beeton, 1861), iii.

190   She must be economic and frugal . . .: Beeton, The Book of Household Management, 3.

190   She should 'thoroughly understand accounts . . .': Beeton, The Book of Household Management, 23.

191   *'the interval that must necessarily elapse . . .'*: Beeton, 'The Doctor', *The Book of Household Management*, 1071.

191   *'Should the palpitation originate from organic derangement . . .'*: Beeton, *The Book of Household Management*, 1080.

191   *'Tickle the top of the throat with a feather . . .'*: Beeton, *The Book of Household Management*, 1081.

191   *'for the most part, in young, nervous, unmarried women . . .'*: Beeton, *The Book of Household Management*, 1078.

191–192   *'Young women, who are subject to these fits . . .'*: Beeton, *The Book of Household Management*, 1079.

193   *'theoretically, about 120 years.'*: Dr Sarah Myhill, *Sustainable Medicine: Whistle-Blowing on 21st-Century Medical Practice* (London: Chelsea Green Publishing, 2017).

193   *'In the course of more than six decades . . .'*: Lauren Collins, 'Was Jeanne Calment the Oldest Person Who Ever Lived—or a Fraud?' *The New Yorker* (17 February 2020).

193   *'Energy borrowed has to be paid back at 300 per cent interest . . .'*: Myhill, *Diagnosis and Treatment*, 261.

194   *'To recover you must be emotionally ruthless and selfish . . . surround yourself with "energy givers" rather than "energy vampires"'*: Myhill, *Diagnosis and Treatment*, 261.

194   *'A hysterical girl is, as Wendell Holmes has said in his decisive phrase . . .'*: Silas Weir Mitchell, *Fat and Blood and How to Make Them* (Philadelphia: J.B. Lippincott & Co., 1882), II, 37.

195   *'I see every week — almost every day . . .'*: Mitchell, *Fat and Blood* , 28–29.

195   *No matter how it came about . . .*: Mitchell, *Fat and Blood*, 30.

'Nor is this less true of men, and I have many a time seen soldiers who had ridden boldly with Sheridan or fought gallantly with Grant become, under the influence of painful nerve-wounds, as irritable and hysterically emotional as the veriest girl. If no rescue comes, the fate of women thus disordered is at last the bed. They acquire tender spines, and furnish the most lamentable examples of all the strange phenomena of hysteria.'

195   *moral degradation . . .*: Mitchell, *Fat and Blood*, 30–31.

195   *Mitchell believed all these women needed was a liberal gain in fat and blood . . .*: [Mitchell's treatment involved the following: 'seclusion, certain

forms of diet, rest in bed, massage (or manipulation), and electricity ; and I desire to insist anew on the fact that it is the use of these means together that is wanted.'] Mitchell, *Fat and Blood*, 35.

196 *'the willing slaves of their caprices . . .*'; *'The self-sacrificing love and over-careful sympathy . . .*': Mitchell, *Fat and Blood*, 36–37.

196 '*. . . endless mischief for one another.*': Mitchell, *Fat and Blood*, 32. 'Another form of evil to be encountered in these cases is less easy to deal with. Such an invalid has by unhappy chance to live with some near relative whose temperament is also nervous and who is impatient or irritable. Two such people produce endless mischief for one another.'

196 *'Only through a great struggle did she break off and become a doctor.*': Virginia Woolf quoted in Elsa Nettels, 'Virginia Woolf's Life and Art', *Women Healers and Physicians: Climbing a Long Hill*, ed. Lilian R. Furst, (Lexington: The University Press of Kentucky, 1997), 252.

198 *'Life is an arms race.*': Sarah Myhill, *The Infection Game: Life is an Arms Race* (London: Hammersmith Health Books, 2018).

198 *'and that the most truthful way of regarding illness – and the healthiest way of being ill – is one most purified of, most resistant to, metaphoric thinking*': Sontag, *Illness as Metaphor*, 3.

198 *'The immune system is everywhere and nowhere . . .*': Donna Haraway, 'The Biopolitics of Postmodern Bodies: Determinations of Self in Immune System Discourse', *Simians, Cyborgs, and Women. The Reinvention of Nature* (Milton Park: Routledge, 1991), 203–230; 218.

199 *'Most of the patients with Giardiasis . . .*': Leo Galland, 'Intestinal Parasites May Be Causing Your Energy Slump', huffpost.com, 25 May 2011.

199–200 *G. intestinalis was first noted by Antony van Leeuwenhoek having examined his own faeces . . .*: Brian J. Ford, 'The Discovery of Giardia', *Microscope* (2005) 53(4): 147–153.

200 *It alters the variant-specific proteins on its surface, confounding the infected body's immune system . . .*: 'Antigenic variation in Giardia lamblia is regulated by RNA interference', César G Prucca et al. *Nature* (December 2008) 456(7223): 750–754.

201 *In 2018, Dr Kevin Tyler from UEA's Norwich medical . . .*: Alex Therrien, 'Scientists discover how giardia parasite makes you ill', BBC News, 29 January 2018.

271

201   'The Allergy Epidemic – And What To Do About It', Goop. [Accessed 13 April 2021.]

201   Norwegian studies . . .: Kristine Mørch et al. 'Chronic fatigue syndrome 5 years after giardiasis: differential diagnoses, characteristics and natural course.', BMC Gastroenterology (February 2013) 13: 28.

202   A comparative study in 2017 . . .: Kurt Hanevik et al. 'Giardia-specific cellular immune responses in post-giardiasis chronic fatigue syndrome.' BMC immunology (Janurary 2017). 18, 5.

205   'I had to my surprise a week ago a call from Mrs Lucian Carr . . .': Alice James, letter to William James (25 November 1889) Death and Letters, 181–182.

205–206 'invalid chair'; 'It has rubber tyres & bicycle wheels so that there is abso-lutely no jar & one can lie out in it like a bed if necessary': Alice James, letter to Catharine Walsh, November 21–24 [1885?], Death and Letters, 110.

206   William James defended the cure: 'life-long invalids have had their health restored': William James, The Varieties of Religious Experience, (New York City: Longmans, Green & Co., 1917).

211   In September 2017, the British Medical Journal's Archives of Disease in Childhood published a paper by Esther Crawley . . .: Esther Crawley et al. 'Clinical and cost-effectiveness of the Lightning Process in addi-tion to specialist medical care for paediatric chronic fatigue syndrome: Randomised controlled trial.', Archives of Disease in Childhood, (February 2018) 103(2): 155–164.

211   Observer bias means participants are more likely to exaggerate their recovery during an unblinded trial compared with blinded assessors: Carl Heneghan, Ben Goldacre and Kamal R. Mahtani, 'Why clinical trial outcomes fail to translate into benefits for patients.' Trials, (March 2017) 18, 122. [Trials that use 'surrogate, composite and subjective endpoints', and report 'rela-tive measures at the expense of more informative absolute outcomes', can undermine the translation of research into practice and policy, therefore failing to improve patient care. And this is not an unusual occurrence; 'relatively few trials make a meaningful contribution to patient care, often as a result of the way that the trial outcomes are chosen, collected and reported.' Reporting subjective primary outcomes in treatment trials is also standard: only 38% of drug intervention reviews studied by Goldacre and

his colleagues reported objective primary outcomes. They found outcome reporting bias in nearly two-thirds of the primary studies they reviewed. Switched outcomes, or 'the failure to correctly report pre-specified outcomes', which presents significant problems in interpreting results was also highly prevalent (31%).]

211 *In the case of the SMILE trial . . ..*: David Tuller, 'Trial By Error: Time to Retract the LP Study; Letter to Archives of Disease in Childhood', Virology Blog, 3 June 2019. [According to Tuller's reporting on SMILE, Crawley promised to verify the self-reported school attendance by request-ing school records, but these – the only objective outcome for the trial – have still not materialised. Tuller doesn't know if she failed to obtain the reports or chose to omit them.]

212 *'much misinformation is spread using social media.'*: Prof. Michael Sharpe, 'Expert reaction to controversial treatment for CFS/ME', Science Media Centre, 20 September 2017.

212 *'that this report will in effect act as positive publicity for a programme that is being proposed for a wide range of physical conditions . . .'*: Prof Dorothy Bishop, 'expert reaction to controversial treatment for CFS/ME', 2017.

215 *'more harm than good . . .'*: Henry James, letter to Catherine Walsh, *The Complete Letters of Henry James, 1884–1886: Volume 1* (18 May 1885), 202.

215 *'What I do experience is a calming of my nerves & a quiescent passive state . . .'*: Alice James, letter to William James (2 December 1891), *Death and Letters*, 199–200.

215 *'K. turned on the hypnotic Tuckey, the mild radiance of whose moonbeam personality has penetrated with a little hope the black mists that enveloped us . . .'*: Alice James, *Diary* (4 December 1891), 222.

215 *'a typical British matron . . .'*: Alice James, *Diary* (5 April 1891), 185.

215 *Dr Ambroise-Auguste Liébeault's 'Treatment by Suggestion'*: Charles Lloyd Tuckey, *Psycho-therapeutics, or, Treatment by Sleep and Suggestion* (London: Baillière, Tindall and Cox, 1889).

216 *'lifting it a little way, as ants carry a blade of straw so feverishly, and then leave it . . ..'*: Virginia Woolf, 'The Mark on the Wall', *Monday or Tuesday* (London: Hogarth Press, 1921), 79.

216 *'physical pain however great ends in itself and falls away like dry husks from the mind . . .'*: Alice James, *Diary* (4 March 1892), 232.

216   'had to get a little worse in order to lose all conscience about absorbing K. as a right': Alice James, Diary (26 April 1891), 200.

217   'Through complete physical bankruptcy, I have attained my "ideel" as nurse calls it'; 'levelled all the rough places and let the sunlight into the dark corners of suggestion'; 'the excellent Louisa': Alice James, Diary (22 March 1891), 181.

217   'simple embodiment of Health'; 'Katharine can't help it, she's made that way.': Alice James, Diary (4 March 1892), 232.

217   'I wish you could know Katharine Loring': Alice James, letter to Sara Darwin (9 August 1879), Death and Letters, 87.

218–219   Quentin Bell's characterisation of his aunt Virginia as a 'sexless Sappho': Quentin Bell, Virginia Woolf, (New York City: Harcourt, Brace, Jovanovich, 1972), 2: 186. [See Eileen Barrett, 'Introduction', Virginia Woolf: Lesbian Readings, eds. Eileen Barrett and Patricia Cramer (New York City: New York University Press, 1997).]

219   'the best of these illnesses is that they loosen the earth about the roots . . .': Hermione Lee, introduction to Virginia Woolf, 'On Being Ill', (xviii).

219   'What Virginia meant by "intimacy" was really the maternal coddling she wanted from Vita': Mitchell Leaska quoted in Patricia Cramer '"Plain as a Pikestaff ": A Response to Recent Biographers on Virginia Woolf, Childhood Sexual Abuse, and Lesbianism', University of Connecticut Open Commons, (November 2006).

219   'Vita wanted to become a male lover . . .': James King quoted in Virginia Woolf: Lesbian Readings, eds. Eileen Barrett and Patricia Cramer (New York City: New York University Press, 1997), 6.

219   'Dearest Honey . . . It gets worse steadily – your being away . . .': Virginia Woolf, letter to Vita Sackville West (28 February 1927), The Letters of Vita Sackville-West to Virginia Woolf, eds. Louise DeSalvo and Mitchell A. Leaska (Jersey City: Cleis Press, 2001), 153.

219   'I wish I knew REALLY how you were . . .': Vita Sackville-West, letter to Virginia Woolf (16 August 1929), The Letters of Vita Sackville-West to Virginia Woolf, 287.

219   '. . . I wish for nothing the world so much as that I might look after you . . .': Vita Sackville-West, letter to Virginia Woolf (4 February 1929), The Letters of Vita Sackville-West to Virginia Woolf, 264.

220   'her death was the greatest disaster that could happen': Virginia Woolf,

'Reminiscences' (1907) in *Moments Of Being: Autobiographical Writings* (London: Pimlico, 2002), 11.

220   *In a letter to Vanessa . . .*: Bostridge, *Florence Nightingale*, 530.

220   *'I need the identity as a weapon, to match the weapon that society has against me . . .'; 'Being queer makes me feel more vulnerable . . .'*: Susan Sontag (24 December 1959), *Reborn*, 223.

221   *'the kind of shimmer of reality . . . the lustre on an oyster shell'*: Virginia Woolf, letter to Vita Sackville West (10 October 1927) in Clare Hanson, 'Imaginary Lives: *Orlando* and *A Room of One's Own*' in *Virginia Woolf. Women Writers* (London: Palgrave, 1994), 95.

221   *'But of course, the Dr and Leonard say it's all the Berlin racketing . . .'*: Virginia Woolf, letter to Vita Sackville West (4 February 1929), *The Letters of Vita Sackville-West to Virginia Woolf*, 266.

221   *'I can't believe it's the "racketing" of Berlin . . .'*: Vita Sackville-West, letter to Virginia Woolf (4 February 1929), *The Letters of Vita Sackville-West to Virginia Woolf*, 266.

221   *'illness often takes on the disguise of love'*: Virginia Woolf, 'On Being Ill', 102.

221   *'queer feminist crip'*: Kafer, *Feminist Queer Crip*, 3.

222   *'The change of sex, though it altered their future, did nothing whatever to alter their identity . . .'*: Virginia Woolf, *Orlando: a biography* (Oxford: Oxford University Press, 2008), 133.

> 'Their faces remained, as their portraits prove, practically the same. His memory — but in future we must, for convention's sake, say 'her' for 'his,' and 'she' for 'he' — her memory then, went back through all the events of her past life without encountering any obstacle. Some slight haziness there may have been, as if a few dark drops had fallen into the clear pool of memory; certain things had become a little dimmed; but that was all '

222   *'delicate embroidery of the most distressing case of nervous hyperesthesia'*: Alice James, *Diary* (31 May 1891), 207.

222   *'enormous relief . . . one becomes suddenly picturesque to oneself'*: Alice James, *Diary* (1 June 1891), 208.

223   *'To him who waits, all things come! . . .'*: Alice James, *Diary* (1 May 1891), 206.

223   *'Poor dear William . . .'*: Alice James, *Diary* (1 June 1891), 208.

223 'fantastic unproductive emotions enclosed within tissue paper'; 'her humiliated appendage': Alice James, Diary (7 November 1890), 151.

223 'an appendage to five cushions and three shawls'; 'little rubbish heap': Alice James, Diary (10 February 1890), 81, 78.

223 '"Will you be my friend, my friend of friends . . ."': Olive Chancellor in Henry James, The Bostonians (London & New York: Macmillan & Co., 1886), 80.

224 'Of what matter can it be whether pain or pleasure has shaped and stamped the pulp within . . .': Alice James, Diary (29 February 1892), 232.

231 'Twice as many people on graded exercise therapy . . .': Trudie Chalder in Sarah Boseley, 'Study finds therapy and exercise best for ME', Guardian, 18 February 2011.

231 '"an overwhelming, debilitating, and sustained sense of exhaustion . . ."': WT Riley et al., 'Patient-reported outcomes measurement information system (PROMIS) domain names and definitions revisions: further evaluation of content validity in IRT-derived item banks', Quality of Life Research, (November 2010) 19(9): 1311–1321.

232 'The term "fatigue" conjures up middle-class sacrifices . . .': Hannah Devlin, 'Behavioural scientists form new front in battle against coronavirus', Guardian, 13 Mar 2020.

233 As early as May, ME Action . . .: 'Researchers Expect Covid-19 will cause Surge of Chronic Illness Including ME', ME Action, 10 May 2020.

234 'Many scientists believe the tests are likely picking up dead virus . . .': Ariana Eunjung Cha and Lenny Bernstein, 'These people have been sick with coronavirus for more than 60 days', The Washington Post, 11 June 2020.

234 callers revealed they had already been ill for up to four months: 5 Live Breakfast: Your Call, BBC Radio 5 Live, 6 July 2020.

235 'You can see people who've recovered who really do not get back to normal . . .': Anthony Fauci, International AIDS Society Covid-19 press conference, YouTube, 9 July 2020.

235 In one 2006 Australian study . . .: Ian Hickie et al., 'Post-infective and chronic fatigue syndromes precipitated by viral and non-viral pathogens: prospective cohort study.' British Medical Journal (September 2006) 333: 575.

'A relatively uniform post-infective fatigue syndrome persists in a significant minority of patients for six months or more after clinical infection with several different viral and non-viral micro-organisms. Post-infective fatigue syndrome is a valid illness model for investigating one pathophysiological pathway to chronic fatigue syndrome.'

235   *In a study of 233 Hong Kong residents who survived the SARS epidemic of 2003 . . . .*: Marco Ho-Bun Lam et al., 'Mental Morbidities and Chronic Fatigue in Severe Acute Respiratory Syndrome Survivors: Long-term Follow-up.' *Archives of Internal Medicine, (December* 2009) 169(22): 2142–2147.

235   *In 2011, eight years after the outbreak, Harvey Moldofsky . . . .*: Harvey Moldofsky and John Patcai, 'Chronic widespread musculoskeletal pain, fatigue, depression and disordered sleep in chronic post-SARS syndrome; a case-controlled study', *BMC Neurology* (March 2011) 11: 37.

236   *This dung heap read is if it were written by Simon Wessely . . .'*: David Tuller, 'Trial By Error: Oxford Health Blinks, Removes Pamphlet on Post-COVID Illness', Virology Blog 20 April 2020.

236   *Paul Garner used his prominent platform . . .* : Paul Garner [Director of the Centre for Evidence Synthesis in Global Health and Co-ordinating Editor of the Cochrane Infectious Diseases Group], 'For 7 weeks I have been through a roller coaster of ill health, extreme emotions, and utter exhaustion', BMJ Blog, 5 May 2020.

237   *'I've had messages saying this is all in your head, or it's anxiety'*: Vonny LeClerc quoted in Ed Yong, 'COVID-19 Can Last for Several Months', *The Atlantic*, 4 June 2020.

239   *'Post-Covid fatigue could represent fertile new ground . . .'*; *'If some or many post-Covid syndrome patients respond to over-exertion . . .'*: David Tuller, 'Trial By Error: NICE on Exercise and Post-Covid Syndrome', Virology Blog, 15 July 2020.

239   *NICE put out a statement warning against using the outdated ME/ CFS recommendations on graded exercise therapy as they may change:* 'Statement about graded exercise therapy in the context of COVID-19', NICE, July 2020.

239   *NICE published an initial version of the revised guidelines . . .:* 'NICE draft guidance addresses the continuing debate about the best approach to the diagnosis and management of ME/CFS', NICE, 10 November 2020.

239   *recommending not to offer graded exercise therapy, structured activity or exercise programmes that are based on deconditioning as the cause of ME/*

CFS.: 'In developing more specific recommendations on the content, approach and delivery of physical activity management, the committee considered the benefits and harms associated with graded exercise therapy that had been identified in the qualitative evidence and their own experiences of these types of interventions. They recommended not to offer any programme based on fixed incremental physical activity or exercise, for example graded exercise therapy or structured activity or exercise programmes that are based on deconditioning as the cause of ME/CFS.' Myalgic encephalomyelitis (or encephalopathy)/chronic fatigue syndrome: diagnosis and management (Draft for consultation), NICE Guideline, November 2020, 63.

239–240   *Do not offer CBT as a treatment or cure for ME/CFS':* ME: diagnosis and management (Draft for consultation), 34.

240   *'I learnt that in convalescence after a severe assault . . .':* Paul Garner, 'Covid-19 at 14 weeks', BMJ Blog, 23 June 2020.

240   *On 25 January 2021, nine months after contracting Covid-19 . . .:* Paul Garner, 'On his recovery from long covid', BMJ Blog, 25 January, 2021.

242   *In April 2021, NICE revised their guidelines for treating chronic pain:* 'Chronic pain (primary and secondary) in over 16s: assessment of all chronic pain and management of chronic primary pain' [NG193], NICE, 7 April 2021.

243   *Scandinavian Journal of Disability Research . . .:* Emma Sheppard, 'Performing Normal But Becoming Crip: Living with Chronic Pain.' *Scandinavian Journal of Disability Research,* (March 2020) 22(1): 39–47.

243   *'I can choose to work from home . . .':* Julie (Interview One) in Sheppard, 'Performing Normal But Becoming Crip'.

243   *'those who fail to perform heteronormative . . .'; 'There could be joy and pleasure in pacing':* Sheppard, 'Performing Normal But Becoming Crip'.

245   *In the late 1960s, the Black Panther group set up nationwide 'survival programmes':* MT Bassett, 'No Justice, No Health: the Black Panther Party's Fight for Health in Boston and Beyond', *Journal of African American Studies,* (November 2019) 23: 352–363.

245   *'Caring for myself is not self-indulgence, it is self-preservation, and that is an act of political warfare.':* Audre Lorde, 'A Burst of Light', *A Burst of Light and Other Essays* (Mineola: Ixia), 130.

245   'It is about finding ways to exist in a world that is diminishing': Sara Ahmed, 'Self-care as Warfare', feministkilljoys, 25 August 2014.

245   'I want to live the rest of my life, however long or short . . .': Lorde, 'A Burst of Light', A Burst of Light and Other Essays, 71.

246   'Sometimes, "coping with" or "getting by" . . .': Ahmed, 'Self-care as Warfare'.

246   'I love you . . .': Sara Ahmed, The Cultural Politics of Emotion (Milton Park: Routledge, 2015), 30.

248   'full of beginnings without ends': Ursula Le Guin, The Carrier Bag Theory of Fiction, (London: Ignota Books, 2019).

249   'And then these doctors tell you that you will die, or recover! . . .': Alice James (diary, 27 September 1890), The Diary of Alice James, 142.

PHOTO © FITZCARRALDO EDITIONS

ALICE HATTRICK is a writer and producer based in London. Their criticism and interviews have appeared in publications such as *frieze* magazine, *ArtReview*, and the *White Review*. With Leah Clements and Lizzy Rose, they are the coproducer of Access Docs for Artists, a resource for disabled and/or chronically ill artists, curators, and writers. *Ill Feelings* is their first book.

The Feminist Press publishes books that
ignite movements and social transformation.
Celebrating our legacy, we lift up insurgent
and marginalized voices from around the
world to build a more just future.

See our complete list of books at
feministpress.org

THE FEMINIST PRESS
AT THE CITY UNIVERSITY OF NEW YORK
FEMINISTPRESS.ORG